"I've never been good at making money. I'm amazed that Mark Haroldsen, a millionaire many times over, is willing to share exactly how to do as he's done. And it works! I'm already $500,000 better off in just 16 months!"

—Jimmy Shea
U.S. Gold Medalist
2002 Winter Olympics

❦ ❦ ❦

"The Next Step to Waking Up The Financial Genius Inside You reinforces the key element for a successful real estate investor, which is to set written goals and focus on those goals. This book reminds all of us how powerful written disciplined goal setting can produce great success when combined with determination and persistence to reach those goals."

—Craig Horton, President
Medford Better Housing Assoc., Inc.

❦ ❦ ❦

"I used some principals from Mark's first book to do the following. I took $25,000 from a previous successful deal and bought into my first apartment complex. Like most beginning investors, I was terrified of losing my money. So I formed a partnership with others where I was the managing general partner...We paid $540,000 for the property. It was a lot of money, but we knew the place had tremendous intrinsic value. Years later, I bought out of all my partners and refinanced out with over $900,000 - all of it tax free since it was a loan. The property, at that time, appraised for $2.6 million. As I have told Mark in the past, and I totally believe it now, **EDUCATION IS A SHORTCUT TO EXPERIENCE.** Thank you, Mark, for writing your first book. I am certain that anyone who follows your new book will find their own fortune in short order, just like I did from following your first book."

—Donald G. Arsenault, CCIM, RECS
Arsenault Realty Advisors, LLC

"Through Mark O. Haroldsen's books, tapes, magazine and seminars, I gained the knowledge to not only become financially independent, but to be able to have precious time to spend with my family. There aren't words big enough to describe my sincere thanks for all he has done to enlighten me on compounding profits through real estate investing...Thanks, Mark, for everything!!!" "P.S. I wish you well and know that your new book will do great. Thanks again!!

> — Jan Talaga, President
> Janco Properties, LLC

❦ ❦ ❦

"I would like to personally thank Mark for being a great inspiration to me in the early eighties through his writings and publications. His updated edition, *The Next Step to Waking Up The Financial Genius Inside You,* has re-inspired my drive, which drove me from a broke 20-year-old to being the president and founder of a $100+ million real estate lending and investment organization operating in twelve states...all from scratch."

> — John Odegard, President
> Seattle Funding Group, Ltd.

❦ ❦ ❦

"Mark, I read your book for the first time when I was only 14-years-old. Although it wasn't until several years later that I got started investing in real estate, your book contributed a lot to my career. Now that I have a few million dollars jingling in my jeans, I am even more appreciative. Thank you!"

> — Garth Johnson

The Next Step to...
Waking Up
the
Financial
Genius
Inside You

by Mark O. Haroldsen

Publisher: Mark O. Haroldsen
                Financial Genius *dba* E-Business Benefits
Association of America, Inc.
                4505 Wasatch Blvd. Suite 350
                Salt Lake City, Utah 84124.

Printed in the United States of America

Cover Design, *Royter-Snow Design*
Book Design, *Design Type Service*

Library of Congress Number 2005905375

ISBN 0-9770792-0-1

CONTENTS

A PRE-FOREWORD
"FINANCIAL GENIUS" CONTINUED

Many, many years ago a newspaper story made the claim that Mark O. Haroldsen's book, *How To Wake Up The Financial Genius Inside You*, probably has helped more people to become millionaires than any other single book.

I'm not sure that statement is true, but I do know that even now I still get many phone calls and letters of thanks for being a guide and a help in someone's financial success. (The book did sell more than two million copies worldwide. In addition my staff and I gave literally thousands of live seminars.)

The letter below kind of says it all as to what people have been saying to me. This letter and others like it really "got to me" – made me feel like I had done something good and made a contribution to people's lives. I don't think there's a better feeling, and it also did something else for me. It motivated me to get off my butt and do some more writing. This new book that you are reading now is a result of that push by some appreciative followers. I thank them and I thank you for taking the time to read this.

Please don't misunderstand me. The letter you are about to read is from **the most successful story** I know of that gives me some of the credit. I'm not claiming Mr. Hansen is the average of all the success stories that I've received. But certainly one that grabbed my attention and all of us can learn from (including the teacher) and get a huge dose of motivation and inspiration!

Mr. Mark O. Haroldsen
4505 Wasatch Boulevard, Suite 350
Salt Lake City, UT 84124

Dear Mr. Haroldsen:

I have wanted to thank you for many years, but like most people I have not until now. When a friend told me you were going to republish your wonderful book "*How To Wake Up The Financial Genius Inside You,*" I saw my chance to return a favor.

You woke up my "Genius" over twenty-five years ago when I had a two hundred dollar VW and a ten-speed bike to my name. I wanted to own real estate to gain cash flow and future value as the mortgage loans paid off, but how? Your simple, straightforward plan allowed me, at twenty-three years of age, with no credit history or capital beyond a two-week paycheck, to buy my first two homes for $200 down. I owned those homes for twelve years and sold them for a seventy two thousand dollar profit plus the years of cash flow I lived on.

When people ask, "can I still do this," I smile. I truly believe it is actually easier today with better information, computers, more cash in the economy, and obviously, a great deal more real estate to choose from. I sincerely think I could do "better" today with an average intelligence and above average desire than twenty-five years ago.

For twenty-five years, I have pursued your principles and continued to grow in economic strength and knowledge. Today the group of friends and family that I lead as chief operating partner own over one billion of real estate in Utah, Arizona, Nevada, and California. The cash flows now exceed my dreams and my friends and family are economically secure and grateful. Life is so fulfilling as my options to travel and do charitable work are part of my every day life.

Thank you a million – or more appropriately, "Thanks a Billion."

Your grateful student,

Dell Loy Hansen
CEO Wasatch Property Management, Inc.

NOTE: For more detailed information about Dell Loy Hansen's phenomenal story, see Addendum "A".

I should also note that I've joined Dell Loy with a few other investors in recent years to purchase an $8.2 million building. Mr. Hansen is indeed paying me back for what he learned from my book to the tune of an automatic completely passive monthly cash flow return of over 19 percent on the $420,000 I put into the deal. (Don't you just love the term "passive income" or "passive cash flow" – in this case, that check for $6,720 comes in like clockwork every month.)

Throughout this book, you'll see deals and examples that seem so very small by your standards, and others that will be in the multi-millions that may seem large by your standards. Don't let the numbers under-whelm you or overwhelm you.

I know it's sometimes difficult not to be overwhelmed when you purchase your first big deal. I certainly remember how scared I was by my first big deal, but once I digested those numbers I was able to move to an ever-higher level – but again, each time I hit a new threshold there was some nervousness in my purchase. Please understand that this is pretty normal for any of us.

In re-reading my own book all these years later, I must say that it is a pretty darn simple and straightforward financial "how to" book that works wonders. It basically told my story of starting with a negative net worth when I was 27 years old and how I, in four years, turned that "less than nothing" into a million dollar net worth—(that net worth has since grown steadily well into the eight figures.)

The basic formula I used was buying beat-up and what I always liked to call "dirt bag" properties with borrowed money—from friends, family, sellers, and banks—then doing some simple basic renovations, which would dramatically lift the value of that property, made even more dramatic by the use of leverage. In many cases I was able to achieve a rate of return of several hundred percent in a few months. Now, if you know about compounding, you know what those kinds of percentage increases can do to even a small amount of beginning capital!

But now comes the huge question...the million-dollar question. Can it still be done today...starting with nothing...in our very different economy? Does this old formula still make people rich? Or does it need to be changed or maybe just tweaked a bit?

Well let me say this right up front—Yes—and that is an absolute, positive, most assured YES! *But*...Yes, there always seems to be a *but*. Some things have changed...the formula needs to be tweaked a bit here and there for maximum profits (sometimes treasures are in the tweaking). Interest rates are down drastically, and banks, with all that cheap money, have layered on the paperwork—which has given birth to many other sources of money that were almost unheard of 25 years ago. Some laws have also changed, and lately it seems there are so many more charlatans out there hawking "how to" real estate seminars — some of these seminars that are taught by speakers who are really only paid salesmen. They have memorized a script and are trying to sell a very, very expensive retreat or upgrade you into another seminar—a BIG BEWARE needs to flash in your mind when you watch the infomercials that make everything sound too good to be true! (My good friend, Bruce Couch, wants to write a book about some of these guys with the title—"*The Manure Spreaders*"—and he certainly knows which ones fit that title inasmuch as he spent many years in the seminar business.)

There is another question that I have been asked a thousand times. Did I make most of my money by writing and selling the books and tapes and subsequently doing seminars? And am I still involved today? In simple words...do I practice what I preach? The brief answer is **no** to the first question and **yes** to the second and third question. I wrote the book *AFTER* I made my first million. The book was very successful and with the proceeds from my book sales I bought more property. Overall, I would have to say that about 75% of my net worth came directly from investing in real estate.

I have been so busy in the last few years with my real estate that I haven't had time to do much writing. As a matter of fact, I believe that I would be much further ahead of the real estate financial game if I had never written a book or given any seminars. But I enjoy writing so very much and sharing my knowledge by teaching others how to become financially free. In addition, I love to share my philosophies of life and healthy living with others.

Do I still buy the "dirt bag fixer uppers" that I started with? No, I don't. Yes, that was a great, quick and simple way to start, and if you are a beginner or have tons of time on your hands that's still the best place to start.

But now, I have moved on to real estate deals that cost much more money, and even though the rate of return on my investment may be a bit smaller, I don't like to spend the time on them that I once did when I was younger. I own office buildings in several states, but my favorite building is the one I office in right here in Utah. I have invested in some very, very great triple net, long-term leased up buildings with national tenants. However, I have recently put on a brand new hat – a developer hat. I have learned a ton of things in the last year about real estate development with my $30 million condo development project in Hawaii, which quickly sold out in a matter of weeks! Wow, was I surprised and delighted!

So, if you ask me if real estate still works all these years later, I will give you the same answer the late, great real estate magnate, Bill Nickerson, gave me years ago at one of our Orlando real estate conventions where he was a guest speaker. Bill, author of *How I Turned $1,000 into Five Million in Real Estate — in My Spare Time*, said to me, "Mark, I had that same question asked of me way back when I started and I still have it asked today, and I am sure it will come up tomorrow, again and again. My answer is always the same— it's a big fat yes."

I would add this to what wonderful old Bill had to say: There is a very logical reason that real estate always works, and it may sound like an over simplification but it really isn't. To paraphrase an old statement that all of us have heard, "GO BUY SOME LAND CAUSE THEY AIN'T MAKING IT ANYMORE." But to make that statement even stronger and more profitable, I'd like to add, "Put some kind of IMPROVE-MENT on that LAND" – or ideally, buy land that has a building or some improvement on it already. Real estate is in limited supply and improvements give it more intrinsic value. Improvements also guarantee its sure and steady increase in value in most markets in the U. S. You can literally build an empire, starting with nothing, using leverage wisely (other peoples' money). It should also be noted (and this is a stunning statistic) that in the last 70 years, according to research recently released, real estate has gone up in value 67 of those years in the United States. I don't know of any other investment that comes even close to this phenomenal record.

Real estate also makes far more fortunes for the average guy compared to small businesses. (Be sure to see the subtitled section contained within Chapter 8 that is entitled *STAY AWAY FROM INVESTMENT TIME SUCKERS.*)

NOTE: The big problem with using leverage in other types of investments—such as stocks or starting a new business—is that they don't have the proven record of a sure and steady increase in value. Thus, non real estate investments are very risky using other peoples' money.

Now the big bonus! When you combine all of this with a little creative thinking, a small miracle—sometimes a big one—can take place. That creative thinking can dramatically improve the property's value, and that combined with leverage pushes the return on your investment into double or even triple digits. (If you don't think you are creative, you can always get great input from other people – borrow their brains.)

Remember this critical part of the formula – and this is the case I made in the original "Financial Genius" book (some of the original *Financial Genius* book is contained within this book because it still works). If you are leveraged (let's say on a 10 to 1 basis – that is you only put up one dollar to every ten dollars that someone else puts up) and you combine that with some of your brainpower and OPB (Other Peoples' Brainpower), using that creative brainpower to make certain improvements which increase the value of the property by – let's say 10 percent – your rate of return on *YOUR* invested dollar leaps up to a potentially *life changing 100 percent. Change the increase in value to 20 percent and your return goes to 200 percent.

I could relate hundreds, even thousands of super success stories of men and women of virtually every age who have put into practice the financial formula and methods that have worked wonders and continue to work wonders. You will find some of those stories in the following pages.

For years I have wanted to expand on the formulas and techniques of the original "Financial Genius" book and I have been asked more times than I can count, "Mark, when are you going to write another book?"

So what I've decided to do in this book is combine the best of what I have learned from my own successful deals (as

---

* *I say "life changing" because with 100 percent return per year you can transform $10,000 into $10 million in just ten years – and to me that is definitely "life changing."*

well as my disaster deals), spanning from 1972 through the present, with what others have done by adding to, changing, customizing, and tweaking…not the basic principles (because they never change)…but some of the methods, and formulas set forth in the original "Financial Genius" book. You see, in all those years since my book came out I have met and talked with thousands of people who have had tremendous success. They did it in many cases by tweaking a bit for the treasures – remember this saying, "Sometimes the treasure is in the tweaking?"

"Tweaking for Treasures" – We can all learn so much from that saying. So, my task then, is to convey to you, in a simple, straightforward, step-by-step manner what you must do – the basics as well as the tweaking – so you will reap the maximum benefits

In my attempt to give you the absolute best financial road map, please forgive me if I sneak in some of my philosophies of life, healthy living and reasons for living — that is, why are you alive and what should you do with your life and will it have any impact at all on the world. I am so totally convinced that the longer I live (I'm 60 now) the more I believe this—PROBABLY THE BIGGEST SINGLE CAUSE OF WHY MOST PEOPLE DON'T REACH THEIR OWN DREAMS AND GOALS IS BECAUSE THEY DON'T HAVE STRONG ENOUGH REASONS—STRONG ENOUGH PURPOSE. Reasons or motivations are so critically important. In fact, I think they are the entire ball game. You and I both need to work on our reasons—WE NEED TO WORK VERY HARD ON OUR MOTIVES—and I'm going to try very, very hard to motivate you with THE WORDS I WRITE IN THIS BOOK, and delve deep into your mind to discover your own reasons and motives for forging ahead to do what you really want to do with your life.

Sure the formulas are important, but without the push, the motive, and the reasons, you know as well as I do it is altogether too easy to give up or slow down — after all we all know how easy it is to just plop down in front of the TV, and what we intended to be 30 minutes of TV time turns into hours and hours and then it's time to go to bed.

Hmmm, I think right now is a good place to try to sneak in just one little tidbit on this TV thing that I think will be very helpful. Here it is—sometime ago a university did a study of the satisfaction levels of about 1500 students while going about their daily lives. They gave each student a pager that the student was to have with them at all times. Then, at random times, they would page the students, asking them what activity they were engaged in at that moment.

Through a series of questions, the researchers would measure the satisfaction level of the student with a particular activity. They then came up with a number that told the researchers what activities gave the greatest satisfaction and which gave the least satisfaction – even to the point of depression. Yes, you guessed it – Watching TV was at the bottom!! Kids were even more satisfied with summer school than with watching their favorite TV program – and you know how loudly kids scream if they even think they have to go to summer school. Bottom line, next time you or I think of parking our big butt in front of the mind numbing machine called a TV…let's think again and go do something else. What else? Almost anything will do, but for our purposes here, how about working on whatever goals you have set for yourself and ways that you are going to bring meaning and purpose to your life. (If you must watch TV—how about working out or lifting some small weights or stretching while you watch— do it and see how much more satisfied you feel when you turn off the TV.)

we want to be happy, is to solve those problems all along the way.

Take the person who thinks life really sucks because they are $50,000 overdrawn at the bank. Nothing can be worse for them and they fret and worry, as they are hating their life. But at the same time, they're thinking—"boy, when this is over my life will be almost perfect." But how would this person feel about that overdraft problem if one year later he were told he had cancer, or some other debilitating disease? Looking back, I am sure he would say to himself, "Wow what an idiot I was not to realize how good I had it back than."

The key to life, I believe, is to work on yourself to have enough discipline to handle whatever life throws at you. If you have the right amount of discipline, that's about the size of the problems, you will be able to successfully tackle and solve. If you have a massive amount of (the not too much talked about) big D word (discipline), then that's the size of problem you will be able to handle.

Again paraphrasing from *Flow*, the reason depression is so prevalent in wealthy and healthy countries according to the author's theory, is because of an ethos that builds unwarranted self-esteem, espouses victimology and encourages rampant individualism. Further, we all tend to have an over-reliance on shortcuts to happiness. Every modern nation builds more and more shortcuts to pleasure: TV, drugs, shopping, and spectator sports. And pleasure does not bring long lasting satisfaction—it should be just the dessert, not just the main course as it has become in the U.S.

You and I both know that work can be a source of great gratification which outstrips the actual compensation.

So why am I preaching so hard on this principle of "Life is suffering" and using its antidote: DISCIPLINE? The simple answer is that if one really truly learns this lesson he or she will lift themselves to a much higher plain of living.

There was an event in my life (actually two events) that easily could have scarred or sunk me forever. Those two events certainly did a big job in rearranging my thinking and my priorities. When I was 15-years-old, living in Ankara, Turkey—my 17-year-old brother literally died at my feet while we were trying out for the high school basketball team. That's a pretty heavy trip for a kid and one that took me more than a few years to recover from.

But unfortunately, that tragedy would become pale by comparison to the sudden and needless death of my 16-year-old daughter. For many years after that mind-altering tragedy, nothing seemed to matter at all—certainly not money. I disconnected from virtually all my business activities.

Finally, after working through my personal tragedies (and believe me, discipline was the only way out of "all life is suffering"), I returned to my passion of turning dirt, bricks, financing and creative ideas into millions. My priorities changed because this round of my passion was directed at deriving more satisfaction from "the doing" and the reconnecting with people.

Now I try to impart to you, the reader, just the right methods so you can achieve your own financial freedom, or if you are already there, the right methods to rise to a higher level. At the same time if I can be even a small force in your life to help raise the level of your "satisfaction, long lasting gratification, and contentment factor," then I will feel like I've made a difference in the world.

Some of my so-called followers or students have made my success look like I'm still in first or second grade, and there are some excellent lessons to be learned from those super students. You see, they did some tweaking of the formulas in the "Financial Genius" book and at least, in some cases, they had a ton or two more ambition that I had.

Tweaking was exactly what Dell Loy Hansen did, but he did it in a major way (that's his letter at the beginning of this book).

Many years ago I worked to help Michael Leavitt get elected Governor of the State of Utah. Sometime after that I was attending a function at the governor's mansion where I met Dell Loy Hansen, when he quickly told me that he had read my book as a young college student at Utah State University and had, thanks to my book, begun his real estate investing career part time while going to school.

Fast forward to the present and Mr. Hansen—the student—is making "Mark's multi-millions" look miniscule. Mr. Hansen's total holdings (and he is much, much younger than I) begin with a B——as in billion. (For those of you who didn't excel in math – let me remind you there are 1,000 millions in a billion.) How did Hansen tweak what he learned in my book to produce those kinds of numbers? I mean after all, that's one heck of a tweak! Here's how – he leveraged himself much, much more than most normal humans, by sharing the wealth with others – partners, that is – and lots of them, and some pretty well heeled ones at that. It takes a lot of courage to believe in yourself and what you think you can deliver to your partners. Then of course, you have to do it, and keep on doing it…and as you do, WOW – the word spreads from your partners' lips to others' wealthy ears. And what are they saying? Those lips are saying, "Here's a guy who really takes care of his partners and delivers what he says he will – and sometimes more." (See Chapter 8 entitled *THE QUICKEST WAY TO A BILLION – BEYOND SUPER LEVERAGE*, and read what I call *The Billion Dollar Hansen Model*.)

And bingo – after a hell of a lot of work and effort, and some passing years, you've got a billion dollars worth of real estate.

Now if I were still in my 30's I would probably be insanely jealous and work 23 hours a day to try to catch up, or pass, Dell Loy—but as an older and (I hope) wiser man, I must say Mr. Hansen's super-sized success makes me proud, not jealous.

And he is just one of the many from whom I have heard. (See Addendum "A" for more details about Mr. Hansen and what he's accomplished.)

Just a few weeks ago I got a call from Steve Thomas in Florida. (a great guy and one of my former real estate speakers). Steve called to tell me that he had just received a call from a guy who wanted to know if that former "real estate guru, Mark O. Haroldsen" was still alive. He didn't seem to know if I was 50, 75, 100 or dead. (That's what happens when you stop writing or speaking in public and just go about doing what you like to do—they think you're dead!) I was very pleased to have Steve report back that I had not yet "assumed room temperature." Let me say this, and I think it's very important — even at the age of 60 — it's as important as ever to continue to set goals and strive toward them. Without that drive for the dream, anyone—especially those of us past 50 and 60—can lose interest in life and begin to give up on it. That "giving up" hits the super successful and wealthy people just as much as it does people who are poor or who have failed.

Goals really do energize the body, mind, soul and spirit for ANY person, of ANY age, in ANY circumstances! So I don't care if you are 31 or 71 or 101, you need to take time to write down your goals, and keep doing it at regular intervals. Don't think about it—just do it!

In this book I will probably push this goal thing into your brain more times than you might care to read, but there is so much good that comes from setting goals, and then relentlessly going after them. I can't say this strongly enough.

In my own life, the setting of goals energized me when I was young and they took me to some very lofty places. When I arrived at those places, I suddenly got complacent by thinking that I had arrived. For a time my life became stale, slow, and sad. That led to some depression and I truly struggled with most everything for a longer time than I care to admit. It wasn't until I began looking forward, by realizing that I HAD NOT ARRIVED AND I NEVER WILL. Slowly with that realization I started to write down some of the things that I wanted to do with my life—with my kids, my grandkids, with friends and what I wanted to achieve in the world. The bottom line was what was the meaning of my life? And then most importantly—if I am going to achieve anything, I must reduce it to paper; both the objective and the plan to reach it—complete with a time frame. There is something magic about the process of writing it down on paper or on your computer.

If you have some doubts about the power and energy of written goals, just go ahead and test the concept on any of your own objectives. You will see its magical power in your life—the process is much more powerful than any drug. But you must write it down, or it won't work!

But enough about me—let's talk about you and what you are going to do with your financial life right at this moment and what it is you want to do—tomorrow, next week, next year, and beyond.

Do you want to be financially average? There certainly is no shame or anything wrong with financially average or average in any area of life, but there is so very much more satisfaction and gratification in doing something in the extreme. Perhaps it gives you a feeling that you have contributed more to this planet we call earth. Whatever it is, I know that it's different than the feeling of average. Just look around you; see how the world celebrates, with great fanfare, above average achievements, from President Ronald Wilson

Reagan's funeral—that we will all remember—to Michael Jordan's incredible athletic abilities, or to the super-human performance by Lance Armstrong in the Tour de France. We read and talk about people of great wealth—especially if they do good works with their money— as if they were from a different world.

There are so many reasons and motives for you and I to try to lift ourselves to a higher plane. WRITTEN GOAL SETTING is the critical beginning ingredient. As someone once said, "if you want to change the world, you must first change yourself". (You might want to read Chapter 9 first entitled *SETTING GOALS AND THE ENERGY THEY CREATE*. In fact, I recommend you read it first, especially if you need some extra motivation and need to contemplate your own personal reasons for what you want to achieve and why.)

But just how wealthy do you want to become? You can shoot for the "M" (million) level or the "MM" (multi-million) level or the big "B" (billion) level. It really is your choice—as you will see in this book, it's really up to you. I've said and proved for years that "making millions is simple— no, not easy, but SIMPLE—all you need is the right formula attached to the right methods at the right time. In other words—the right road MAP and I know that MAP inside and out—front to back. I have spent the last 25 years perfecting and tweaking the basic FINANCIAL GENIUS FORMULA. That formula has been tested thousands of times by myself, and the tens of thousands who learned and then did something with my first book, and I don't mean just reading it! (Two million people read it, but I estimate only 10 percent of those really put it into practice.)

In the pages that follow you will see how simple it is to become the master of your own millions. Again I must emphasize, I didn't say it would be easy—BECAUSE it does take a lot of work and effort on your part (and therein is where your great satisfaction and gratification will lie). The formula is SO SIMPLE to follow.

So let's get started!

FOREWARD

by Paul J. Meyer

Mark Haroldsen and I are true kindred spirits.

I first met Mark in the 1970's. Real estate investment was one of my key interests at that point, and I read Mark's book and newsletter. I put Mark's formulas into action, and helped my son, Larry, move into the real estate business.

Thirty years later, Larry and I are developing another $100 million project using the same wealth formula ... and our development efforts offer daily proof that no one knows how to make money in real estate like Mark Haroldsen. The same methods Mark and I have used to make our fortunes will work for you as well, providing you read his book with an open mind and have the courage to succeed.

I first heard Mark talk about courage to succeed back in 1977. I read his article on the subject, and it inspired me to add a lesson on courage to one of our best-selling self-improvement courses. Mark's speech on courage offered up a profound truth: Successful people are not any smarter or better prepared than most others ... they just know the wealth formulas and have the courage to succeed.

People who lack the courage to succeed seldom become millionaires . . . in fact, they seldom do anything at all. Witness the hundreds of people who attend Mark's seminars again and again without ever taking action. Once, when Mark asked an audience of a thousand people how many had been to the same seminar previously, he was amazed to see nearly 20% of the crowd raise their hands. Mark then asked a crucial follow-up question: "How many of you have followed the system and bought property?" All the hands went down.

Do you have the courage to succeed? If you do, you'll learn more from this book than from any dozen books on real estate investing. But if you lack courage, and aren't willing to develop it, you'll probably never put into action the wealth-building formulas contained in this book.

Remember: Success comes to those who *act*. Nowhere is this fundamental truth more evident than in the success of the thousands who have used Mark's methods as stepping stones to riches. The ideas in this book are infinitely transferable ... all you need to do is follow Mark's lead. That's why I gave copies of this book to the 100 top leaders of my companies.

Today I'm 77 years young. I remember with fondness the many times in years gone by when Mark and I met in Acapulco to play tennis and exchange ideas. I'm not sure which I enjoyed most – the tennis or the talk! Actually, even though I'm Mark's senior by more than a decade, I've beaten him at tennis more times than he has beaten me.

Of course, Mark claims otherwise. But that's okay; I want him to know that I'm magnanimous enough to accept his version of the story. Besides, I'm incredibly grateful for the opportunity to know and learn from Mark Haroldsen. I'm content to keep making millions in real estate and let him win on the tennis court.

Paul J. Meyer, Founder
Success Motivational International, Inc.
Founder of more than 40 companies
New York Times best-selling author
Real estate millionaire

INTRODUCTION

When I was 25 years old, my wife and I, while living in Denver, found ourselves in a desperate financial situation. I had just lost my job and my wife was expecting our second child and we hadn't a dime's worth of insurance to cover it. We even had to borrow money from my father and father-in-law in order to pay the rent and bills and buy a few groceries for the two of us and our one-year-old son.

It was then that I determined never to suffer this way again, and even at the time when everything seemed hopeless, I was presumptuous enough to dream and scheme and set my goals to become a millionaire. I said to myself— and even had the gall to write it down—that by the time I was 30, I would retire. The fact is well documented that six short years later, I had achieved that goal.

A year later I wrote and published a book about what I had done to achieve my financial independence. The book is entitled *How to Wake Up the Financial Genius Inside You* and has sold over 2,000,000 copies.

I chose to sell my book myself using newspaper ads and mailings, plus TV and magazine ads. I was very fortunate to be able to sell 1,700,000 on my own. Then, New York Bantam Books picked it up from there and sold another 300,000 copies.

At this printing, I have really made this a totally new book, but I have kept in most of the material from the old book. The new material makes the old book material even more applicable to the real estate market today. Even though

I must emphasize the basic concepts of the old book are time-less and will work virtually at any time and in any market.

Real estate investment is the tool I've found to be most beneficial and suitable to achieving my goals.

Many people have felt that I made my money through the sale of my book and the result of the publication of my nationwide magazine, *The Financial Freedom Report*. I'm not at all embarrassed to state that I've done very well from the proceeds of the sales of these two publications. However, my personal focus is real estate investment and here is a little recap of what has happened since the first printing of *How to Wake Up the Financial Genius Inside You*, in 1976. Prior to publishing the book, through the purchase of real estate, my net worth had risen to over a million dollars during my 31st year. For the next year, I concentrated on getting my book published, starting up my magazine, *The Financial Freedom Report*, and launching a nationwide seminar program. In late 1977, I renewed my effort to acquire property; and then something happened that I had not counted upon, which was a pleasant surprise. The many hundreds of thousands of people in that period of time who had purchased my book and subsequently subscribed to my magazine and attended my seminars, began sending me the deals they could not handle. Having a healthy net worth and some cash to work with, I was able to make bargain purchases of property all over the country. Since that time I have purchased property in California, Colorado, Idaho, Illinois, Kansas, Michigan, North Carolina, Pennsylvania, Texas, Puerto Rico, Hawaii, and of course, Utah. These have been major multi-million dollar purchases that have greatly enhanced my investor position.

Two of the properties have been successfully converted into condominiums, bringing in over a million dollars in profit in both cases.

If someone were to ask me today what success has done to change me, I would have to say the major area of change has been the great appreciation I have for time, and the great part it plays in achieving my goals through good utilization of it. Just as important, if not more so, the great satisfaction of having helped other people and touched their lives in financial and motivational ways. That strikes at the very core of my being.

So what does this all mean to you? Here's exactly what it means. If I can do all that I've done, so can you. Success is a process; it is not an end result, for there are greater and greater successes awaiting those who apply for themselves the success principles of planning, following a game plan, and sticking to the financial goals that you've set for yourself. Do this and you'll wake up the FINANCIAL GENIUS inside you.

Finally, and probably most importantly, I have learned time and time again that if I am fair and honest with people and really try to give them what they want, then the rewards come flowing back to me – not just in cash, but in a deep soul touching feeling that lasts, and lasts, and lasts.

ACKNOWLEDGMENTS

I acknowledge all those men and women throughout the world who are self-made millionaires and billionaires. I acknowledge you, the reader, for taking the time and trouble to buy and read this book. That time and effort sets you apart from the majority, and you are one who *can* succeed in the ambition to make a million.

Most people don't succeed in a big way because they take the easy road. They are the "**watchers**." They watch other people's lives. They know all the characters of the many TV shows. They know all the players of the sporting events by name, etc., etc. Their reality is acted out in watching reality shows so they live vicariously through other people rather than living their own life. Remember: the mere reading will only give you direction. It will give you a solid formula and specific recipes for success. But you must act and follow those directions. As you do, you will not only prosper financially, but you will learn a wealth of information about this financial endeavor that will allow you to give directions to others who can follow your example and act on your direction.

SPECIAL THANKS

To those who have put so much time and effort in to editing and connecting this and past editions—to Vicki Williams who years ago edited my first rough (very rough) draft to Virginia Fackrell who spent countless hours using her great skills to improve the first edition. More recently, I want to give great thanks to Michael D. Hansen and Carolyn Tice who pushed me to keep working on this new version of "*Financial Genius.*"

Also, many thanks to the many, many great people who give me ideas, encouragement, and inspiration. At the top of the list there is my staff, George Winquist, Marina Miles, my son, Mark E. Haroldsen, and Brittany Peters. They are the best and always there for me, and they are my other family. Others who need to be mentioned because of their influence and inspiration to my life are Joe Land, Steve Blaser, my sons, David O. Haroldsen, Marcus Haroldsen, George Poulton, my daughters, Nichol Haroldsen, Camille Haroldsen, and Lindsey Poulton Machan. Additionally, I must give huge credit to my brother, Scott Haroldsen, and my sister, Sue Kenny, who always resisted calling me "nuts" for pursuing some of my seemingly unachievable goals.

There are so many people who have been such good friends through the highs and lows of my life that they are too numerous to mention, but I do want to mention a few more. Larry Pino, Paul J. Meyer, Lois A. Haroldsen, David Craig, David Shamy, Guy Scribner, Dennis Johnson, Jerry C. Higginson, Frank Suitter, Kelly Hansen, William A. King, Ed

Beckcom, Richard Harvey, Radd Berrett, Mike & Ileana Delaney, and Seldon Young.

I especially want to thank the fantastic and helpful, supportive woman in my life, my wonderful companion, Kimberly Wangsgard.

LIFE-CHANGING

Sometime ago I spent a long session with a great man whom I admired. This man has reached great heights. Financially, he was a millionaire, but that is just the beginning. He was a very serious man, a humble man, yet a great leader in business and in religion. He was the author of more than 30 books and was heard on radio and television hundreds of times.

He was a wise investor, investing in everything from real estate to stocks and bonds, and many things in between. He has also backed many young, ambitious men in their private ventures. He is truly a grand, old gentleman who has the energy and enthusiasm of a man one half his age.

During our session, I asked him for his secret for success. He answered that when he was quite young he decided if he wanted to be a great man, achieve much, and reach the height of success, he would have to know what the great men of the world thought. He set upon the task of reading about the great men of the world, reading the words they had written, and then re-thinking each of their thoughts in an attempt to make their great thoughts his own. From each one he attempted to find something of benefit. Next, he made a habit of always carrying two books, one to read from and one to write in. As he read great thoughts, he would write down his own thoughts that were stimulated by the reading. Later, he published many of his thoughts into his own books.

What I learned from this *great man** is that probably the shortest route a person can take in the quest for excellence and struggle for financial success is to study thoroughly the great men and women and their lives. I began to study the great financial fortunes of the world, the men who made those fortunes, and how they did it. I investigated their thoughts, read the principles, formulas, and recipes they felt were important, discovered their thought processes, gained insight from their personal habits, benefited from their experience, and saw how they actually made their millions.

Some of these great people I met face to face and sat down with them and picked their brains and got to know them and their families. Most of these great people, however, I got to know through their books and writings, or in some rare cases, tapes that they had dictated – or books written about them.

Contained in this book are both a summary of what I learned from these great people and also how it changed my life and financial condition through the general laws of success applied to a specific formula for accumulation of wealth.

---

* *Sterling W. Sill was my mentor back then. He gave my life so very much in the way of direction and purpose....and still, even after his death in 1994 he leads and inspires me through his books and the notes that I took from our many sessions together.*

HOW TO READ THIS BOOK

At the end of each chapter, there are blank pages entitled "Notes and Thoughts." These pages are for you to write your thoughts, ideas, and goals as per Sterling W. Sill's advice. Do not write my thoughts; write the thoughts that are stimulated in your mind from reading my comments.

You will find as you read this book, particularly the second and third times, that your own ideas multiply. Consequently, you will find yourself writing many of your own great thoughts.

My task is not only to show you the formulas and methods that will lead you to success, but also to stimulate your mind and bring out great thoughts and ideas that are and always have been in your mind. Those thoughts, along with a little direction and guidance that will help you form a game plan, will bring rewards and riches you once thought came only to others.

Note: Throughout this book you will see various examples of actual deals with prices for houses and apartment buildings – some of those prices may seem very, very cheap by the standards of most markets today. Just keep in mind that everything is relative. Whereas I might have been negotiating a price on a house for $15,000 or $20,000 and end up buying it for $12,000 many years ago, and most likely there may not be a single income producing property in your entire state for under $250,000, remember that back when I wrote parts of this book, all prices of homes and apartment buildings were much, much lower, but so also were the rents.

Prices of virtually all income producing properties are valued and bought and sold based on the potential income stream of that property. Please keep this in mind.

The principles, however, and the formula remain essentially the same. Also, keep in mind that many years from now your kids, grandkids, and great grandkids may be looking at home prices that will be a million or even ten million dollars or more. Once again, everything is relative.

I am also acutely aware that in certain markets, and during particular timeframes, prices of properties rise so quickly and so high that it is very difficult to buy a property where the rent is enough to cover the mortgage and expenses and still give you a decent rate of return – California and Hawaii have fit into this category many times.

When faced with markets like this, there are several things that can be done. First and foremost, as you will see later in the book, the key to vastly increasing the value of a property is through the improvements you make, both physically and through better management of that property. So, if you are in a market where virtually all properties are selling for prices that are not supported by the rental income – that same inflated ratio will no doubt remain stable. Therefore, as you raise rents (after fix-up) you will also usually raise the value by the same percentage increase.

Additionally, there are other ways around the problem that some people are faced with in these highly inflated markets. For example, you can take advantage of the fast rising prices by becoming a builder and building and developing for quick sales at much higher prices to take advantage of such markets.

Other ways to capitalize on these markets is by doing some major shopping and comparison of overpriced properties and buy any under-priced property you can find (and you can always find some) that can be subsequently marketed aggressively and sold for a profit.

Of course, another alternative is to look at other markets in other cities, and even other states. This is not the easiest way, but the rewards can be huge. And with access to the Internet, the task is much simpler now than it was twenty years ago.

CHAPTER 1
MAKING MILLIONS
FROM PENNIES

If I gave you a choice of working for me for $1,000 a day for a period of thirty-five days, versus working for yourself for one cent the first day and doubling the amount each day for thirty-five days, which job offer would you take?

Obviously, if you were to take the first choice, at the end of thirty-five days you would have $35,000. A wage of $35,000 in thirty-five days is phenomenal. Had you chosen the alternative of working for one cent the first day and doubling the amount each day for thirty-five days, you would be compounding your money at 100 percent per day.

When I use this example in lectures, usually about half the people prefer the first job offer and half the second. Without the aid of a pencil or calculator, decide which choice you would make.

OFFER 1		OFFER 2	
Amount in		Amount in	
Day	Dollars	Day	Dollars
1	$ 1,000	1	$ .01
2	1,000	2	.02
3	1,000	3	.04
4	1,000	4	.08
5	1,000	5	.16
6	1,000	6	.32
7	1,000	7	.64
8	1,000	8	1.28
	$8,000		$2.55

Okay, it's been 8 days now. Have you made a decision yet? Would you take the sure $1,000 per day, or 100 percent compounded from a beginning penny?

Total Days 1-8 $2.55

OFFER 1 Amount in			OFFER 2 Amount in	
Day	**Dollars**		**Day**	**Dollars**
9	$1,000		9	$ 2.55
10	1,000		10	5.10
11	1,000		11	10.20
12	1,000		12	20.40
13	1,000		13	40.80
14	1,000		14	81.60
15	1,000		15	163.20
16	1,000		16	326.40
	$16,000			$652.80

How about now? Which choice do you favor? What if I said I would continue paying you $1,000 a day for an entire year? Would that push you over the top for a quick decision?

Total Days 1-16 $652.80

OFFER 1 Amount in			OFFER 2 Amount in	
Day	**Dollars**		**Day**	**Dollars**
17	$ 1,000		17	$ 650.00
18	1,000		18	1,300.00
19	1,000		19	2,600.00
20	1,000		20	5,200.00
21	1,000		21	10,400.00
22	1,000		22	20,800.00
23	1,000		23	41,600.00
24	1,000		24	83,200.00
	$24,000			$166,402.80

Not much of a problem to decide now. And you have eleven days to let your money grow.

Total Days 1-24 $166,402.80

OFFER 1 Amount in		OFFER 2 Amount in	
Day	Dollars	Day	Dollars
25	$ 1,000	25	$ 165,750.00
26	1,000	26	331,500.00
27	1,000	27	663,000.00
28	1,000	28	1,326,000.00
29	1,000	29	2,652,000.00
30	1,000	30	5,304,000.00
31	1,000	31	10,608,000.00
32	1,000	32	21,216,000.00
33	1,000	33	42,432,000.00
34	1,000	34	84,864,000.00
35	1,000	35	169,728,000.00
	$35,000		$339,456,652.80

Note: These figures have been rounded off for ease of calculating.

Most people find it almost impossible to believe that one-penny compounded at 100 percent per day is worth over a third of a billion dollars on the thirty-fifth day.

Sure, that is an exaggerated example of the fantastic effects of compounding interest, but the use of compound interest is virtually the only way to make millions today. Try changing days to years (more on that later).

LEVERAGE MAKES YOUR MONEY WORK HARDER

I was extremely fortunate in that I was given some good advice early in my career. A man of great wealth told me to get to know and fully comprehend interest rates, leverage, and how to compound investment capital through good investments. Although his advice did not sink in at that time and he did not elaborate on the types of investments to make, a few years later when I started making small investments, what he had said came back to me. And the results from using his philosophy have been amazing.

As with many young men, my goal had always been to become a millionaire. Like most, I became frustrated. I worked hard, but there didn't seem to be enough hours in the day to make a million. I reasoned that there had to be a way; I knew people who had achieved that goal, many of them still young. I studied the lives of more than two dozen millionaires and finally realized that the only practical way of making a million was to have your money work as hard for you as you work for yourself. Later I learned that with the wise use of leverage your money can literally work ten times harder than you can. I was on the way! The next step was to learn as much as I could about money, interest rates, and the use of leverage and compounding.

Even though I was busy at the time, I took time out to really learn and understand everything there was to know about the compounding of money. I particularly focused on the wise use of leverage. What leverage could do for you and to you astounded me. It has to be the most incredible tool in this era of inflation.

Virtually all of the financial wizards, industrial giants, and self-made millionaires now and in times past have realized the profound effect of the compounding of money.

SIMPLE COMPOUNDING

Compounding, of course, simply means that you earn interest on top of interest. For example, if you invest $1,000 for one year at 15 percent return, at the end of the first year you have $1,150, or 15 percent over and above the amount you started with. Your profit is $150.

The second year the entire $1,150 would earn at the rate of 15 percent for a total of $172.50 interest. This $172.50 interest added to the $1,150 brings your total to $1,322.50.

Whereas money experts agree that it is not realistic to compound money at 100 percent per day for thirty-five days, as in our example, most would agree that it is possible to compound money at 100 percent per year for thirty-five years. It is possible, and indeed not difficult, to compound money at 30 percent per year. In fact, there are many examples, including my own, where people have compounded their assets at over 100 percent per year. In Chapters 6, 7 and 8 on leverage, you will see how easily this can be done on sums as low as a couple hundred dollars, and on several hundred thousand dollars. This is less difficult to accomplish in the early years of an investment program when you are not dealing with large amounts of capital.

Even with the less dramatic figure of 30 percent, the results are amazing. For example, when $10,000 is compounded at 30 percent for eighteen years, the result is an accumulation of capital in excess of $1,124,000. Would it surprise you to know that many people compound their assets at the rate of 30 percent per year, particularly those with a net worth of less than $1 million? In Chapter 6 you will find out exactly how to consistently compound your money at 30 percent (and higher!).

Even though I felt I knew and understood interest rates, compounding, and how to use leverage, at that point I lacked the proper investments to try out my newfound knowledge. I tried stocks and bonds (in fact, I used a $1,500 government-backed school loan to experiment), only to find that because I lacked control over the investment I consistently lost money.

I thought some control could be gained if I were closer to the investment, so I joined a stock brokerage firm, and lost more money. It was then, as a stockbroker, that I found the type of investment that could give me a consistent, dependable, and at the same time, a high return.

THERE HAD TO BE A "GOLDEN GOOSE"

While trying to get my feet wet as a young, green-as-grass stockbroker for Paine, Webber, Jackson and Curtis, I met a client (an account I inherited when a broker left the firm) who showed me what I had been searching for.

*Larry Rosenberg** worked as an accountant for the Public Service of Colorado. He used to call for stock quotes; and once in a while he would buy 400 or 500 shares of a stock. At first I couldn't figure out where he was getting all the money. (His stock picks weren't bad, but nothing great.) I knew he couldn't be getting it from his salary, so I concluded he had either inherited it or was embezzling!

I finally got up the nerve to ask Larry what and where his "golden goose" was. He told me it was apartments in northeast Denver. The real shocker was the number of apartments he owned, and where and how he started.

Mr. Rosenberg not only had acquired more than a thousand units, but he had started with nothing only twelve years before. He did it in a part of Denver that was going downhill. Larry and his brother, Lew, have not only made themselves a fortune, but they have made a great contribution to an entire section of Denver. They have improved and upgraded buildings and grounds to the advantage of everyone.

---

* *Larry Rosenberg is still in Denver, Colorado at this time and remains a very good friend. We talk on the phone a few times a year and compare investment ideas and strategies. He graciously agreed to spend time with me recently as I filmed the story of my life. What a wonderful face-to-face reunion after all these years. (My story is available in DVD format. For more information email me at moh@reincome.com. or moh@networld.com .*

I had found an investment I could control, one where I could apply leverage and compounding. I was excited because I could begin immediately by buying small units.

HIGH RATES OF RETURN

If you are a small investor or just beginning, you really have a big advantage in many areas of investing. Whether you are shooting for a rate of return of 15 percent, 30 percent, 50 percent, or 100 percent, you can compound your money at these higher rates more easily because of the amount of money you are working with. The reason is that many large investors are not interested in some of the areas that you as a small investor are interested in. Consequently, while you still have small sums to invest, you can increase your average annual return dramatically.

For example, you can invest in a small real estate property — a duplex, four-plex, ten units, or thereabouts, where your only competitors in buying such units are people in similar situations, people without a lot of capital. Additionally, these people don't generally have a vast amount of experience or knowledge, so with a little extra effort you can surpass your competition.

Later, as your assets begin to build to around $800,000 or $900,000 you will find it harder to get the higher return every year. However, another thing will happen at this point — your abilities as an owner and investor will have compounded and it will be possible to continue at a high rate of return. The point is that your brain actually has a similar power to compound itself. In "Can Exercise Improve Your Brain Power?" *Reader's Digest,* May 1973, the author (Edwin Diamond) indicated that through physical and mental exercise your brain size can actually increase.

Each of us begins life with roughly ten billion brain cells. There are literally tens of billions of connective glia cells that can increase the size of the brain and the mental capacity of the person who does those things to stimulate or "compound" it.

Conversely, a person who does not exercise both brain and body, but who does the same things every day and stays in a narrow routine, becomes less alert and his brainpower diminishes, or at best stays the same. As one broadens his horizons and packs many and varied experiences into his life, he finds that a compounding effect takes place — the more he learns the more he wants to learn; in fact, the easier it is to learn. The more experience one has the more he wants to have, and he finds it easier to comprehend and benefit by these added experiences. I call this brain compounding. It is just as important as money compounding, and the two principles should be used jointly. It was said of J.P. Morgan that he had the genius to focus all of his mental powers - and concentrate on one thing for five minutes.

REAL ESTATE AND BRAIN COMPOUNDING

As you read this next example be sure not to get hung up on the numbers in the examples. Yes, they are low – I mean who could ever buy a house with $10,000 these days. But remember, everything is relative. Back when I did this deal not too many people made more than $28,000 a year. To make this example fit more closely in today's market just add a zero, or maybe even two zeros depending on where you live. The average price of houses in Kauai in 2004 for example, hit more than $500,000. That's the average! Can you still make money in markets like that? Absolutely. As you will see, I've been doing just that – read about it in an upcoming chapter. Remember, it's the concept that you and I need to continue to learn from and duplicate.

Let me give you an example of combining the two types of compounding. I had been building my asset base slowly for a little over a year. At the same time my mental abilities, at least when focused on investments, began to compound. A real estate agent through whom I had bought several properties came to me all excited about a fantastic little investment he had found.

My first question: "Why don't you buy it if it's so great?" He brushed this aside, saying he was too old to get involved in buying single-family houses.

I told him that single-family units were not in my game plan and that I didn't have any extra investment cash. He insisted on showing me the house. I went along out of curiosity and was surprised to find a modest, well-kept home in a lower income area in tip-top condition. It was obviously worth the $14,500 asking price. But the Realtor had described it as a "fantastic bargain." Sure enough, the seller's wife said they had to sell it that week and were lowering the price to $10,000. Within an hour I had written an offer to buy it for $10,000 cash.

I made the offer with less than $500 in the bank. But my brain had been working fast from the moment I saw the house. I wasn't going to let that bargain slip through my fingers. I was sure I could borrow the money somewhere. If I couldn't, I would only lose $100 earnest money. The odds were attractive.

The minute I had the seller's signature I went directly to the largest bank in town. Because my credit was good, I secured a $10,000 loan on my signature. Two days later I picked up the money, went to the closing, paid the money, and took title to one of the few properties I have ever owned free and clear. But that state of affairs didn't last long. I went to another bank with which I had been dealing for some time and asked for a long-term real estate loan on the property. Within three weeks they had appraised the property and loaned me $10,000, which was 70 percent of their appraised value (a low appraisal, incidentally).

Of course, I took the $10,000 from the mortgage money and paid off the first bank. My wonderful tenants were now paying off the mortgage. After all expenses were paid, more than $700 was left over each year. That extra income was tax free (see Chapter 17), and with inflation the house was eventually worth several times what I paid for it.

In the chapters on leverage, you will find several other examples of this type of leverage and financing with much larger properties.

This example has two points: (1) In spite of prevailing market conditions you can find attractive rates of return and make your money compound quickly. In this example you can't even determine the percentage rate of return on my initial investment, since I really didn't have anything invested in the property. And (2), if you are actively engaged in seeking investments and comparing financial data, appraisals, and methods of financing, your mind works overtime and starts to compound. You think of ways of getting the job done that never would have crossed your mind earlier. This is brain compounding.

Let me give you another great example – another real live case. This one's not mine, but from a young man who's on his way to many millions. He's going to pass me up quickly – and at my age now, I love it! And get this…he is the grandson of the first real estate agent I ever used. The late Elmo Higginson was that man who helped me so much way back when I began. And now I've been able to help his 26-year-old grandson who is well on his way. (Talk about what goes around, comes around.) Here's one of the young Jeremy Higginson's recent (2004) deals:

> I have been buying and selling real estate for about three
> years, using mostly conventional financing. My first no

money down deal was a home I bought with a 5% down payment and 95% conventional financing. We found this home while we were in the neighborhood looking at another property.

When we drove by this home we noticed that the lawn was totally dead, there were beer cans on the front porch, and most obvious were the two huge windows in the front that had been boarded up.

I remember saying to my wife as we drove by, "boy that house looks cheap." We did some investigation and found out that it was a HUD home. A HUD home is a home that was financed via FHA that had gone to foreclosure. When buying a HUD home here in Utah, you have to bid on it via the Internet.

HUD was asking $96,000 for the property. We were using a real estate agent who was also a general contractor and we figured that the property would be worth $125,000 if it were all fixed up. The agent figured that it would cost us about $3,000 for fix up costs. We offered $92,000 with HUD paying our closing costs and they took it.

The 5% down payment came from a cash advance on two or three of my credit cards (other peoples' money.) Once we closed, we got to work.

Because the Realtor just made a commission on the purchase of the property, we worked out a deal wherein he and his partner would help me remodel the property, but I only needed to pay my agent's contracting partner while we were working. The agent would wait until we sold the property.

Well, like always it costs a little more than expected and it ended up costing us $3,400 for labor and materials to fix up the place. At the time I knew very little about remodeling, and as the contractors remodeled I tried to help, but I mostly learned. If they were doing something that I didn't know how to do, I asked a lot of questions. I basically paid the contractors to remodel the place and teach me how to remodel.

I had the property on the market for a few months and finally sold it for $125,000 with me paying the closing costs.

economy would dive-bomb to the bottom of the economic ocean. (Countries tend to prosper to the extent their citizens spend, and spend, and spend their hard earned wages.) But this next part is huge. If you practice religiously the big "S" – that is save, save, save – you will end up with a gigantic prosperous financial economy or financial net worth of your own and live life as if you were your own country.

That, at least for my life and money, is a pretty powerful thought! We all want our [little] lives to mean something when it's all done and finished. And money, whether we like it or not, counts for something. It can be used for good or evil. Money can be used for enhancing humankind or tearing it down. It's all up to you. So don't kid yourself or put money down. Money is damned important and has hundreds of ways to influence our lives, and that will always be the case.

So why not accept that fact and go get some of it and make your mark – and then do some great good with it.

Using the PSIC formula, you can most assuredly make your mark financially. PSIC has been proven to work over and over again, and not just in my experience, but with thousands of others who read my first book. It really is against all rational thought to question the basic formula. The only real challenge is do you really want to do it? Do you really want to start, and stick with it? It's really a very simple formula to follow.

So why don't most people "just do it"? The answer to that question is not unlike that of why most people don't have success and stay with dieting. There's a temptation for all of us to set a goal and start with enthusiasm, only to get off track later. For an easy trick to use to keep yourself on track for virtually any goal you set, read Chapter 9 on *SETTING GOALS AND THE ENERGY THEY CREATE*. Go ahead, read it right now even though it's out of order.

One last parting thought about money and its value. Michael F. Roizen, M.D., who wrote a fascinating book entitled *Real Age*, published by Cliff Street Books, said, "Health is like money. At first the comparison sounds crass. How can you equate money with something as precious as life? But how can you not? Money as money isn't worth a dime. Money is only as valuable as what it buys. Money is really about potential. It provides possibilities, choices, and freedom. It also allows you to place a value on your choices and to make decisions."

I just had to add this exciting and uplifting story. I just got back from a month-long trip to Europe, visiting several countries. Quite accidentally, while visiting the city of Szczecin in the North of Poland, I met the 40-ish Krzysztof Fialkowski. I spent a delightful day with him, he was so very giving and generous with his time – and wow, how very proud he was of Poland and the huge economic strides that it has made since it broke away from the Soviet Union and returned to a free-enterprise system and democracy.

But get a load of this…Kristoff (as I call him) in addition to his full-time job has been applying the good ole PSIC formula, and with great success. Among other deals, he bought an old beat up building, fixed it up, financed it, and leased it to a bank and made a tidy sum of money doing it. And Kristoff is just beginning. He has several other real estate projects started and looking fantastic. In one of his current deals he is using a partner – a very wise move, as you'll see when you read Chapter 8.

See Chapter 8 entitled *THE QUICKEST WAY TO A BILLION – BEYOND SUPER LEVERAGE,* and note that Kristoff used many of the seven required steps to the real big money and net worth.

NOTES AND THOUGHTS

_____

_____

_____

_____

_____

_____

_____

_____

_____

_____

_____

_____

_____

_____

_____

_____

_____

_____

_____

_____

_____

_____

CHAPTER 2
ACTION ONE —
PLANNING YOUR FORTUNE

The line between planning and dreaming is fine but real. Planning is a dream with the addition of action.

Conrad Hilton, founder of probably the greatest hotel empire in the world, did a lot of dreaming in his younger years, but he didn't stop with a mere dream. He added that all-important extra ingredient — action.

In his autobiography, Mr. Hilton entitled his first chapter "You've Got to Dream," and states:

Why, when I saw my first photograph of the recently built "new" Waldorf in 1931, read of such luxuries as a private railroad siding in the basement, a private hospital for guests, a golden rivet in her innards where her construction had started, six kitchens, two hundred cooks, five hundred waiters, one hundred dishwashers, not to mention two thousand rooms, I was beating my way around Texas half hidden under a ten-gallon hat, existing on a voluntary loan from a bellboy. My laundry was in hock and a gun-toting constable was trying to find places to hang up the court judgments against me.

It was presumptuous, an outrageous time to dream. Still I cut out that picture of the Waldorf and wrote across it, "The Greatest of Them All." As soon as I had won back a desk of my own I slipped the dog-eared clipping under the glass top. From then on it was always in front of me.

Fifteen years later, in October, 1949, "The Greatest of Them All" became a Hilton Hotel.

It had taken a lot of work, four years of delicate negotiation and even before that, careful planning. It had taken a lot of prayer. During the final crucial days I had attended church at six-thirty each morning. No matter how late we worked into the night, I started the day on my knees. *(Be My Guest* [Englewood Cliffs, N.J.: Prentice-Hall, Inc., 1957], p.18.)

DREAM BIG!

Conrad Hilton started with only a dream — no money — just a big, big dream. But he did what most people are not willing to do. He added action, and turned his imagination into a plan. He gave the plan details, scheduled the details, and made alternate plans in case the first plan failed. Most importantly, he put his plan into action and made it come true.

In Chapter 11 of the same book, he asks, "How Big Can You Dream?" If you don't dream big, you certainly won't achieve much. It is against the basic laws that govern man. Unless you can visualize something, you cannot attain it.

Amazing as it sounds, the great majority of people in the United States don't spend even an hour a week, pencil or pen in hand, planning the strategy for their financial future. Someone once said, "Most people are so busy earning a living, they never make any money." And it's true! Most don't take the time to lift their heads from a mundane, routine life to do more than *dream* of financial security and independence.

They delude themselves into thinking they are happy, that their future is secure because they have a secure, salaried job.

That is not security. Their only security is two weeks' notice and, if they are lucky, some severance pay.

PERSISTENT PLANNING

Action one then in the PSIC formula has to be *persistent planning.* And it has to be done! There is no getting around it. So do it, and do it first.

Can you imagine the builders of the Waldorf Hotel beginning construction without a plan? That would be absurd. They would not only begin with a plan, but the plan would be in the greatest detail and would be written down, even to the last light switch and toilet seat. *IF* detailed plans were not made, the building would be a catastrophe beyond imagination. By the same token, doesn't your financial future deserve, even demand, the same kind of attention and detailed planning?

Of course, a person can't make all his plans in one night, or one week, or even in one month. He must begin where he is. Then he must add to his plans, refine them, and even change them from time to time.

Take the time right now to put your plans on paper. (The following two pages have been left blank for this purpose.)

First, list your goals, both short range and long range, but don't try to be too specific, at least not for now. State your goals in general terms at first. Then break them into more specific actions.

NOTE: See Chapter 9, entitled *SETTING GOALS AND THE ENERGY THEY CREATE,* on how and why goal setting energizes your life.

NOTES AND THOUGHTS

_____

_____

_____

_____

NOTES AND THOUGHTS

_____

_____

_____

_____

_____

_____

_____

_____

_____

_____

_____

_____

_____

_____

_____

_____

_____

_____

_____

_____

_____

_____

FIND YOUR NET WORTH

Now that you have your goals listed, take stock of your resources. List all your assets. List all your liabilities. Then subtract your liabilities from your assets, and you will have an idea of your total net worth.

Now that you know your net worth, use the compound tables in the appendix to start making some hypothetical projections. (See Appendix A.) You will be surprised, even astounded, at what compounding your net worth can do in a few years.

Check your net worth again. See what kind of liquid assets (cash or near cash, such as savings, bonds, etc.) you have and what assets could be quickly and easily turned into cash. Don't overlook what is probably your largest asset — the equity in your home.

PROJECT YOUR FINANCIAL FUTURE

Now, go back, and using the compound tables, make projections again. At this point you should use only the liquid assets you have as a base to begin your investments.

Once you have established a financial goal for yourself, you are on your way to achieving it. But you must not lose sight of that goal. Remember that where one person succeeds because of genius or brilliance, ten people succeed because of persistence. Persistence is a rare commodity today. However, that makes it fortunate for anyone who is persistent. His persistence will be noticed much more readily.

According to Edward Eggleston, "Persistent people begin their success where others end in failure." So first, put your financial goals in writing and look at them often. Next, be sure to be persistent in your pursuit of those goals.

Recalculate on paper the yearly compounding of your initial investment until it takes you to your goal. Do this as frequently as necessary to keep it fresh in your mind.

At least once a month I use a calculator to make all kinds of projections, using different compound rates and different periods of time. In addition, I make out a new balance sheet (assets minus liabilities equals net worth) every two months, in order to measure my progress. This review helps me see where I am making mistakes and gives me an early warning system against lagging behind in my projections. It also motivates me when I review my past successes and helps me dream bigger dreams.

Way back in April 1970, an article "Little Cash Needed on Road to Wealth" in the *Denver Post* quoted Marvin Naiman, then president of the Sherman Agency, "Average people, people able to raise $5,000 to $10,000 cash, have it within their power to become millionaires in real estate within twenty years." Naiman was counseling people with absolutely zero money who he was sure would be rich in a few years. In his view, "Imagination is the essential ingredient — imagination and a little bit of daydreaming."

This is even more true today. People without imagination allow themselves to feel stymied by talk of recession, high interest rates, and tight money. When, in fact, because so many are afraid to venture, opportunities are actually more plentiful.

My friend and mentor, Larry Rosenberg, said recently as we were filming the same thing he said to me more than twenty years ago. He said, "Mark, many times, if not most, it's a disadvantage to have a lot of money to start with. After all, it takes no imagination or creativity to start buying properties if you start with several million dollars. " Just take a look around you and you'll see all the mistakes that are made and all the fortunes lost by the second and third generation of wealth because they don't have to push themselves, they don't have to think creatively.

My other mentor friend, Paul J. Meyer, was talking about a friend of his who recently retired and is making

$15,000 to $20,000 a month from his investments in real estate. He's a millionaire many times over. Quoting from Paul's wonderful little book entitled *Being Smart with Money*, published by Paul J. Meyer Resources of Waco, Texas, "What is even more amazing is that he has never made more than $75,000 a year in his entire life! He never struck it rich , won the lottery, or inherited money from an uncle. **Instead, he is wealthy today because he was smart with his money.**" Paul goes on to tell about another friend who made $200,000 a year for many years but spent it all and as he approached retirement, he didn't own his car, his home, and he had no money in savings.

I hope the point is well made that starting with a bunch of money is not an advantage. Creative thinking combined with dreams is the answer.

Dreams put into action through planning are essential to the accumulation of wealth, regardless of changing economic factors.

ONASSIS

Probably my favorite biography is *Onassis,* the story of Aristotle Socrates Onassis, written by Willi Frischauer [New York: Meredith Press, 1968]. The author gives the reader insights into the dreams, desires, and motivations of Aristotle Onassis in his climb to financial success.

Aristotle Onassis was a dreamer, a planner, and probably more than anything, a very persistent person. Mr. Frischauer states:

> *More than anything else, Aristotle Onassis wanted to own and run ships; and from the dream and the idea it was only a short step to the intention and the plan. To persuade himself that his plan was sound, he went in for what he called "a little mental gymnastics."*

> *In his mind's eye he visualized a ship with a*
> *capacity of half a million cubic feet of grain, which*
> *might have cost one million dollars to build in 1919*
> *or 1920. [p. 56.]*

Keep in mind that this was before Onassis had even bought his first ship, but he could visualize it in his mind, had done some dreaming, and later set a definite plan of action to acquire such a ship.

At the age of seventeen, without a passport, Onassis arrived in Buenos Aires and lied about his age in order to get a job (for the British United River Plate Telephone Company at twenty-five cents an hour). In his spare time, Ari planned and thought about the feasibility of importing tobacco from Greece to Argentina. He envisioned a market there because Argentina was importing tobaccos primarily from Brazil and Cuba, with only a small percentage of Oriental brands.

PERSISTENCE AND PLANNING

After receiving tobacco samples from his father in Greece, he contacted each of the tobacco companies in Buenos Aires and was turned down by each in turn. The plans he set into motion after that failure were those that only one person in forty million would have tried. That very kind of planning and persistence made Aristotle Socrates Onassis what he was.

> *Choosing the firm that seemed to offer the best*
> *chance of a sale, he made it his business to track down*
> *the managing director, a Senior Juan Gaona, who*
> *became the young tobacco salesman's principal target.*
> *Early mornings he posted himself at the entrance of*
> *the Senior's office, standing there without saying a*
> *word, looking at Senior Gaona when he arrived and,*
> *incidentally, looking rather sorry for himself.*

On alternate days he transferred his lonely vigil to the important man's home, taking up his position at the door. Wherever the hapless Senior Gaona went, Aristotle Onassis was waiting for him, a sad and silent youngster. After a fortnight of this exercise, Senior Gaona would not have been human had he not begun to wonder what it was about. If it was a battle of perseverance between two unlikely protagonists, Aristotle Onassis emerged as the clear winner. His strange sales campaign was about to enter the third week when Senior Gaona could no longer restrain his curiosity and confronted his silent pursuer.

"Who are you?" he asked in a tone of mixed sympathy and exasperation. "What are you doing here? What do you want?"

"I am trying to sell tobacco," was the simple answer. Aristotle complained that he had not been given a fair chance; the tobacco he had to offer was of excellent quality. Senior Gaona was amused. "You ought to go to my purchasing department," he told Onassis.

This was all the unorthodox tobacco salesman wanted to hear. It was one thing to call on a buyer off his own bat but an entirely different matter to be in a position to say that he had been sent by the managing director, [p. 48.]

Onassis presented his wares the next morning and secured a $10,000 order, from which he made a commission of $500. This must have seemed a fortune to him, compared to the twenty-five cents an hour he was making at the telephone company.

A short time later he received an order that netted him $2,500 in commission. This was only the beginning in his rise to the top. He had understood and used the powerful ingredient of persistent planning.

In case you didn't know, by the end of Aristotle Onassis' career, he was better known (other than marrying Jacqueline Kennedy) in the business world for his multi-billion dollar fortune he had amassed starting with nothing, and he was arguably the largest ship owner in the world.

So, in summary it's not enough to merely have a dream – you must add overall planning to that dream. Get specific with your planning and boil your thoughts down to specific goals. Both long-term and short-term goals must be made. Then put time frames on those goals and add action items to drive yourself to the fulfillment of those goals. (Be sure to read more on goals in Chapter 9.)

Persistence must be added to the formula. Begin by figuring your net worth so you know what you have to work with. As an added benefit to figuring your net worth and doing frequent updates to that statement, you will find that it will motivate you as your net worth grows. (Studies have shown that by simply measuring almost anything we do, our performance improves.)

NOTES AND THOUGHTS

_____

_____

_____

_____

_____

_____

_____

_____

PLANS AND GOALS

_____

_____

_____

_____

_____

_____

_____

_____

_____

_____

_____

_____

_____

_____

_____

_____

_____

_____

_____

_____

_____

_____

_____

PLANS AND GOALS

_____

_____

_____

_____

_____

_____

_____

_____

_____

_____

_____

_____

_____

_____

_____

_____

_____

_____

_____

_____

_____

_____

CHAPTER 3
ACTION TWO —
SAVING THE MAGIC 10 PERCENT

To belong to that exclusive group of millionaires — the one out of a thousand — you must begin by following the 10 percent rule. Any increase in the 10 percent rule speeds you on the way to making your fortune.

William Nickerson* in his book *How I Turned $1,000 into Five Million in Real Estate—in My Spare Time* [New York: Simon and Schuster, 1969] states, "Starting with average funds can speed the way to financial success. The hardest task on the road to a million dollars is saving a nest egg." (p. 23.) As soon as the typical American has a small amount of money saved, he is tempted to spend it on depreciating assets such as a car, a camper, boat, trailer, or an exotic vacation.

Most people spend their entire lives saving up just enough money to buy something to keep up with their neighbors. They never have enough left over to make any meaningful investments. You know that old saying, **"Everyone has two choices: Play now and Pay later – or – Pay now and Play later."** And believe me, if you choose to

---

* *William Nickerson passed away in the year 2000 after having made a huge contribution to the world through his books, his investments, his donations, and his very charming speeches and presentations. I am honored to have been able to call him my friend and am so very grateful that he agreed to speak at our conventions many times – what a delightful person. I place huge personal value on the interview and discussion between Bill and myself that the late Dick Hamilton, acting as moderator, taped in Bill Nickerson's home in Aptos, California many years ago.*

Pay now and Play later, the level of your play will be at infinitely higher levels with not a money worry in the world. And to those of us who thought we would not enjoy playing nearly as much when we got old, I say – WOW, were we ever wrong! I absolutely love to play and I play all the time now.

PAY YOURSELF FIRST

The 10 percent rule is a simple one, but a difficult one for some to follow. You must save a minimum of 10 percent of your gross earnings. The second part of the rule is that you never, never, never, never spend that savings. Your savings is your capital, and your capital must never be disturbed. Let me repeat, NEVER spend your savings! Now, spending is different than investing.

Many claim they cannot save money. They say it is impossible on their income and constantly rising expenses, that when the end of the month rolls around there is nothing left. The solution is simple: Pay yourself first. If you do this, faithfully, religiously, and without ever missing a single paycheck, you will find that this 10 percent of every dollar you earn will (with careful and astute investing) mushroom into a sum that will far exceed your total lifetime earnings.

The Bible talks about the importance of the 10 percent rule in a different way. Early Christians were encouraged and even commanded to pay one-tenth of their annual increase to the Church. In modern times, The Church of Jesus Christ of Latter-day Saints (the Mormons) uses this ancient biblical doctrine of the tithe.

The amazing thing about the Mormons and tithing is that, notwithstanding the large donations made by many of the Mormons, it is estimated that there are more than three thousand millionaires in that small church. From first-hand observation, many of the Mormon Church members enjoy a pretty good standard of living and all of this after they have given 10 percent of their gross earnings to their church. No wonder the Mormon church is one of the wealthiest churches in the world (on a per capita basis) I am not saying it's bad to give to charity, but you should at least know how much you are really giving——and in the case of you saving that sacred 10 percent, you must understand what you are really giving to yourself!

MORMONS CAN! CAN YOU?

The Mormons claim that by giving 10 percent to their church they are better able to plan ahead and use wisely the balance of their money. Even poor widows and retired people on dwindling incomes caused by inflation seem to be able to make this contribution without crimping their life style. This contradicts the belief that expenses always rise to meet the income.

Mormons stress that payment of tithing should be done first, before bills and expenses. Likewise, as stated before, in your financial program you should always PAY YOURSELF FIRST.

In the Summer of 2004 the subject of paying yourself first came up as I was talking to a bright young physical therapist who happened to be a Mormon. As Rick Lybbert was pushing and pulling on my legs, bringing tears to my eyes, I shocked him by telling him how much he was really giving to his church. (He was working on me after I had a bilateral hip resurfacing operation – that simply means I had two new hips installed.)

As I started telling Rick about the mind bending power of saving ten percent and then letting it compound, he was aghast at the compounding amount he, as a tithe paying Mormon, was giving to the Church over his lifetime.

As I went through the numbers with Rick he said, "I don't think I want to hear this." I explained to Rick that if he only made thirty thousand dollars a year starting at age twenty-five, and paid ten percent of that to the Church, that donation, by the time he turned seventy-five, would be worth over six million dollars – and that's assuming he invested his money at only a fifteen percent rate of return. Plus, that's assuming he stopped making those ten percent donations when he turned thirty – or just five years after he started.

But wait! Stop and think this concept through completely. If that six million dollar return is yours and your family's, I think Rick – and you and I – really do want to hear this.

But again, let me say, because it's worth saying twice, that I am not against charitable and religious giving. All I am saying is that you need to be aware of how much you are really giving. Believe me, institutions on the receiving end of your donations understand what is being given. And, of course, institutions don't usually die so they can go on compounding for a hundred, two hundred, or five hundred years. As a giver to good causes, we all know the great feeling of satisfaction we get from giving and the good it can do for others. And, of course, that is a very good thing. But always be aware of how much you are really giving and give yourself at least that same amount, if not more – and be sure to give it to yourself first.

If you still don't think you can achieve the 10 percent savings goal, try this line of reasoning: What if you worked for a troubled corporation that was going downhill financially, at least temporarily, in an industry that was faced with a recession? Your boss tells you that he has been ordered to cut your department by 10 percent. Rather than firing 10 percent of the employees, he is giving you all the choice of taking a 10 percent pay cut until the corporation gets on its feet again. What will your choice be? Remember that there is a recession in progress and unemployment is soaring. You know that it would be difficult to find another job.

It is a good bet that you would conclude that you could somehow get by on 10 percent less income. No, it won't be easy, but with a little effort it can be done. It means cutting out things you don't really have to have. (By the way, this became cold reality for some 7,000 Delta airline pilots who voted on taking a 32 percent salary cut, which was necessary in order for the airline to survive. That took the average captain's salary from $286,800 per year down to $194,000 per year – a $92,000 pay cut.)

ADD TO THE 10 PERCENT

Once you have control of your income and are saving 10 percent, the next time you get any kind of an increase either through a salary raise or through a decrease in deductions, put all the extra you receive into your savings program. This will speed up the achievement of the million-dollar goal.

If you look back at the compounding of a penny in Chapter 1, you will see that in the early stages of compounding with such a low sum the total accumulation of money is very small. If you were to take out even a small amount in those first few steps (for example, take out twenty-five cents on the sixth day), the results are devastating. However, if you take out large amounts in the last few steps, you could spend literally millions a year without even denting your total assets. (What would be the effect if from the thirty-third day on, you spent $5,000,000 each day?) Likewise, if you add money in the beginning stages, that addition has a tremendous effect, especially toward the end. Just for fun, try starting with $10,000 versus one penny on a thirty-five-step basis.

RETIREMENT: TRAGEDY
OR CAPITAL INVESTMENTS

The importance of saving to get started on your way to a million should be the most glaringly simple deduction to anyone who has commonsense and reasoning power. But obviously it is not that apparent to most men and women.

I believe it was Earl Nightingale who quoted some tragic statistics regarding a hundred average people at the age of retirement. In this sample, pre-suppose that all had started work at the age of twenty-five; all received encouragement from parents, teachers, and friends; and all shared the dream of success and wealth. After forty years of hard work, only one of the hundred would be rich, truly rich; four would be financially independent; five would still be working; thirty-six would be dead; and fifty-four would be broke. This is a sad situation in a country with so much opportunity and so much wealth.

The reason for these tragic statistics is that people don't save, they don't begin at the beginning. They don't even acquire what is known as *capital*. Virtually every wealthy individual has begun his fortune by first saving until he had enough capital to begin investing.

JOHN D.

The granddaddy of super wealth, John Davidson Rockefeller, born in Richford, New York, 8 July 1839, realized and utilized this principle.

At sixteen years of age, John D., with probably America's most determined ambition to build up a large and useful business — and therefore successful — set out for a job. The firm of Hewitt and Tuttle hired him for $50 for services from September 26 to December 31 inclusive — about $3.74 a week. The firm handled grain, produce, coal — in fact, every commodity that passed through Cleveland going east or west.

It shipped by rail, canal and lake and offered an ideal training ground for the young man. He studied every phase of the business. He checked in every detail every bill before it was paid. Argued with dealers for better prices. Knew just exactly where the business stood every night.

And Hewitt and Tuttle knew they had a find in young Rockefeller. Nothing distracted him from the affairs of the business. No boisterous fun for him. No cigarettes; no cards; no pool; no girls. Just plenty of work and plenty of Sunday School. His soft voice, and his quiet clothes and his devotion to the Baptist Church early earned for him the nickname of Deacon.

He stayed on this first job two and a half years at a meager salary although he had been rapidly advanced in responsibility. He finally asked for a salary of $800 a year. The employers held out with an offer of $700. During this deadlock, a chance came to John D. to join in a partnership and he was lost from the firm of Hewitt and Tuttle.

This partnership was formed before John D. was nineteen, with a young Englishman named Clark who had $2,000 to put into a commission business and who wanted two partners with equal capital. Even on a low income, the youthful Rockefeller had managed to put aside $1,000. He was to receive another $1,000 from his father when he turned twenty-one. He asked his strict parent if he might not have his $1,000 then so that he might not lose his opportunity. The father consented but only on the condition that he pay him 10 percent interest per year until he was twenty-one.

Rockefeller is not an isolated incident. There is example after example of people on meager salaries saving faithfully and religiously until they have a nest egg large enough to make that initial investment. Each one realized, as everyone must who is going to make substantial sums, that capital must work for you as hard or harder than you work, in order to reach the million-dollar goal. Cornelius Vanderbilt is one of many who had saved $1,000 by the time he was eighteen years old and $9,000 by the time he was twenty-three. Those savings came from meager amounts of income.

Whether your income is $20,000 or $200,000 a year, it is still possible to apply the 10 percent rule and become part of a distinguished group, the one out of a thousand who reaches the million-dollar mark.

Remember that for every $10,000 you can save, given eighteen years and 30 percent annual compound rate of return (which is not difficult to achieve if you are involved with a "hands on" types of investments that I've been talking about), you will have $1,124,000.00.

NOTES AND THOUGHTS

_____

_____

_____

_____

_____

_____

_____

_____

_____

_____

_____

_____

_____

PLANS AND GOALS

_____

_____

_____

_____

_____

_____

_____

_____

_____

_____

_____

_____

_____

_____

_____

_____

_____

_____

_____

_____

_____

_____

_____

PLANS AND GOALS

_____

_____

_____

_____

_____

_____

_____

_____

_____

_____

_____

_____

_____

_____

_____

_____

_____

_____

_____

_____

_____

_____

_____

CHAPTER 4
ACTION THREE — HIGH RATES OF RETURN THAT MAKE YOU RICH

A famous and wealthy man said, "Ninety percent of all millionaires become so through owning real estate. More money has been made in real estate than in all industrial investments combined. The wise young man or wage earner of today invests his money in real estate." That statement is truer today than it was when Andrew Carnegie made it.

There is a multitude of different types and sizes of investments. And there are even more people representing these investments, vying for our investment dollar. But of the hundreds of available investments I know of none that offers as many basic advantages as real estate. These advantages put the odds overwhelmingly in your favor for succeeding in the pursuit of wealth. The four basic advantages of real estate, which we talk about in detail later, are:

(1) Cash flow that is usually higher than in other investments.
(2) Equity buildup that can dramatically increase the overall return.
(3) Inflation, both natural and forced.
(4) A tax shelter that very few other investments offer.

THE ODDS ARE HEAVILY IN YOUR FAVOR

William Nickerson thought real estate is the best investment because it is so easy to use other people's money. As he puts it:

> Most forms of investment pay only the paltry leavings after others deduct their expenses and fair compensation for using your money. You lend your savings to banks, and insurance companies, and they capitalize on your money for their profit.
>
> Investment in business and income property puts you on the real money-making side of the capital fence and pays you for courage and imagination. You profit not only from your own savings but also from the savings of the timid, the uninformed, and the satiated who already possess all the money they want.
>
> Every venture presents an element of risk, but with rent-producing income property you take negligible risks and your chances for success are 1,600 times better, for example, than your chances if you start in business. With each, however, you follow the freeway that leads to wealth by harnessing the secret force of capitalism — which is the pyramiding power of borrowed money. Regardless of how wisely you invest, you can't go far on your own money. Your greatest expansion is assured by making maximum use of the other fellow's money.
>
> The road to riches is paved with borrowed money. Big-time real estate operators buy properties worth millions without putting in a penny of their own. Multi-million-dollar deals are made by borrowing the utmost from mortgages and the balance on personal and collateral notes. (*How I Turned $1,000 into Five Million in Real Estate—in My Spare Time*, p. 13.)

Nickerson got his figures — the odds of 1,600 to one — from the Department of Commerce which states that four out of five new businesses fail within eight years. Additionally, 50 percent go out of business within two years. The overall odds are four to one that a new business will not make it. He contrasts those four-to-one odds against real estate investments, where only one out of four hundred properties is foreclosed, establishing the odds of four hundred to one in favor of you succeeding. By combining these two sets of statistics, he came up with 1,600 to one odds for success in income property. In addition to the four basic advantages of real estate, two others reduce the risk of loss. First, housing is a basic necessity. Most investments, such as stocks, bonds, motels, hotels, resorts and miscellaneous businesses, do not have this advantage. Those investments normally are made when basic necessities have already been taken care of. Virtually every person in this country wants to upgrade his housing by moving into something nicer, thus creating a constant demand and a demand that only moves upward.

This demand is increased by the birth rate and by new families formed through marriage. In some areas there is the added benefit of the movement of people from one state to another. The Western states and the Sun Belt in the last fifteen to twenty years have benefited most by such migration. Current statistics show this pattern continuing with these states having the greatest percentage increases.

With this advantage it is difficult to fail by ownership of income properties. Even without the advantage of migration of people into your state or community the odds of success are heavily in your favor.

The second big advantage is the control one has with income properties. With stocks, you not only do not control the market and the fluctuation of the market, you do not even control the corporation in which you have invested. If the president of the corporation makes an unwise decision, you have no recourse (assuming you do not have controlling interest). In the ownership of income-producing properties, you do not have absolute control over the market; however, through the management of your property over which you have 100 percent control, you can influence the market and better your position if necessary.

Your primary concern in projecting the growth of your net worth should be the return on equity (the return you get from investing whatever dollars you have). Specifically, all you care about is the overall return you receive when you add up the four advantages of real estate: (1) cash flow, (2) equity buildup, (3) inflation, and (4) tax shelter or tax advantages.

CASH FLOW - TO REINVEST, NOT SPEND

First of all, *cash flow* in real estate investing can be very high and has consistently been higher than other types of investments. Cash flow can make a tremendous difference in the rate of growth in acquiring a fortune.

It is simple to calculate the cash flow figure. You need only two answers: (1) How much out-of-pocket money did you put into the investment? (2) How much money did you get out of the deal (put in your pocket) in one year? If you put in $5,000 cash and took out $1,000 in one year, your cash flow was 20 percent ($1,000 \div 5,000 = 20$ percent). Cash flow is the first thing you should look for in evaluating a real estate investment. Remember, if you get an extremely high cash flow, you can take that cash and reinvest it in another similar investment. This gives the compounding effect to your money and can work miracles in a short period of time.

In older real estate, cash flow should be at an absolute minimum of 10 percent, after all contingencies, vacancies, and other costs, both expected and unexpected. Whereas 10 percent is the minimum, many times a much higher rate of return on a cash flow basis can be achieved. I have had real estate investments where the cash flow exceeded 100 percent; in two cases the cash flow actually exceeded 200 percent per year. With a little calculating, you see how quickly you can rise in the early years if you find this type of investment. It is important to look for the proper investment vehicle. Your hours of searching for the super bargains in real estate will be amply rewarded. I have never known anyone who put in the hours looking for bargains that didn't find at least a few good deals.

EQUITY BUILDUP —
ADDS TO YOUR WEALTH MONTHLY

The second advantage to real estate investments is the *equity buildup* or the amount of principal payment made to reduce the mortgage loan. This payment, of course, is made from the gross income (rental income from tenants of your buildings). When the equity buildup is calculated as a rate of return on the initial equity you put into an investment, the return can vary widely depending on the length of time of the mortgage, the interest rate, and the amount of the beginning equity (down payment). If you paid all cash for a $90,000 property and financed it at a 6_ percent rate, your return on that investment in the first year from equity build up would be $2,268 or 2.52 percent – on the 10th year, because of the maturity of the loan, your equity return for mortgage pay down would be $4,066 or 4.52 percent.

But wait, look what happens to those numbers if you buy the property with a lot of leverage. Let's say a 10 to 1 ratio, and again, if the numbers are too small for your thinking, just add a zero to each figure. Let's assume you bought a $100,000 property with $10,000 down and the $90,000 borrowed at 6-1/2 percent for 20 years. Now watch the numbers jump.

The first year equity build up through mortgage pay down would be the same $2,268 – but your return on your cash down (your equity) would be 22.68 percent because of the leverage, and a whopping 40.66 percent return on the 10th year alone.

And that's before we take into account the next two factors of inflation and the tax advantage.

INFLATION — THE KEY THAT WILL DOUBLE YOUR NET WORTH YEARLY

Inflation or appreciation is the third ingredient that adds to the overall return of investments in real estate even when inflation is seemingly a very low two or three percent. There are several causes of inflation. Without trying to debate who and what causes inflation, there is no question that continued deficit spending by our government is a prime factor. But whatever the causes, there can be benefits to inflation if the investor realizes proper and wise use of leverage. Let me illustrate with a simplified example. Say you bought a $100,000 piece of income-producing property. Assume you paid $10,000 down, with the $90,000 balance owing to either the seller or through a mortgage to a bank, and possibly a second mortgage. You would begin making monthly payments on the mortgages. These would be made from the rents you collect each month.

Even if you didn't have any cash left over at the end of each month (cash flow), what would be your situation, assuming that this particular piece of real estate inflated for whatever reason by 10 percent in one year? First of all, what would be the worth of that building at the end of the year? With simple mathematics, it is obvious the building would be worth $110,000. By subtracting the $90,000 mortgage or slightly less because of payments toward the principal (equity buildup), the balance would equal your new net equity in the building. What has this 10 percent inflation done to your return (assuming you were to sell the building)? The magic of leverage can be seen in this simple example. Even though the building only grew in worth by 10 percent, your return was an astounding 100 percent. (See Chapters 6, 7, and 8 for detailed explanations and examples of leverage.)

It is not likely that real estate by itself will appreciate or inflate at a 10 percent rate per year. Depending on the area of the country and locations within particular towns, the rate of so-called natural inflation has been anywhere from 1.5 percent to 4.5 percent per year.

There is another kind of inflation, however, that really should not be called inflation, but that's what I call it. What I call *forced inflation* could probably more properly be called *appreciation through improvements.* Forced inflation can be used over and over again in virtually every city and also in concert with natural inflation. What forced inflation does is simple: it creates higher worth of a particular real estate investment (income property), brought about by improvements to that property. Using the former example of a $100,000 building that improved in value by 10 percent in one year, if this building were to actually inflate in value only 2 percent in a given year and your program called for an increase in net equities of 100 percent, you would have to do something to bring about an increase. And you could! That would be to bring about forced inflation or improvements to the property to increase the worth of the investments to the desired level. (See Chapter 16 on improvement to sell or manage to keep.)

Even if one plans on only the natural inflation and assuming that inflation is a 2 percent factor on the $100,000 property, this is still a 20 percent rate of return on the original $10,000 investment (2 percent on $100,000 equals $2,000 annually; this $2,000 would be a 20 percent return on the original $10,000 down payment). The extra rate of return derived from inflation when added to cash flow and equity buildup makes our real estate investment an unusual and attractive way to invest money. Of course, if we stop after one or two investments in real estate, we don't get the compounding effect. (See Chapter 5 on compounding or reinvesting our return.)

TAX SHELTER: SHORT CUT TO WEALTH

The fourth fact that makes real estate investments so attractive and adds immensely to the overall return is *tax shelter* or tax advantage. Let me ask a simple question: How long would it take a person to make a million starting with $10,000 and investing the money at a consistent 25 percent compounded rate of return? I will even help you out by providing a chart at the end of this chapter. By using the chart, the obvious answer would be twenty-one years. Right? Wrong! Why? Because of that government agency we are all familiar with — the IRS. Yes, Uncle Sam takes a big part, an ever-growing part of our income.

To answer the above question we must know two additional facts: What income tax bracket is the person in and what type of investments is he making? Let's make two assumptions: This person is in a 50 percent tax bracket* (this also assumes these investments are not held long enough to

---

* *One of the greatest tax inventions given to us was the IRS designation of the 1031 Exchange rule which allows a real estate investor to pay zero tax on the sale of a property as long as that investor follows the 1031 Exchange rules very strictly and invests the proceeds from the sale into another "like kind property" within the prescribed time limits. That is you must put the proceeds from the sale of a property into what is commonly called an exchange company (the actual name the IRS uses for this type of company is Qualified Accommodator). The proceeds are deposited into the exchange company directly from the closing of the sale of your property. The proceeds can never be in your control. You must then identify up to three other properties that you may buy using the proceeds from the sale of the first property. You have 45 days to identify the three properties and notify the exchange company in writing of those properties. Then you have another 135 days to close on one or more of the three properties you identified using the proceeds being held by the exchange company. The bottom line is that you don't have to pay any capital gains tax – you simply defer it. You can defer subsequent capital gains should you sell the new property by following the same 1031 Exchange rules into another new property. In fact, you can do this over and over through the end of your life, and even beyond that if you do some smart tax and estate planning. So, in theory, you will never have to pay tax on those properties if you do it right.*

be long term capital gains and the 50 percent rate is the State tax rate added on top of the maximum federal tax rate) and is making general types of investments in stocks and bonds and various small businesses. OK. And now the question again: How long would it take this person to make $1 million with $10,000 compounding at 25 percent? If you want to take the time to figure it, the simple way is just to compound $10,000 at an annual rate of 12.5 percent. The answer could be stated this way: If the person were thirty years of age when he began this program, made the investments we mentioned and paid average taxes, he would be seventy years old by the time he reached the million-dollar mark. It would have taken him forty years.

Now, compare the man who made real estate investments, paid no tax because of the preferential treatment he can take advantage of, and he reaches the goal by age fifty-one, or in twenty-one years. Through the wise use of current tax laws, one person was able to enjoy his fortune nineteen years longer than the one who did not take advantage of the same tax laws.

This fourth advantage of real estate investing adds anywhere from 2 percent to 3 percent advantage on the low side on the overall return on equity up to 40 percent or 50 percent on the high side, all dependent on the person's tax bracket and the particular real estate investment.

In addition to the advantages mentioned, income property investments can shelter income from other sources such as salary, commissions, fees, other capital gains.

When the four basic types of return in a real estate investment are tabulated, the total potential seems almost unbelievable and unachievable. Whereas it is difficult to find real estate investments that have the high side of the range in all four categories (225 percent), it is not impossible and can be done regularly if enough effort is put into the task. Below is a tabulation of the four ingredients to real estate investment:

Type of Return	Annual Percentage Rate of Return on Beginning Equity
Cash Flow	5% to 25%
Equity Buildup	3% to 45%
Inflation (mostly forced)	10% to 105%
Tax Advantage	2% to 50%
	20% to 225%

To many people, the range of 20 percent on the low to 225 percent on the high side seems too optimistic for the total return on equity. Believe me, these are not pie-in-the-sky figures. These are down-to-earth figures and are achievable on a consistent basis. Where you end up on that scale is up to you and depends on how much effort you put into locating the right investment, bargaining for the price and terms, buying the property, making necessary changes, and disposing of the property in a way that is advantageous from a tax standpoint.

Some might question whether it is worth the effort to try to reach the higher end of the scale — 225 percent. If that is your attitude, I suggest you sit down with a calculator and find the results on any size investment with a 225 percent compound rate of return. I think you will find enough motivation from your calculations to answer whether it is worth the effort to you.

In my program I have not yet reached the high end of the scale. I have come close with an overall return of a little better than 160 percent. On individual investments I have reached the 225 percent mark. I know others who have hit the high mark consistently, so I know it can be done. If you are the ambitious and persistent type, you might well be one who can do it. Even if you only muster out at a 20 percent or 30 percent return and stick with it, your million-dollar daydream will become a reality.

And those returns can be pumped even higher for you if you bring in partners. (For more information on the wise use of partners, read *BEYOND SUPER LEVERAGE* in Chapter 8.)

ACCIDENTAL FORTUNE

When it comes to investments, some research shows that most people make more money by accident in real estate than they do on purpose in almost any other type of investment.

Over the years I have observed that this is especially true when it comes to real estate vs. stocks.

And there is a simple reason for real estate working out very well for most people vs. stock investments.

The answer lies in the nature of all of us humans – we all think pretty much alike when it comes to risk and reward – and fear and greed.

HUMAN NATURE AND THE STOCK MARKET

For example, let's say a person buys $10,000 worth of stock and it goes up in value to $20,000 or $30,000 – what would most people do? What would you do? Most people would sell it thinking that they don't want to see it fall back to where they bought it. (Yes, some people might hold it until it was worth maybe $40,000 or $50,000 before selling – but in any case, the higher it rises the more pressure the typical human mind feels to sell).

But the point is that most humans reason in their mind that they've got to sell it and lock in their profit. But many times those stocks are the very ones that turn out to be the Microsoft companies of the world – and ten or fifteen years later, that $10,000 investment is worth a half million or even a million dollars. But of course, they didn't profit from the rise because they sold their stock.

I think it would be pretty safe to say that there are very, very few people who bought Microsoft on the initial public offering who held it through the years to its very pinnacle or even close.

And guess what? When most people buy stock and it goes down in value, once again they usually do the exact opposite of what they should do. They hold on to it! Not only because of ego and not wanting to admit they were wrong, but because they hope that if they hold on to it long enough it will go back up to where they can at least break even. (I guess people think "what goes down, must go up" – Hmmm, go figure that one.).

In both cases it's a big mistake – a huge mistake!

By selling stock that goes up too early, and holding on to the ones that go down, eventually and inevitably you will end up with a portfolio full of "losers".

But why don't people make the same mistake with real estate?

REAL ESTATE FITS YOUR MINDSET

Overall, it's because of the nature of real estate – especially developed real estate with income flowing from it, or real estate as a place to live, which fits in or blends in with the emotional and mental makeup of a typical human being.

What do I mean by that? Here's what:

First, we like and can identify with what we can drive by, see, touch, admire, maybe live in, fix up, take pictures of, collect rent from, and show to our family and friends.

Second, we don't easily know on a day-to-day, or week-to-week, or even a month-to-month basis exactly what that real estate is worth, so we don't have a thought or an urge to sell it.

Third, even if we think it's worth more, it takes a lot of effort to sell it. We must advertise it and/or list it. Get it ready to be shown. Show it – usually many times. And go through lots of other hassles.

Bottom line – since we don't easily know the short term market fluctuations, and it's cumbersome and time consuming to sell real estate, we tend to hold on to it for a very long time – and that usually turns out to be a good thing.

Consequently, more people make more money in real estate by accident than they do on purpose in most other investments.

FROM OLYMPIC GOLD MEDAL
TO GOLDEN REWARDS

Now here's a true-life, incredible story of a super real estate success caused by the factors I've just mentioned above:

Recently, I was talking to my very dear friends, Stein and Francoise Eriksen, about my new book on real estate that was ninety-nine percent finished and just a few weeks from going to press.

Now, Stein and Francoise and both super successful, fun, and dynamic people. But their success stems   from Stein's Olympic Gold Medal and World Cup Skiing   Title years ago (he was the first superstar of skiing). As well as from Francoise' fiery Frenchwoman's drive and personality that has created some great successes in the retail world of ski apparel.

These two people, along with a great third partner – their very bright and energetic son, Bjorn – make a terrific trio!

But what I didn't know until my recent conversation was what a **HUGE** contribution to their overall financial success came from a little real estate investment made many years ago – and made almost by accident.

First, I'll give you the monthly bottom line – (which I think will make you want to read on) – That bottom line is $50,000 that comes in automatically each and every month. That's a pretty nice bottom line – and that's pretty nice passive income that started somewhat by accident.

It started in Aspen, Colorado where Stein had a ski shop and was paying $2,000 a month in rent. Out of the blue, a friend who owned one-half interest in a building on the main street of Aspen called Stein and asked him if he wanted to buy his one-half interest. It seems that Stein's friend wanted to do some major traveling through Europe and other parts of the world.

Stein told him that he would love to buy the building but he couldn't afford it. Not to be deterred, his friend said, "Wait a minute…how much in rent are you paying each month now?" "What if you could move your shop into my building and pay me the same on the purchase of my building rather than throwing money away on rent.?"

That sounded pretty good to Stein, but what about the down payment? Where would that come from?

A $25,000 down payment was worked out and Stein had to scramble hard to put that much money together, but finally managed to do it.

And now, many years later, through the up, down, and sideways markets, Stein still owns the property and gladly collects his hassle-free $50,000 net income per month from his free and clear building. (He did buy the other half interest in the building three years later for the same price that he paid for the first half.)

But here's the $50,000 question. If that had been $25,000 worth of Microsoft stock (plus a $2,000 per month payment), do you think Stein, or you, or I might have been tempted to sell our position along the way – maybe when it doubled or tripled, or quintupled in valued? Especially if we could have made that sale by simply picking up the phone and calling a broker, or hitting a few keys on our computer to make the sale?

I'm not sure about Stein's answer, or yours – but I think I would have sold way too soon! And to think, some people have called me a "Financial Genius".

No, I'm just an ordinary semi-idiot, but I chose an extraordinary vehicle called improved real estate that makes me look like a "Financial Genius" as it makes my bank account bulge.

EXAMPLE OF COMPOUNDING
($10,000 at 25 percent for 21 years)

Years	
0	$ 10,000
1	12,500
2	15,600
3	19,531
4	24,414
5	30,500
6	38,125
7	47,656
8	59,500
9	74,375
10	92,969
11	116,125
12	145,156
13	181,445
14	226,250
15	282,812
16	353,515
17	441,259
18	551,562
19	689,453
20	861,250
21	$1,076,562

NOTE: Several of the above figures have been rounded off for ease in figuring.

NOTES AND THOUGHTS

PLANS AND GOALS

_____

_____

_____

_____

_____

_____

_____

_____

_____

_____

_____

_____

_____

_____

_____

_____

_____

_____

_____

_____

_____

CHAPTER 5
ACTION FOUR —
REINVEST TO COMPOUND

The story is told about a visitor to an older New England town of great affluence. The town was conservative, with most of its residents middle-aged, retired gentlemen and their wives. While walking one day with one of the town's well-known residents, the visitor noticed a stately old gentleman walking down the street. As he walked, it seemed that everyone went out of the way to avoid him, even if it meant going to the other side of the street. Puzzled, the visitor asked his host who this seemingly undesirable man was and why the people were avoiding him. Whereupon the host stopped abruptly, looked in all directions to make sure he couldn't be heard, leaned over and whispered in the visitor's ear, "HE DIPPED INTO HIS CAPITAL."

Obviously, these people, men of great means, fully understood the seriousness and potentially dire consequences of spending one's capital. A cardinal rule with wealthy families of the past was, "Never, never, never touch your capital." A rule that you must incorporate and follow to the letter if you expect to attain your million-dollar goal is; never, never, never spend or touch your return on investments in the beginning years of your investment program. And, of course, you must follow the rule of never touching your capital.

Take a minute and turn back to Chapter 1. Look at the example of one penny compounded at 100 percent. Note what a devastating effect could come from touching the capital or return on that capital in the first few days. For example, see what happens to the end result if twelve cents is spent on the fifth day or $5.10 is taken out on the tenth day. How many days would you lose? How much money would you lose in the overall investment plan? If we change the days to years, then how much time or money are we losing by dipping into our capital in the fifth or tenth year? How does this affect the total in later years?

If you took the time to figure it out, you saw that the results were disastrous in the early years. On the other hand, would it shake your fortune very much to take out a million dollars after thirty-two, thirty-three, or thirty-four years? Would it result in much of a change in your overall net worth? As you can plainly see, the effect would not be worth mentioning. Isn't this the obvious reason that the rich and the super rich can afford to be so generous with their wealth, and it never seems to flicker their financial light? (Of course, there are also tax advantages to making these large donations.)

Early in my investment program, I began saving at least 10 percent of my income, then investing that 10 percent, and reinvesting the income from the investment. It wasn't until much later that my secretary told me about an interesting book that expounded the virtues and the necessity of using these principles to accumulate great wealth. The book was written by George S. Clason (*The Richest Man in Babylon* [New York: Hawthorn Books, Inc., 1955]). In this delightful book a man by the name of Arkad who is not only very wealthy but known for his generosity to charities, family, and friends, is asked by his friends how he became the richest man in all of Babylon while they were still struggling for their very existence. They were puzzled because Arkad had been one of their playmates and they had all attended the same school. They pointed out to Arkad that in neither athletics nor studies did he outshine them. Why had he become so wealthy and they hadn't? Here is Arkad's answer to his contemporaries:

"Being, as you know, the son of a humble merchant, one of a large family, with no hope of an inheritance, and not being endowed, as you have so frankly said, with superior powers or wisdom, I decided that if I was to achieve what I desired, time and study would be required.

"As for time, all men have it in abundance. You, each of you, have let slip by sufficient time to have made yourselves wealthy. Yet, you admit, you have nothing to show except your good families, of which you can be justly proud.

"As for study, did not our wise teacher teach us that learning was of two kinds: the one kind being the things we learned and knew, and the other being in the training that taught us how to find out what we did not know?

"Therefore did I decide to find out how one might accumulate wealth, and when I had found out, to make this my task and do it well. For, is it not wise that we should enjoy while we dwell in the brightness of that sunshine, for sorrows enough shall descend upon us when we depart for the darkness of the world of spirit?

"I found employment as a scribe in the hall of records, and long hours each day I labored upon the clay tablets. Week after week, and month after month, I labored, yet for my earnings I had naught to show. Food and clothing and penance to the gods, and other things of which I could remember not what, absorbed all my earnings. But my determination did not leave me.

"And one day Algamish, the money lender, came to the house of the city master and ordered a copy of the Ninth Law, and he said to me, 'I must have this in two days, and if the task is done by that time, two coppers will I give to thee.'

"So I labored hard, but the law was long, and when Algamish returned the task was unfinished. He was angry, and had I been his slave, he would have beaten me. But knowing the city master would not permit him to injure me, I was unafraid, so I said to him, 'Algamish, you are a very rich man. Tell me how I may also become rich, and all night I will carve upon the clay, and when the sun rises it shall be completed.'

"He smiled at me and replied, 'You are a forward knave, but we will call it a bargain.'

"All that night I carved, though my back pained and the smell of the wick made my head ache until my eyes could hardly see. But when he returned at sunup, the tablets were complete.

" 'Now,' I said, 'tell me what you promised.'

" 'You have fulfilled your part of our bargain, my son,' he said to me kindly, 'and I am ready to fulfill mine. I will tell you these things you wish to know because I am becoming an old man, and an old tongue loves to wag. And when youth comes to age for advice he receives the wisdom of years. But too often does youth think that age knows only the wisdom of days that are gone, and therefore profits not. But remember this, the sun that shines today is the sun that shone when thy father was born, and will still be shining when thy last grandchild shall pass into the darkness.

" 'The thoughts of youth,' he continued, 'are bright lights that shine forth like the meteors that oft make brilliant the sky, but the wisdom of age is like the fixed stars that shine so unchanged that the sailor may depend upon them to steer his course.

" 'Mark you well my words, for if you do not you will fail to grasp the truth that I will tell you, and you will think that your night's work has been in vain.'

"Then he looked at me shrewdly from under his shaggy brows and said in a low, forceful tone, 'I found the road to wealth when I decided that *a part of all I earned was mine to keep*. And so will you.'

"Then he continued to look at me with a glance that I could feel pierce me but said no more.

" 'Is that all?' I asked.

" 'That was sufficient to change the heart of a sheep herder into the heart of a money lender,' he replied.

" 'But *all* I earn is mine to keep, is it not?' I demanded.

"Far from it,' he replied. 'Do you not pay the garment-maker? Do you not pay the sandal-maker? Do you not pay for the things you eat? Can you live in Babylon without spending? What have you to show for your earnings of the past month? What for the past year? Fool! You pay to everyone but yourself. Dullard, you labor for others. As well be a slave and work for what your master gives you to eat and wear. If you did keep for yourself one-tenth of all you earn, how much would you have in ten years?'

"My knowledge of the numbers did not forsake me and I answered, 'As much as I earn in one year.'

" 'You speak but half the truth,' he retorted. 'Every gold piece you save is a slave to work for you. Every copper it earns is its child that also can earn for you. If you would become wealthy, then what you save must earn, and its children must earn, that all may help to give to you the abundance you crave.

" 'You think I cheat you for your long night's work,' he continued, 'but I am paying you a thousand times over if you have the intelligence to grasp the truth I offer you.

" 'A part of all you earn is yours to keep. It should be not less than a tenth no matter how little you earn. It can be as much more as you can afford. Pay yourself first. Do not buy from the clothes-maker and the sandal-maker more than you can pay out of the rest and still have enough for food and charity and penance to the gods.

" 'Wealth, like a tree, grows from a tiny seed. The first copper you save is the seed from which your tree of wealth shall grow. The sooner you plant that seed the sooner shall the tree grow. And the more faithfully you nourish and water that tree with consistent savings, the sooner may you bask in contentment beneath its shade.'

"So saying, he took his tablets and went away.

"I thought much about what he had said to me, and it seemed reasonable. So I decided that I would try it. Each time I was paid I took one from each ten pieces of copper and hid it away. And strange as it may seem, I was no shorter of funds than before. I noticed little difference as I managed to get along without it. But often I was tempted, as my hoard began to grow, to spend it for some of the good things the merchants displayed, brought by camels and ships from the land of the Phoenicians. But I wisely refrained.

"A twelfth month after Algamish had gone he again returned and said to me, 'Son, have you paid to yourself not less than one-tenth of all you have earned in the past year?'

"I answered proudly, 'Yes, master, I have.'

" 'That is good,' he answered beaming upon me, 'and what have you done with it?'

" 'I have given it to Azmur, the brick maker, who told me he was traveling over the far seas and in Tyre he would buy for me the rare jewels of the Phoenicians. When he returns we shall sell these at high prices and divide the earnings.'

" 'Every fool must learn,' he growled, 'but why trust the knowledge of a brick maker about jewels? Would you go to the bread maker to inquire about the stars? No, by my tunic, you would go to the astrologer, if you had power to think. Your savings are gone, youth, you have jerked your wealth-tree up by the roots. But plant another. Try again. And next time if you would have advice about jewels, go to the jewel merchant. If you would know the truth about sheep, go to the herdsman. Advice is one thing that is freely given away, but watch that you take only what is worth having. He who takes advice about his savings from one who is inexperienced in such matters, shall pay with his savings for proving the falsity of their opinions.' Saying this, he went away.

"And it was as he said. For the Phoenicians are scoundrels and sold to Azmur worthless bits of glass that looked like gems. But as Algamish had bid me, I again saved each tenth copper, for I now had formed the habit and it was no longer difficult.

"Again, twelve months later, Algamish came to the room of the scribes and addressed me. 'What progress have you made since last I saw you?'

" 'I have paid myself faithfully,' I replied, 'and my savings I have entrusted to Agger the shieldmaker, to buy bronze, and each fourth month he does pay me the rental.'

" 'That is good. And what do you do with the rental?'

" 'I do have a great feast with honey and fine wine and spiced cake. Also I have bought me a scarlet tunic. And some day I shall buy me a young ass upon which to ride.'

"To which Algamish laughed, 'You do eat the children of your savings. Then how do you expect them to work for you? And how can they have children that will also work for you? First get thee an army of golden slaves and then many a rich banquet may you enjoy without regret.' So saying he again went away.

"Nor did I again see him for two years, when he once more returned and his face was full of deep lines and his eyes drooped, for he was becoming a very old man. And he said to me, 'Arkad, hast thou yet achieved the wealth thou dreamed of?'

"And I answered, 'Not yet all that I desire, but some I have and it earns more, and its earnings earn more.'

" 'And do you still take the advice of brick makers?'

" 'About brick making they give good advice,' I retorted.

" 'Arkad,' he continued, 'you have learned your lessons well. You first learned to live upon less than you could earn. Next you learned to seek advice from those who were competent through their own experiences to give it. And, lastly, you have learned to make gold work for you.' " (*The Richest Man in Babylon,* pp. 23-29.)

After you have taken great efforts to plan, save and invest, remember the words of Algamish to Arkad when he found that Arkad was having a great feast each time he received a return on his investment, "You do eat the children of your savings. Then how do you expect them to work for you? And how can they have children that will also work for you? First, get thee an army of golden slaves and then many a rich banquet may you enjoy without regret."

Within this story of Arkad lie all of the basics in general form of the PSIC formula. All that needs to be added to this story are the specifics of how to invest and what to invest in to bring the highest possible return on your investment. Then it will be up to you to achieve your million-dollar goal in the shortest possible time. The following chapters give you the specific instructions.

NOTES AND THOUGHTS

_____

_____

_____

_____

_____

_____

PLANS AND GOALS

_____

_____

_____

_____

_____

_____

_____

_____

_____

_____

_____

_____

_____

_____

_____

_____

_____

_____

_____

_____

_____

_____

_____

PLANS AND GOALS

_____

_____

_____

_____

_____

_____

_____

_____

_____

_____

_____

_____

_____

_____

_____

_____

_____

_____

_____

_____

_____

_____

_____

CHAPTER 6
LEVERAGE — MOST POWERFUL TOOL IN YOUR BAG

Archimedes, the Greek mathematician and physicist, calculated the law of the lever. He is reported to have said that if he had a lever long enough and a place to stand, he alone could lift the world.

In real estate the same principle applies: If you have a long enough lever, you can lift or buy properties that are so large that you heretofore have not even dreamed of such purchases. The OPM formula — Other People's Money — is the formula for using leverage. In real estate, leverage is implemented by using borrowed money. You use leverage when you buy, for example, a $100,000 piece of property with $10,000 of your own money. The financing or $90,000 is in effect the lever. Your $10,000 is the weight that pushes the lever down in order to lift the $100,000 piece of property. Leverage is the most powerful tool in your entire investor's bag of tools. If wisely used, this tool can and will, regardless of your starting position, make you as rich as you have the energy to follow through and continue to purchase properties.

HENRY FORD DIDN'T INVEST A PENNY OF HIS OWN MONEY
Leverage can also be used in a myriad of business and other ventures, in addition to real estate. Henry Ford

mastered the use of leverage. In fact, in building his auto empire, Henry Ford did not invest even one cent of his own money. His contribution was "sweat equity" so named by Arthur Cohen who, starting with $25,000 in 1954, has done in real estate what, to most, seems utterly impossible. Mr. Cohen now controls in excess of $1.7 billion of U.S. real estate. Quoting from the book *The Young Millionaires* by Laurence A. Armour, "The basic 'play' in real estate is to make money with other people's money — e.g., mortgage money." ([Chicago: Playboy Press, 1973], p. 186.) (More of Mr. Cohen in Chapter 7.) As a matter of fact, a large percentage of businesses today incorporate leverage as a basis of increasing their growth rate.

CASH VERSUS LEVERAGE

The biggest advantage of leverage in real estate lies in entry into the market. If you did not have a big nest egg or a great amount of assets, you would have a difficult time using the 10 percent leverage in starting your own business or even in buying a corporation or small business. By comparison, someone just starting out in real estate can use 90 percent leverage, and more, particularly on income property. For example, if you were planning to start your own business and had saved $20,000, you would have a very difficult time borrowing more than $20,000 additional from a bank to leverage your business into an increased growth rate. True, friends with money might possibly loan you additional funds to increase your leverage.

But compare this situation to an investment in real estate. Even if you have no prior experience in buying properties and have scrimped and saved $10,000, without much difficulty you could find and purchase an income property valued at $80,000 to $100,000. If you looked hard and ended up with a property valued at $100,000, your leverage factor would be 90 percent. That means 90 percent of your investment would come from other people's money (probably in first and second mortgage money). In the previous example of starting your own business, your leverage factor would be 50 percent.

You may say at this point, so what? Why such a fuss over the amount of leverage? Couldn't borrowing all that money hurt me? And even if it doesn't hurt me, how can it help me?

Well, let's answer these questions with an example. Assume that you have $20,000 and you have decided that your odds are greater in real estate. You're to the point of comparing two pieces of real estate. They are both income-producing properties, but their sizes are different. One is $200,000 in multiple units. The other is a $20,000 single unit. The $200,000 property can be purchased on a favorable leverage basis — $20,000 down and first and second mortgage money (the seller has agreed to carry a second mortgage). On the other hand, the small unit is to be sold for $20,000 cash.

Before the hypothetical purchase, let's make another assumption. Assume that inflation continues as in the past. After purchasing the property we would get lucky and have a big jump in inflation. For example, if we had a 10 percent inflation in buildings, one year later the purchase you made would be worth 10 percent more than you paid for it. For the time being, completely forget about the cash flow, equity buildup, and tax benefits you would inevitably receive from such a purchase. Without these extra benefits, from inflation alone (assuming you sold the building for the new increased value), what would be the rate of return on your investment?

First, had you chosen the smaller investment, the 10 percent return or increase on the building would bring the value to $22,000, making a profit of $2,000. However, had you chosen the highly leveraged investment, the value at the end of the year would have increased to $220,000. Since your investment would have been $20,000, with a return of $20,000 your rate of return would be an amazing 100 percent. Remember, that was with an increase of only 10 percent. You would have actually made 100 percent on a 10 percent increase in the value of the building! In this simplified example (I have had many deals that have been just this simple) you easily can see why leverage is the most powerful tool in real estate investments because even if it took two years, or even five, to increase in value by 10 percent, you have made a tremendous return on the appreciation of the property. (Start adding in the other three factors — cash flow, equity buildup, and the tax advantage — and your rate of return becomes phenomenal.)

What if inflation stops? First, don't stand on one foot until that happens. Second, in periods when it slows down, you could always implement that extra ingredient — forced inflation or planned property improvement — and increase the value, regardless of what inflation has or has not done to it. (See Chapter 16.)

Let me tell you about a deal that I'm just finishing and it will show you how a little extra leverage can push even a normally boring cash-on-cash rate of return of a triple net lease property up by 100 percent! I know it's not the kind of deal a beginner would do, but I think it's still instructive because if you keep it in the back of your mind, you could very possibly use it for later deals.

Note: Be sure to read the last section of this chapter that tells how a "beginner" turned a $3,000 student loan into $1 million in just a few years.

So here's the deal I'm talking about. Let's call it "a hunk of dirt with a desirable dividend" – and by the way, I found it at the tail end of my frantic search to place some 1031

Exchange money. Yes, this is an example of the IRS pushing me with a deadline to do something good for myself. Keep in mind that this example is mainly showing how I increased only the cash rate of return as a percentage of my cash into the property – or what is called "cash on cash" rate of return.

FACTS

- The property is 3.27 acres of land off Interstate-15 (it has a couple of small buildings on it, but the company leasing the property is primarily using it for a convenient place to ship and receive large containers)
- A national tenant just signed a 7-year triple net lease (at $6,732 per month, or $80,784 per year, with escalation clauses that pushes the lease rate to $7,581 per month by the 7th year)
- Price: $975,000
- Cap Rate: ($80,784 ÷ $975,000) = 8.28%
- Cash-on-cash rate of return, assuming you pay all cash = 8.28%
- Cash-on-cash rate of return, if you put $300,000 down (which is what I was originally going to do from my 1031 Exchange money) and borrowed the balance of $675,000 at 6.5% for 30 years (this assumes an amortizing loan with payments of $51,197.51 per year) = 9.862%

So far the deal looks like an average deal. Nothing special, a fair return without any work or effort other than depositing the check every month…and I can do that even on a lazy day. Please note that by leveraging it with long-term 30-year money, the rate jumps up by about one and a half percent, or really a 19 percent increase in your cash-on-cash rate of return.

But here's where it gets very interesting!

By simply using my prime rate line of credit (and I know everybody can't do this), I quickly and easily moved the "cash on cash" rate of return from 8.2 percent to 17.36 percent.

THE NEW HIGHER RATE OF RETURN

- Lease income: $80,784
- Current prime rate:
  4.25% x $675,000 = <$28,688>
- Net cash-on-cash return: $52,096
- Rate of return on my $300,000: 17.36%

Note: As prime rates move up, which it probably has done by the time you read this, my percentage rate of return will go down – but even a full one percent higher, that is 5.25 percent will still yield a rate of return of 15.2 percent. *(Just before final printing time, I decided to lock in a 6.25% long-term fixed rate.)*

And here is some icing on the cake. The chances of this property going up in value in seven years is very high – the bottom line – it's a perfect way to have cash flow from basically just "dirt" while you wait for a big gain.

EVEN A BAD BUY CAN MAKE MONEY

One of my earlier investments, and the smallest one I have ever made in real estate, looked at one time as though it were a disaster. I bought a single family unit in a poor location of Salt Lake City; in fact, the exact location was 542 South 10th West in a mixed neighborhood of dubious reputation. I had bought the home in a hurry, believing it to be a real steal because of the price and terms. The owner was asking around $9,000 for the home; I made a quick offer of $7,500 with only $700 down and the balance on a uniform real-estate contract at 7 percent interest at $80 a month. From a leverage standpoint, it was a very good investment. Much to my surprise and delight — at the time — the owner accepted my offer. On closer inspection, I found the property was structurally unsound. The house had been built many years before, on the dirt without a foundation. The dirt settled and moved, and the corners of the house had sagged until there wasn't a level floor in the house.

Undaunted, I forged ahead with planned renovations. I brought in a crew of young men, fifteen and sixteen-year-olds, on a hot summer morning. I don't remember how many, but we had quite a crew. Some were painting, some cleaning, some sweeping, some cutting the grass, trimming hedges, or laying carpet. There I was orchestrating the activities in an attempt to avert a disaster. Well, somehow we managed to get the job done. When the bills rolled in, I had spent another $1,300 on renovations. That didn't bother me, because with its new paint, carpets, and drapes the house looked neat and tidy. I quickly rented it for $155 a month, giving after all expenses a $50 spendable income. Based on the rent I was receiving, I estimated the worth of the house around $12,500.

Disaster struck. The results were an undesirable tenant and a clogged toilet. The first Roto-Rooter man who went down to clean it out informed me that the sewer tile was broken and would have to be replaced. The bid on that work was close to $1,000, and seemed like $10,000 to me. I began to wish I had never got involved in real estate investments!

Things got worse. The tenant got impatient, ran to the City Health Department, and I was summoned to come to the property. I did. I found three people from the tenants union with blood in their eyes, one representative from the City Health Department, and two from the City Building Department. They advised me that the house was unfit to live in and they would have to tack up their condemnation paper that very day.

To that point I had been arguing the merits of the building. At that point, I realized that was the wrong approach. I quickly reversed field. Rather than arguing, I asked them for time to make the needed corrections. Amazingly, their attitude changed as quickly as mine did. They softened and granted me the needed time. (As it turned out, the sewer line did not have to be replaced, a more experienced Roto-Rooter man was able to dislodge the blockage, and the City Health Department didn't press the other items.)

I had learned a lesson. I was shaken by the experience, and I was determined to sell the property as quickly as possible. One reason for my haste was that I was told if I sold to an owner-occupant, the city would not give them any trouble. I got rid of the problem property in about a week. It went fast because I sold it without any down payment. Remember that this was one of my poorer investments. But let's reconstruct what happened on the financial side of this investment.

First of all, the person who bought the home from me sold it within six months for a profit. A few months later, the second buyer decided to refinance it. When he obtained his loan, he cashed all the underlying contracts and mortgages out of the picture. When I figured up my return on the property, I was startled.

I had invested $700 on the down payment, plus $1,300 on improvements, for a total investment of $2,000. I had received $960 in rents after expenses and payment on the uniform real-estate contract.* I received an additional $4,200

---

* A uniform real-estate contract (called a land contract, contract for deed, or just a contract – or various other similar names depending on the state) is merely a contract between a buyer and a seller. These contracts can be ideal for both buyer and seller because of the flexibility both have in customizing terms.

in capital gains, $350 of which was the amount the original seller agreed to knock off from what I owed him, in order to be cashed out from the second buyer's loan. The total income to me was $5,160 on a $2,000 investment in eighteen months! THAT IS A RETURN OF APPROXIMATELY 172 percent. Keep in mind again that this was one of my poorer investments and one of the first when I really didn't know what I was doing. True, I had some beginner's luck, but the more deals you make and the more experience you gain, the luckier you become.

Two months earlier in that same year, by using the principles of leverage and forced inflation, I bought a small cottage on Sherman Avenue in Salt Lake City for $7,925.

After spending $1,500 on improvements, bringing the total cost to $9,425, I secured a $12,000 first mortgage on the property, putting $2,575 in my pocket without any investment. The $1,500 improvements, changes anyone could make without specialized training, included basically cleaning up and painting of the exterior, painting part of the interior, and adding a small amount of wallboard and some inexpensive nylon carpeting. My return on the investment? Well, it's not possible to figure as I didn't have any cash invested.

VERY LITTLE CREDIT REQUIRED

Many of the best buys with high leverage, especially in small properties, can be made with uniform real-estate contracts. This usually gives the guy with fair to poor credit a break. With all the properties I have bought, only two sellers have checked my credit.

Remember the physical therapist, Rick Lybbert (Chapter 3) and his shock in learning what happens when you compound relatively small amounts of money over a lot of years?

Well, it just so happens that Rick and his wife, Margo, are the two people in the story below that took a $3,000 student loan and turned that small amount of money into $1 million worth of equity.

Here's Rick's story in his own words – what a great beginning for a young couple:

In 1996, Margo and I purchased our first home in a newly developed area of West Jordan with a down payment of roughly $3,000 that I got from a subsidized student loan. Because it was subsidized, we did not have to make a payment, nor did interest begin accruing, until six months after graduation from physical therapy school. We actually closed on the home and moved in one week before I graduated from physical therapy school. Despite the fact that I was unemployed at the time, the bank qualified me for the loan on a letter from my future employer which stated my future salary.

In 1996, the year we bought our first home, the real estate market was slowing down as compared to a couple of prior years. I remember thinking to myself that I missed the window and that I was buying "high" and it would be many years before I gained any equity. I perceived my $130,000 mortgage on a 30 year amortization schedule to be overwhelming and almost depressing. Little did I know what the future would hold. Little did I know how the concept of leverage would drastically change my financial position.

Three years later, in 1999, Margo and I fell in love with another newly developed area built on the shore of Utah Lake called Saratoga Springs. We put our West Jordan home up for sale and to our surprise, it sold in two weeks. Because we purchased the least expensive home in the neighborhood, the more expensive homes "pulled" up our value. To our surprise, we gained $20,000 of equity from our $3,000 investment three years prior. This equity gain was immediately rolled into our new home in Saratoga Springs. I was especially pleased at the time because our new mortgage and monthly payment was approximately the same, yet we had a nicer, more valuable home. This was the first time I experienced the benefits of investing in real estate first hand.

Still, I had no idea or concept of how beneficial real estate investment could be.

Two more years went by and in 2001 I found an extremely undervalued lot for sale in our neighborhood. It was undervalued because it was priced as an interior lot despite the fact that it had unobstructed lake views. I knew that if I purchased this lot that I would be able to sell it within six months and possibly make twenty or thirty thousand. My plan was to apply that money towards my mortgage. I was excited! I purchased the lot and then disaster struck! My wife fell in love with the lot and was determined that it would be the site of our future dream home. My vision of reducing my mortgage, and thus improving my financial position, was vanishing before my eyes. I now perceived this new lot as a curse that would increase the size of both my mortgage and monthly payment and definitely move me away from my goal of financial freedom. I could not have been more wrong.

As desired by my wife, we set out to build our dream house on our newly acquired lot. Because we could not afford to pay a general contractor, I became the general contractor for the project. The only problem was that my prior construction experience was sparse, or should I say non-existent. Nevertheless, my price was right so I got the job.

To make a long story short, building our own home turned out to be the most valuable financial experience of my life. It was during this experience that I was introduced to the concept of leverage. I was initially introduced to leverage while initially funding the project. I learned that the bank will loan eighty percent of the total appraised value of the project. Because I was doing much of the work myself, my total cost for the project was less than eighty percent of the appraised value. Subsequently, we built our dream home with absolutely no money out of pocket. The bank financed it completely.

The real financial lesson was learned at the completion of the project. As expected, our mortgage and monthly payment went up and I did not have the twenty to thirty thousand dollars I would have otherwise had if we had sold the lot. What we did have, however, was over $100,000 in equity according to the appraisal of the home at its completion. It was then that I began to understand the power of leverage. I quickly learned that having the ability to borrow $100,000 was tremendously more valuable than actually having $30,000 in my pocket.

I speak of building our own house as the most valuable financial experience of my life because it unlocked the door to $100,000 worth of borrowing power which in turn unlocked the doors to significant investment opportunity that would have otherwise remained locked.

I first tapped the equity in our home when I was given the opportunity to become a minority partner at the physical therapy clinic where I worked. This investment allowed me to receive a portion of the company's profits. My return on investment was significant enough to pay back my initial investment in the company as well as give me additional cash flow.

I again used our home equity to purchase a small rental house for $89,000. I fixed up the place with an additional $5000 and found renters. The property appraised for $120,000 so I refinanced it and again replaced the money in the equity in our home.

Most recently, the "perfect" building for my physical therapy clinic came available for purchase. The asking price was $425,000, way out of my personal price range. Nevertheless, I went for it! I ended up getting in a bidding war with two other parties and eventually won and put the building under contract for $485,000. Now I needed to figure out how to pay for it. I figured that my physical therapy company, of which I was a minority partner, could likely qualify for the loan. I approached my partners with a Win/ Win proposition. I offered them the opportunity of purchasing half of the building if they would give me the opportunity to purchase up to half of the physical therapy business. My partners immediately saw the value in owning half of the building and decided that it was worth allowing me to purchase additional shares up to fifty percent of the physical therapy business. We then utilized the business to qualify for financing of the building. And again, I utilized the equity from our home to satisfy my obligation in purchasing the additional shares in the business as well as purchasing half of the building. Had it not been for my wife's desire to build our dream home on the lot I would have otherwise sold, I would not have had access to borrow the money necessary to do these deals. Most importantly, I would not understand the tremendous value of leverage.

To summarize, the initial $3000 investment from student loan money eight years ago has grown to close to $1,000,000 in net worth when considering our equity in our home, our rental house, the commercial building, and the physical therapy business. I never would have believed it possible had I not personally experienced it.

While my deals thus far have been relatively small in comparison to most, I suspect that the fundamental principles remain the same for small and large deals alike. I look forward to applying these principles to bigger and bigger deals with time. I no longer see my financial future as overwhelming and depressing, rather, I see it filled with great opportunities to achieve financial freedom.

With these high leverage investments, one can see that it doesn't take much money to get started. Once you get started with several deals like this, you can have a fairly good-sized capital base to move into the bigger properties and into super leveraged situations, as outlined in Chapter 7.

PLANS AND GOALS

_____

_____

_____

_____

_____

_____

PLANS AND GOALS

_____

_____

_____

_____

_____

_____

_____

_____

_____

_____

_____

_____

_____

_____

_____

_____

_____

_____

_____

_____

_____

_____

_____

_____

_____

_____

_____

_____

CHAPTER 7
SUPER LEVERAGE — SPRINGBOARD TO MILLION DOLLAR PROPERTIES

Conrad Hilton's mother gave her son this advice, "If you want to launch big ships, you have to go where the water is deep." *(Be My Guest,* p. 120.) Deil O. Gustafson, a man who is still virtually unknown and yet whose net worth is between $20 and $30 million dollars, knew that he also had to go into deep water in order to launch big ships. He also realized that if you don't have any money and still want to launch big ships, you must figure a way to do it. Like many others, he learned that big projects can be launched through the use of leverage. Quoting Mr. Gustafson, "Anyone who says you have to have it to make it doesn't know what he's talking about." He says, "If that [you have to have money to make money] were true, I'd still be back teaching school."

SUPER LEVERAGE WILL PUT CASH IN YOUR POCKET

When Deil Gustafson first waded into the water, he did it in a big way, using leverage as only the professionals and the most experienced real-estate operators would dare to use it. Quoting from the 3 January 1974, *Wall Street Journal,* front page, Gustafson's "first venture into real estate also was accomplished without the benefit of cash. In 1963, he and a partner, whom he has since bought out, learned that Nicolette Village, a development of 160 townhouse-type apartments in the Minneapolis suburb of Richfield, was available at a bargain price. He went to a bank in search of the financing.

" They asked me what I was paying for the property. I told them to go out and appraise it and tell me how much they'd put up.' They did and said they'd give me $1.3 million which I guessed was 80 percent of what they thought it was worth. I said fine. The actual purchase price was $1.1 million. I used the $200,000 that was left to start some other things. It wasn't income, so I didn't have to pay taxes on it. When you're young and need funds, that's a great way to get it.' He says that the development has been profitable almost from the outset and that it's currently worth 'at least twice' his purchase price."

My definition of super leverage is when you buy a property and at the closing, or within a relatively short period after closing, you can take out all of your own equity money and have cash in what is sometimes called the "Hip National Bank," or your own wallet.

I have used the Deil Gustafson example many times in lectures and in consulting with people. Most are skeptical that such deals can be found today. I go on to explain the many deals that I've had with this so-called super leverage. Even after my explanation, most think I was as lucky as Gustafson in finding the deals. But I do not think it is possible for you or anyone else to go out and look at a hundred potential deals (possible purchases of income property) without finding at least three to five bargains. At least one and possibly two will be super leverage situations.

Now if you expect these super leverage investments to be labeled that, you are kidding yourself. If they were labeled "No-cash investment with a positive cash flow" or "No-cash investment plus cash in your pocket of $100,000 or $200,000," they wouldn't last two minutes. No, they don't come labeled; it takes study, creativity, and some foresight. I said *some*, and

I don't mean a lot. If you are a person of average or near-average intelligence, you will be able to make this kind of deal.

MY FIRST SUPER LEVERAGE DEAL
NET $48,000

For example, in mid-1975 the Coventry Hearth, a twenty-two-unit apartment building, was brought to my attention by a real estate agent. This building had been for sale for some time. In fact, it had been listed in the real estate book that is published weekly. No offers had been made. Looking at the bottom line or net cash flow, it seemed like a poor deal, but the total price of $110,000 for twenty-two units was attractive. On closer inspection, it was quite apparent that expenses were extremely high and for the size of the apartments the rents were on the low side.

Realizing there was potential in the building, I restructured the income statement provided by the seller to see what the picture would be if certain changes were made. These were mostly cosmetic improvements in painting, carpeting, drapes, curtains, and a minor face lift. The result was that after improvements were made and expenses cut, the new cash flow would be extremely attractive. In fact, after those changes and all contingencies, the cash flow would be 27 percent cash return on my investment (down payment plus improvements). Of course, after I added equity buildup, put in an inflation factor, and added the tax advantage, the total return on my investment would be 47.8 percent (The inflation factor was only 2 percent.) Pull out your calculator and see what a beginning investment of $10,000 will do over eighteen years at a 47.8 percent compound rate. The results will surprise you.

As it turned out, this particular deal was even better than I had expected. To begin with, I bought the building for

$102,000 with $10,000 cash, about what I projected, after three weeks of negotiation. Next, I found there were actually twenty-three units rather than twenty-two. The owner had been using one unit as a storage room. I spent an additional $25,000 (some from rents and some borrowed) in upgrading the building, everything from painting, carpeting, draping and face lifting, to landscaping.

At this point I had $35,000 cash invested in the property, not to mention many hours spent planning and arranging for the things to be done. With an overall return of almost 50 percent, should I be satisfied with my investment? Well, I was for a while. Then I looked at the situation again and saw a way to turn this attractive leverage situation into a super leverage deal. (Some brain compounding was taking place!) Let me back track and present all the facts in this, my first big super leverage deal.

Shortly after I purchased the Coventry Hearth and began renovation, including a change-over of 95 percent of the tenants, I found that the bad tenants were moving into the building next door, the Copper Crest. This didn't completely solve my problem because the undesirables were still in the neighborhood. As I moved new tenants in, the old tenants were harassing my new tenants.

I approached the owner of the Copper Crest and explained the problem. He knew something was up because his problems had multiplied greatly in the weeks since I had bought my building. During this conversation, I found that he was in the insurance business and really didn't want to be a landlord. I asked him if he would consider selling his building. He said he wasn't interested in selling, and I let it go at that. He told me he would alert the manager to screen the renters more carefully.

A few weeks later when the problem had not abated, I approached him again with the same basic problem and the same question: Would he sell his building to me? Finally on the fifth visit, he agreed to sell the building. I prepared an offer. Before delivering it, I called to tell him I had the offer ready. He had changed his mind and didn't want to sell. Since I had already prepared the offer, I told him I wanted to bring it to him anyway; and he agreed.

As I hung up the phone, I was in a dilemma. The offer I was about to present was a low offer because of the problems I would face in buying the building and unknowns that were ahead in the deal. However, I had expected him to counter with a higher offer that I probably would accept. Now that he had changed his mind and didn't want to sell, I didn't know how to alter the offering price for the building. I finally decided to keep the offer as it was and I delivered it to him, leaving before he had a chance to open it. (I wanted to give him time to think about it. Also, I didn't want him to read from me that I knew it was a low offer.)

Two days later he called me. I held my breath, wondering what his decision was. He stated flatly, "The offer looks fine except for a few minor points. Let's get together and discuss it." Needless to say, I was in shock, but delighted. I hustled down to his office and discussed what turned out to be very minor points. We both made some compromises, and he signed the offer.

The deal turned out this way: for the ten apartment units, most of which were one bedroom; a very nice office in the front of the building which he agreed to lease back from me at $500 a month on a five-year lease; and a small print shop in the basement, the total price was $90,000. Terms were $5,000 down and the balance on a twenty-year 8.5 percent contract.

So, from the purchase of the first building, I accidentally walked into a deal that did two things for me. First, the second building made it a super buy and gave me a fantastic return on my investment. Second, it solved the problem of the undesirable tenants being in the neighborhood.

As we closed the deal on the second building, a humorous situation developed. Upon finding that I was the purchaser of the building, the tenants who had just moved in from Coventry Hearth didn't wait to be asked to leave; they left, and in a hurry.

After the cleanup and repairs to the building, and change-over in tenants at an investment of more than $5,000, rents were increased enough to give me a 50 percent cash flow on my invested dollar and a whopping 88 percent total return on my investment!

For the seller, the deal was good also. The building had been a headache to him. It was a distraction from the insurance business he knew best and was obviously very successful in. A few weeks after the sale, he told me what a relief it was not to have the problems of the apartment building.

Now, with the two buildings sitting side by side and both giving excellent returns on the cash flow basis alone, I was receiving approximately $14,450 annually or an overall return of 32 percent on a cash investment of $45,000. Sounds like a deal that I would and should continue to hold just as it was. Of course, I could have done that. In fact, I could have held that property for the rest of my life and maintained the income by raising rents to keep up with inflation.

Depending on how high you want to rise and how aggressive you are, this is the kind of situation to try to turn from an extremely good deal into a super deal by using super leverage. That is what I am currently doing. This type of a deal can be found and consummated by following a few basic steps. (See Chapters 10 and 16.)

First, I approached the person who sold me the Coventry Hearth on a wrap-around uniform real-estate contract. The underlying or first mortgage loan was approximately $68,000 with me paying him on a $92,000 contract. In other words, his equity was $24,000. The terms of the sale were structured so that the interest on his $24,000 was accruing but would not be paid until the entire $24,000 plus interest became due and payable in five years.

My approach was to ask this man if he would discount what I owed him by $4,500 and take approximately $20,000 and subordinate his interest in the property in the form of a second mortgage, thus allowing me to put on a new first mortgage in the amount of approximately $120,000. He said he would not discount his interest by $4,500, but he would subordinate about $20,000 of what I owed him. The next step was for me to get the bank to make the first mortgage loan. OK, now what was my position when all this was accomplished? At the time that I received the $120,000 loan on the building, based on the new market price of $175,000, I paid the former owner $4,000 and executed a $20,000 second mortgage to him.

From the proceeds of the $120,000 new first mortgage loan, we deducted the $68,000 old first mortgage and the $4,000 prepayment to the former seller — the inducement to get him to subordinate his interest. (To subordinate means he would take a second mortgage position or a subordinate position to the first mortgage.) My position was that I had $140,000 in loans on the building and I had essentially a break-even cash flow basis, because the second mortgage loan was a short-term, five-year note. But the real bonus was that I had $48,000 in my pocket, $48,000 that I earmarked for an attractive investment in a $500,000 building.

Even without the benefit of forced inflation — increasing the value by improvements — this potential investment had a 20 percent cash flow, giving me almost $10,000 cash yearly on my $48,000 down, a $10,000 yearly inflation factor (or 2 percent on the total price), a big tax advantage, plus the equity buildup of approximately $5,000 annually, or an annual total return of about 50 percent on the $48,000, or $24,000. Remember that I still owned the Coventry Hearth, the first building. From it I received approximately $9,114 in benefits each year: $1,200 from equity buildup, $2,204 from inflation at 2 percent, and the balance from tax benefits.

COVENTRY HEARTH BENEFITS

	Before Refinance		After Refinance
Cash Flow	$ 9,450	27.0%	0
Equity Buildup	836	2.4	$1,200
Inflation (2%)	2,204	6.3	2,204
Tax Benefits	4,240	12.1	5,710
Total Return	$16,730	47.8%	$9,114
(on cash down payment plus improvements)			

REINVESTMENT
OF $48,000 CASH
FROM REFINANCE

$500,000 Building
$48,000 Down

	Dollars	%
Cash Flow	$10,000	20.0
Equity Buildup	3,000	6.2
Inflation (2%)	10,000	21.0
Tax Benefits	2,000	4.1
Total Return	$25,000	51.3

In summary, I gave up $16,730 in benefits from the Coventry Hearth (47.8 percent of my $35,000 cash equity) to receive approximately $34,114 in benefits ($25,000 from the new purchase without the benefit of forced inflation and $9,114 from Coventry Hearth). By implementing so-called forced inflation and increasing my equity at a faster rate, the benefits were much greater than the $34,114 I received without any improvements. (See Appendix B)

$60,000 NET FROM THE SECOND SUPER LEVERAGED DEAL

I approached the insurance man who sold me the Copper Crest with the same basic question I had asked the man who sold me the Coventry Hearth: Would he subordinate part of the interest he currently had in the building if I made certain concessions to him? The concessions I offered him were as follows: I would agree to pay him $20,000 of the $85,000, reduce the pay off time from 20 years to 11 and increase the interest rate from 8.5 percent to 9.5 percent.

Additionally, I would make improvements and increase the value of the property, raise the rents and thus increase the value of the building even more. He agreed, and I proceeded with a first mortgage of $90,000 on the property. The cash from this mortgage was used as follows: $20,000 of the $90,000 went to the seller of the Copper Crest for the agreed prepayment. From the balance of $70,000, $10,000 was used to make the agreed improvements. This left $60,000 in my pocket to reinvest.

Bear in mind that the Coventry Hearth and Copper Crest were made into super leveraged deals at a time when bank refinancing enhanced their overall success. Interest rates have risen, mortgage terms have changed, and our whole economics environment is a new ball game. But basic success approaches such as super leverage remain the same. It is up to you, the sharp investor, to adapt your strategy to conditions as they are today. You can live with much higher bank rates but better terms must be negotiated with the seller—which of course can be done by finding a seller who is *very* motivated!

THE SKY IS THE LIMIT
WITH THIS SPRINGBOARD

Do you begin to see how this so-called super leverage can be a springboard?

On the smaller properties, I get the contract or mortgage holder to subordinate his interest to allow me to put a first mortgage on the property. By using this method, you can get all or most of your equity out and still own the property. Besides putting extra cash in your pocket, this can give you some very distinct and large tax advantages. Sometimes you can get more than your equity out and still own the property. These are cases where the person holding the mortgage or contract will subordinate his interest and his second mortgage, and the first mortgage you place on the property totals more than the value of the property. (See Chapter 15 on creative financing to show you how you can do this on your very first purchase.)

By using this type of creative financing and super leverage, you not only are able to generate cash for reinvestment, but you reduce your tax liability. You also do the impossible; you borrow second mortgage money at extremely low rates. As you probably know, second-mortgage money is expensive, 18 percent to 21 percent. By using this method of financing, you borrow second-mortgage money for as low as 8 percent or 9 percent. Of course, this depends on your original contract or mortgage arrangement with the seller and what you negotiate from that point. Using this method, I have had several situations where the second-mortgage loan was at lower rates than the first mortgage loan.

SWEAT EQUITY IS AS VALUABLE AS CASH

Arthur Cohen, mentioned in the last chapter, is a master of the art of creative financing. "Even when he cannot mortgage out [mortgaging out means completely financing out of a deal so you have no cash equity in the deal], his ideal is to minimize the amount of money he must put into a project. Cohen tries to limit his investment to his own efforts and creativity — 'sweat equity' as it is sometimes known in the trade.

"In Arthur Cohen's case, sweat plus leverage is the basis of his fortune. "My greatest asset," he says, "was the added value from my sweat equity and that generated all the capital I needed." (Laurence A. Armour, *The Young Millionaires* [Chicago: Playboy Press, 1973], p. 186.)

Quoting further, "The fundamental talent is the ability to select property that has a potential for an increase in value." (*Young Millionaires,* p. 186.) (In Chapter 10 you will see that the talent or ability to select properties with the potential to increase in value can be learned and duplicated. After you learn the basics and begin to apply them, you will be amazed at your success.) With creative financing (using super leverage and by the use of sweat equity being able to mortgage out of deals), you can continue to progress. When you get all your money out, you can go on to buy, and buy, and buy. The only factors that can slow you down would be your energy and your ability to find the deals.

YOU CAN FOLLOW COHEN IF YOU UNDERSTAND HIS SYMBOL

Cohen is mainly concerned with big deals now. However, he has held onto one small deal from his beginning years in the real estate business, because of its symbolism of what can be done, and what was done by Arthur Cohen.

"The love that Arthur Cohen bears for the Burroughs Building is something of a standing joke around the Manhattan headquarters of Arlen Realty and Development Corporation. It's a joke because the object of Cohen's affection is a one-story office building in the New York City suburb of Mamaroneck. The property earns only $1,500 annually — hardly worth, on the face of it, a passing glance from the chairman of a corporation that controls some $1.7 billion of U.S. real estate. In fact, the Burroughs Building isn't even owned by Arlen. It is one of Cohen's private holdings, a leftover from his early real estate career, which he began with a $25,000 stake in 1954.

"But Burroughs is also a serious symbol of how he parlayed that stake into a personal fortune amounting to about $200 million. They laugh at me,' says Cohen, laughing himself, 'but I love that building.' He built the 2,300-square-foot property in 1957 without putting a penny of his own toward its $130,000 construction cost. For fifteen years he has received a steadily increasing income from the building, and to Cohen that kind of deal is what real estate is all about. Everyone at Arlen understands the symbolism. 'The quality on the return is there, and that is what I always look at,' Cohen explains. The little ones and the big ones are all judged on the same formula.' " (*Young Millionaires,* pp. 184-85.)

There are many, many super leveraged deals around both large and small in every city of the United States, regardless of size of the city. How to find these properties is the subject of the next chapter.

The best part of the "super leveraged" deal is that average people can have the same kind of super multimillion-dollar results. As the old sub-head in my ad said years ago, and is as true today as it was twenty-five years ago when I wrote it,

"Millionaires are not ten, fifty, or a hundred times smarter than you and me, they just know the wealth formula."

Quite early in my career I came up with a deal that was a bit treacherous, but in the long run "super leverage" really worked for me and made it a super winner.

IT'S A DEAL!

In any career there are certain moments that make all the long hours, days, and years of hard work worthwhile. For a salesperson, it is the moment when the customer puts pen to paper and signs a hefty order.

Real estate investors are no different. They too have their shining moments, and those moments usually occur when a seller agrees to sell them the property they want for the price and terms they were hoping they'd get. But the road between finding the right income property and hearing those marvelous words, "It's a deal!", can be long and treacherous.

THE KISS THEORY OF REAL ESTATE...

One time I bought a marginal property in a pretty tough neighborhood in Charlotte, North Carolina. I paid a little over $900,000 for it with $100,000 down. I did about $65,000 worth of renovations, increased the rents and occupancy levels, and sold it for $2.375 million.

A SLICK TRICK?

Sounds easy, right? But there is a big problem that this kind of deal can cause for many readers. First of all, the above facts are absolutely accurate. I did, without exaggeration, make $1.310 million on this one deal. But it wasn't as easy as it would appear at first glance. That's what causes many big problems for others in that they are so easily discouraged because their deals don't seem to work out as slick and easy for them.

You see, so many lecturers and writers make it sound easy – even to those legitimate practitioners who know what the real world of investing is like. So why do they make the process sound so easy?

THINK ABOUT IT!

The comments at the beginning of the paragraph entitled *THE KISS THEORY OF REAL ESTATE* for example, takes only 19-20 seconds to read (if you are a slow reader). But, the deal took several years to do and those years included some months of high vacancy, a couple of small, but upsetting fires, a sudden extra vacancy caused by a shotgun death (no accident) of a tenant, a fight with the city over right-of-way, several threats directed at the manager, and several manager changes in mid-stream.

What I'm saying is that there was a lot of worry, fretting, work and pain. But through it all there was growth. Personally, from a human standpoint, it was self-development, better discipline, better planning, etc., and finally big growth as in turning $165,000 into $1,310,000. The growth (both financial and personal) made the pain well worth it.

The next time you are discouraged and ready to quit when things seem to be falling apart, remember, it will only take you 19 or 20 seconds to tell someone how well you did on a deal that was giving you fits. And even if you attempt to tell your listener about the tough times, you probably won't be able to come close to explaining how tough it really was and how you worried, fretted and worked to get the job done.

NOW FOR THE KISS...

The KISS principle is one of those time-tested concepts that really works. I was first introduced to the KISS principle

(Keep It Simple Stupid) with the additional syllable of SIB added on the front, or in other words, SIB-KISS, which simply stands for "See It Big – Keep It Simple", with the last S for Stupid being optional, of course.

As I've said before, it's simple to make a million dollars, but it's not easy. You need to follow those simple concepts that make money, but you do have to work your tail off applying those concepts or absolutely nothing will happen.

Keeping it simple will work, but if you want to make a fortune, you have to add the SIB – See It Big. After all, doesn't that ability to visualize the big dream energize you when you work on that problem property, problem tenant, or problem of financing? It sure does the trick for me. It gives me the necessary mental and physical energy to do exactly what I need to do at the right time.

My old friend, and mentor, Sterling Sill, put it this way, "Genius is the ability to clearly visualize the objective". That's genius all right, but visualizing a big objective is also to energize yourself mentally and physically. Energize your brain with the big vision. We all need more of it from time to time.

When you're telling people how simple it was to turn your $5,700 into $77,000 in five and a half months, or whatever your numbers turn out to be, be sure to tell them it's a lot easier to tell about it than it is to do it. Then they'll realize how very human they are when they get discouraged and bump up against a seemingly immovable object.

And finally, don't let the phenomenal fact that $165,000 was turned into a $1,310,000 profit pass you by. (That works out to be almost an 800% return on my money – and a major part of the reason for that very high return was leverage.) Although, it took a lot of work and effort, $1,310,000 can set you up for life, or at least for a month or two depending on your spending habits.

Go out and do it! You can!

NOTES AND THOUGHTS

_____

_____

_____

_____

_____

_____

_____

_____

_____

_____

_____

_____

_____

_____

_____

_____

_____

_____

_____

_____

_____

CHAPTER 8
THE QUICKEST PATH TO A BILLION
BEYOND SUPER LEVERAGE

Not many people set goals to become a billionaire. That's an awfully big number – one I only briefly thought about for myself. For me there were too many other things I wanted to do with my life. BUT...

I know that I could have done it if I had wanted to and I know how to do it and what it takes to get there.

For the very, very few who want to get to that rare and lofty place, I will tell you what it takes to get there, but let me make two points first.

One – The strategy and steps I'm about to disclose can certainly be used by anyone regardless of how large of fortune they want to create – whether it's a few million or one hundred million, it works just as well.

Two – Just a comment to let you know how truly rare it is to reach that billion dollar mark. As of 2003, there were only 269 billionaires in the United States, and only 497 billionaires in the world. That's only one out of every 12,877,263 people on the planet who have ever reached that status.

So how does a person starting with nothing reach the rarified air of a billionaire or even one tenth of that amount?

Here's how: It's what I call **beyond super leverage**. But it must be done by leveraging both money and people.

It's all well and good for you to buy an income producing piece of real estate with 10 or 20 percent of your own money and 80 percent of borrowed money, which will make you a ton of dough if you buy right and manage the property well. But to move to a much higher level and in short order, you need to do more.

Most people, once they've figured out how leverage can lift their net worth so quickly, go to the next step that can help a lot but is very risky. They not only borrow the 80 percent that the bank lends them, and in some cases the seller finances for them, but they borrow the 10 or 20 percent that is the down payment. This, of course, puts them in a 100 percent financed position. That's all well and good as long as everything goes almost perfect with the property. But it is so "high risk" that a slight hiccup with the economy or that particular property will cause you to lose it all.

If you want to go for the tens of millions level, or a hundred million, or yes, even a billion, you need a better plan.

THE BILLION-DOLLAR HANSEN MODEL

The Hansen model is an ideal model for such a goal. Instead of borrowing the down payment and using that kind of super leverage (and risk), you simply have partners put up all or part of the down payment. If you take time to cultivate good, wealthy partners and treat them well, you will have a never-ending, and actually increasing source of equity capital.

In many cases, Hansen and his partners used a much larger down payment than 20 percent. Why? First of all, people with a lot of money usually don't want a high-risk investment. The quickest way to scare off big money people is to try to sell them a deal that "promises them" a ridiculously high return for their passive investment – for example: "You're going to double your money in the first year." So by using larger down payments with partners' money, you decrease the overall risk for everyone. Yes, the overall return for the partners is less, but if the deal is structured right, and fair I should add, **your** return can be much greater. Of course, the reason for your high return is because you have less of your own money in the deal and maybe not even any cash in the deal. It's not that you haven't put anything into the deal. You've put time, energy, and effort, along with your skill and know-how to find the deal and put it together.

People with a lot of cash usually are satisfied with lower returns that are paid regularly and consistently. They know that very high rates of return without hands-on efforts are virtually non-existent.

Remember, whereas those kinds of returns are certainly possible for those of us who work our tails off, the passive investors (those who just put up the money and wait for their monthly check) normally cannot get those kinds of returns.

To offer them those kinds of numbers (the 100 percent per year), even if you think you can deliver them, is a huge mistake.

You see, Hansen has learned that lesson. If a big money investor goes into one of his deals with a projected cash return of...let's say, 9 percent...and that investor knows that the total down payment of all the equity partners totals 40 percent, that investor feels pretty darn safe. Then when Hansen delivers a cash return of 12 or 14 percent, or even 19 percent, WOW! That investor is calling all his friends, and making sure he puts his kids' trust money into the next deal...and Hansen doesn't have to look too far for investors on his next deal. In many cases, Hansen always puts up some of his own money into each of his deals, but if he wanted to he could legitimately give himself a fair piece of each deal without putting any cash. Either way, that's what I call **beyond**

super leverage. And that's exactly the first step toward the multi, multi millions or even a billion.

However, I should note that by Hansen putting up at least some of his own money, it does send a very good message to all the investors and makes it much easier to get partners into his deals, especially if it's the first deal a new partner has with Hansen.

So with that basic overview of the general plan of what can be done, let me give you the exact steps of how to go about it – and then a list of the human traits, skills, and qualities that a person needs to have to get the job done. And remember, you can use the following steps to end up with a million, ten million, or a hundred million – those numbers being far short of the billion dollar mark, but still pretty darn satisfying in anyone's book.

STAY AWAY FROM INVESTMENT TIME SUCKERS

Before we go to the required steps, let me make a comment about the best types of investments that will most likely serve your purposes of reaching the extreme levels of net worth. Most people don't realize one of the critical ingredients to super success, especially in the investment arena, is this thing we call "time." It's a must, if you really want to hit it big, to stay with investments that don't suck your time. If you stay with investments that are not "time suckers," then it frees up your time so you have more time to add to your investments. I know so many people who go out and invest in small businesses which almost inevitably take enormous amounts of time, thus they are "time-tied" to those small business and don't have time to add to their portfolio and hence never rise to the next level.

But now, let's look at the human traits, skills, and <u>desired qualities</u>, and the <u>required steps</u>:

The Desired Qualities are:

(As you read this list and compare yourself with this ideal person, or what we'll call the "Billion-Dollar Man or Women", keep in mind that no one rates a perfect 10 on each of these attributes, skills, or qualities. But on the other hand, if you rate yourself a 1 or 2 on each of these qualities, you'd better not quit your day job just yet.)

1. High energy level.
2. High honest and integrity level.
3. Ability to explain and excite people about potential (selling).
4. Very good to "super" organized.
5. A firm grasp of the numbers as it relates to the property's return and potential return.*
6. Jack-of-all-trades and master of none.
7. A good reader of people and not only an ability to negotiate without showing all the cards, but also ability to recognize people's talent to hire and keep as employees or associates.
8. Must be good at delegation and following up on those who are delegated to make sure the job is done.

The 7 Required Steps are:

1. Find it.
2. Negotiate it.
3. Tie it up.
4. Package it.
5. Share it/Sell it.
6. Manage it (very well).
7. Duplicate it.

---

* Dell Loy Hansen is a near genius when it comes to his grasp of the numbers and putting together proformas as to a property's potential.

A few words about the 7 Required Steps:

1. Find it. Within this book I've given you a number of ways to locate properties. If you use everyway of finding properties, from the "shotgun" approach to using topnotch brokers and agents, then you will have plenty of properties to choose from. Now don't forget, one of the quickest ways to find properties of virtually any type, from apartments to office buildings, is to go to the Internet. Just go to *Google*, or any other good search engine site, and type in "real estate listings" or "apartments for sale" or "homes for sale" or any words that might lead you to the kind of properties you're looking for. Most sites you will be directed to will allow you to go to any city in the United States and then enter in the price range you desire.

Concerning brokers or agents, I think you will be amazed, as I have, once you find and connect with those rare high volume, high quality producing brokers and agents. And you'll be amazed at how many great properties they seem to uncover and bring to you.

2. Negotiate it. Once you've found a property that fits your approximate criteria, and one of course that you know can deliver the numbers to keep your partners very satisfied, you must push as hard and as smart as you possibly can to get the best price and terms. There are a lot of different negotiating strategies to use and generally you need to use the one that fits your personality best. Some people, like Dell Loy Hansen, (who, by the way, is an excellent and tough negotiator), like to, and is good at, negotiating face-to-face. Personally, I don't do as well with the face-to-face negotiations. My face gives too much away – in other words I am not a good bluffer in person. However, I do very well on the phone or even better on paper with the broker or agent acting as a go between and doing the face-to-face for me.

You need to know yourself well and use a negotiating style that fits you. But remember this – negotiating the deal is a huge part of the battle, and if you do it well, you'll be able to deliver the rate of return that will keep partners knocking at your door and wanting in on your next deal. And I don't care what a seller or buyer says about "this is my final price." Virtually, every price is negotiable. Having said that, however, if you know that asking price is truly a deal and will give you the return you need, don't be greedy because you just might lose out to another buyer. (See Chapter 13, entitled *NINE NEGOTIATING HINTS FOR HIGH RETURN ON INVESTMENTS.*)

3. Tie it up. By now you should know how to tie up a property. Here's a few more hints and reiteration of those ways: Tie it up with "subject to" language. The standards of course are these:

This offer is subject to:
a. Inspection within so many days – the longer the better.
b. Review of the income and expenses and acceptance of same.
c. Financing that is acceptable to buyer.
d. My partner's approval within 3 or 4 weeks (or more if you think the seller will agree). (This is my favorite "subject to")

By using any of the above or maybe all of the above and putting as long a timeframe on it as possible, this gives you time to package it and share it (sell it).

4. Package it. Now that you have the property "tied up," you want to put what you've tied up into a package that makes it simple for the investor to see what he's going to "buy into."

This package would include the numbers and the pictures. Numbers such as the income and expenses as they are now – plus a proforma (projection) of several years into the future. That is what can reasonably be done to increase income and decrease expenses, and therefore increase the rate of return to your investors.

These numbers, put together with a well thought out summary and description of the property, along with photos that show off the property of course, is a critical part of the package.

5. Share it/Sell it. The packaging done in step 4 is critical. But even more critical is your energy, integrity, and ability to excite people and convince them you can and will deliver what you so promise.

Just about anyone can figure out where the big money people are, but if you don't have the qualities listed above, you won't get past the receptionist.

Networking is key here. If you have friends who are CPAs, tax attorneys, real estate agents or brokers, and CEOs or VPs in different companies, you've got the basis of a great start. Each one of them has friends and clients they can refer you to, but only if these people trust your judgment, your integrity, and your ability to deliver what you say. If you do your first deal right (and your first deal will no doubt be your toughest), the world will beat a pathway to your door.

6. Manage it. This step is the hardest one, and one that, for many – including myself – is not a lot of fun.

That step is the hard knock, day-to-day, every single day school of good consistent property management. With more and more property coming in on the plan I've outlined above, you must learn to tap very good people to help with the management of all those properties. You must delegate, delegate, delegate, and to keep those good people you must have very attractive incentives for each one of them in order for them to produce and keep them happy.

Dell Loy Hansen has hundreds of young, ambitious, and well-trained people managing all of his properties. Sure, some of them leave and some are sent packing – and it's a constant battle. But it's a battle that needs to be fought both in money rewards and in the rewards of great satisfaction and contribution.

7. Duplicate it. Great fortunes are made again and again by doing "what works" again and again. Once you've built your mold (and realize it's never a perfect mold and you're always tweaking it) keep using that mold over and over. If you can buy one great deal, package it, share it, and manage it, you certainly can do it a second and third and fourth time.

So many people buy one great property – think they were just lucky and stop there. Then years later, they look back and say, "Wow, look what I've done with this house, or duplex, or small office building – Gee, I wish I had bought ten of them back then." Don't be that person. Keep on keeping on – duplicate your successes.

It's fascinating to me that all these years later I am now writing about what it takes to be a billionaire. Why? Because back in November of 1976 *Fortune Magazine* ran a story on "The Last of the Billionaires" which talked about how five different billionaires made their money.

I read very carefully every word of that story because I was very interested in how they did it. Then, in 1983 when I wrote *Goals, Guts & Greatness*, I boldly stated on page 135, that I thought *Fortune Magazine* was dead wrong. They had concluded that we'd seen the last of the billionaires because of the tax laws and various other factors that would stop others from doing it now or in the future.

You see, one of the reasons I disagreed is because by then I was personally being coached by a billionaire by the name of Curtis Carlson.

In addition to our talks on the phone and meeting him on one of his cruise ships, I flew to Minneapolis for more coaching and a huge shot in the arm of motivation.

Here's what I said followed by Curt Carlson's advice to me as I put it in the book *Goals, Guts & Greatness*:

"*Fortune Magazine* suggests that we've seen the last of the billionaires. But I disagree. I feel that the human will is powerful enough to achieve even that great goal, if the desire and motivation are great enough. If a man can set a goal to make a million dollars and accomplish it, he can set a goal to make ten million, or a hundred million, and accomplish it. Why can't he go for a full billion?

Now, I'm not recommending that you set your goal to be a millionaire, or a billionaire – unless that's what you really want. What I am recommending is that you believe in yourself enough to set a high goal. Then, formulate your game plan, just as these billionaires did. Combine that with enough motivation and determination to execute the game plan and hit that goal.

Believe in yourself enough to take the steps required to achieve whatever goal you set. If you can do that, you can reach – and exceed – your every dream."

Here's some of the advice that Curt Carlson gave me that day in Minneapolis way back then that he also attributed to his superior success for his kind of superior success – and notice as you read it that it's just as pertinent today as when he said it more than 20 years ago.

"CARLSON'S ADVICE"

After you've got yourself going and have met your first goals, Curt Carlson said, "There are two things you should do to obtain super success."

"First, he said, get the very best people you can find to help reach your goals. Especially, find the best attorney and the best accountant that money can buy – and use them."

"Second, learn to delegate well. Don't try to do everything yourself. Match the right people with the right jobs and then give them the power of authority they need to carry out their responsibilities."

This advice may seem to be relatively insignificant. In fact, I myself may not have paid too much attention to it – if it weren't for the fantastic record that Curt Carlson has behind him.

He started with nothing 40 years ago, his companies are privately held but exceeded one billion dollars in assets in 1981.

Do you think Curt Carlson believed in his goals? The game plan? Motivation and determination? Action? Himself?

One last word about Curtis Carlson, whose fortune was in the multi-billions when he finally passed away a few years ago. And this last word says it all.

In my first face-to-face meeting with him he was so very proud to pull out of his wallet a tattered piece of paper with his very first written goal on it. And that goal was to make $100 in a single week – yes, Mr. Carlson truly started at the very bottom and rose to the rarified air of a multi-billionaire.

Fortune Magazine certainly had it all wrong. They didn't know of the driving spirit of Mr. Curtis Carlson and the many others who are following him.

NOTES AND THOUGHTS

_____

_____

_____

_____

_____

_____

_____

_____

_____

_____

_____

_____

_____

_____

_____

_____

_____

_____

_____

_____

_____

_____

_____

CHAPTER 9
SETTING GOALS AND THE ENERGY THEY CREATE

You're lying in bed – just waking up – your mind is a bit hazy. Slowly you're becoming more aware of the every day waking, working world, full of mundane duties and tasks. Suddenly, seemingly from nowhere, comes an **idea** – a **thought** of something you want to do – maybe something fun – something exciting – or maybe something you want to do for someone else – a surprise, a kind deed – it could be one of a thousand different things. The point is it's your unique and exciting and driving idea or thought. Sometimes it's only a fleeting thought, but it did create some actual energy inside you. Yes, just energy in your brain at first, but many times if you follow through on the fleeting thought, it excites you enough to fully act out the thought. It can create enough energy to "move your world," and sometimes it can move the world around you!

THOUGHTS PRODUCE ADRENALINE
If your hiking in the mountains and you are confronted by a grizzly bear, suddenly your body has a huge surge of energy that can assist you in doing some almost supernatural things. You and I somewhat understand that brain/body connection and how that type of confrontation will create a thought in the brain that immediately produces adrenaline in the body.

We all understand how quickly the brain can cause the body to create that kind of energy. Energy we must have in a case of dire emergency. It's a brain induced bio-chemical reaction that pumps adrenaline into our system and almost instantly gives us a huge amount of energy and strength.

So it's pretty obvious that the brain can produce actual energy and it's the thoughts we run through our minds that stimulate the brain to create <u>that real energy</u>. Some of those thoughts are just a reaction to an unusual or sudden traumatic experience. **But other thoughts we have on purpose are created by the brain and can have a specific objective in mind – it's our choice.**

Apparently what happens is that the neurons in your brain are wired to respond to novel and new events and not wired to fire if the events do not provide new and different information. So when we have a new thought, and hence a new idea that leads us to setting goals, actual energy is created that moves us physically toward our goal.

At the other end of the "brain/energy connection" spectrum we all know a quick way that our energy is drained is when we mentally get down or depressed, especially now in our fast moving, high-stressed world. Psychiatrists tell us that depression is running at an all time high and can hit almost anyone. If we want to maintain maximum energy so we can carry out our goals and live a more productive and happy, fulfilling life, there are some mental paths that will help us out.

According to Martin Seligman, in his book *Authentic Happiness*, many people as soon as they detect any sadness going on in their mind, begin to ruminate and dwell on <u>how they feel</u>. Then, they start projecting those feeling into the future. This, in turn, increases the sadness and affects all of the person's activities – then, BANG! Immediately, it drains their physical energy to the point that they really don't want to do anything.

As an antidote, David Burns, in his book *Feeling Good,* says, "Every time you feel depressed about something try to identify a corresponding negative thought you had just prior to and during the depression, because these thoughts have actually created your bad mood. By learning to restructure them you can change your mood." Then you see a return to your energy.

THE MAGIC OF WRITING IT DOWN

Yes, you can actually generate energy by simply running certain thoughts through the gray matter of your brain. But if you want to make a quantum leap forward to ensure those goals are reached, there is one single step you need to take.

And that step is actually writing down on paper or your computer what you want to achieve and when.

You, no doubt, already know that – but do you believe it enough to do it? Maybe the next paragraph will persuade you that a written goal really makes a difference.

Now please pay extra attention to what Richard Wiseman, a British Research Psychologist and Ph.D. discovered. In his book, *The Luck Factor,* he tells of the study of the Class of '53 from Yale University and the goals that some of them wrote down. Only 3% of that 1953 class actually took the time to write down their goals. 20 years later, it was discovered that the success of those 3% totaled more than the other 97% combined!

Now if that isn't a wake-up call to those of us who want to achieve something big in our lives, then we'll just have to stay asleep, and I guess we'll just have to accept mediocracy and being average.

This Yale study is just one of many proofs that writing down your dreams, goals, and plans to some great objective you want to achieve in your life really does work. The writing or recording of your goals dramatically increases the odds of your success.

STUCK ON GOALS

In addition to the great mental and physical energy that setting goals can bring you, on top of the obvious factor of accomplishing a lot of good things, there are two more good reasons why I am so stuck on goals. I think when you hear them you might get your mind fixated on goals also.

Last Christmas morning, as I sat watching all my kids and grandkids so content and involved in giving and receiving gifts and enjoying each other so much, I was suddenly struck by a thought! What filled my brain was how fortunate I am and how far and high my goals have taken me and lifted my life, **and anyone can achieve the same thing.** No, not just the stuff – the things – the material wealth – but the great sense of accomplishment and satisfaction.*

To know that your mind could focus on an objective – some mountain to climb, and then to be able to do it is so deeply gratifying and satisfying. I'm sure you know what I'm talking about. We've all done it, and it feels so good. But we don't do it enough.

---

* *In fear of sounding self-serving, or even boastful, I would like to mention some of the great rewards of my goals setting, which have been so very diverse. Setting and achieving my goals have allowed me to do so many things, including traveling the world and taking all my kids and their spouses and my grandkids on trips to all kinds of foreign countries for extended vacations. It has also allowed me to spend time with and talk to world leaders, which has been very fulfilling inasmuch as they have listened to my opinions and maybe even changed some of their thinking. That list not only includes the President and Vice President of the United States, but many other world leaders such as Lech Walesa, the solidarity leader of the revolution in Poland – His Holiness, the Dalai Lama – Shimon Peres, former President of Israel – and an electrifying exchange with Mikhail Gorbachev and his wife with two of my sons standing at my side. To me, these events have been life-long dreams and were made real when they were attached to some of my specific goals. Setting and achieving my goals have also allowed me to become the benefactor of charitable organizations, such as the Granite Education Foundation. The satisfaction one receives from giving to others is one of the best feelings in the world.*

And here's the second additional reason I think goals are so critical to our lives – and this one is easy to miss. Many young people are missing it, and many of us, as we age, miss it. First of all, get a load of this shocking statistic and I'm sure it's true, I see it everywhere I go and I especially see it in the news with movie stars and famous people. Since 1960, "in every wealthy country on the globe, there has been a startling increase in depression. Depression is now <u>ten times</u> as prevalent as it was in 1960!" Now that is shocking!

And even worse – and look around you and I think you'll be able to see this yourself – "the mean age of a person's first episode of depression 40 years ago was 29.5, while today it is 14.5 years." [Quotes by: Martin Seligman, PhD, author of *Authentic Happiness.*]

I must add one critically important comment about depression. I believe a huge additional factor to the horrendous rise in depression America today is also intimately connected to our terrible diets. Specifically, science tells us, and is continually learning more, that the serotonin levels in our brain that produces the feeling of wellbeing and satisfaction are stimulated and produced by carbohydrates.* Especially "complex" carbohydrates. But our diets are loaded with fat, meat, and simple carbohydrates – all of which makes us fatter and more depressed…and at the same time does not stimulate the serotonin in our brain.

You might be saying to yourself, what is he talking about and what does it have to do with goals? Believe me, it has a lot to do with it – here's how.

When we set a goal for ourselves and totally immerse ourselves in it, we not only experience a temporary euphoric state of mind as we are totally involved in the process, but our self esteem rises as we move closer to achieving our goal.

---

* *Lack of certain vitamins and minerals are associated with depression. Go to Goggle.com and search for **depression, carbohydrates.**.*

Not only that, but that "wonderful sense of well being" and lifted self esteem stays with us for quite some time. But there are two distinct critical keys if we want to raise the probability of our success!

First, the goals that we set for ourselves must be difficult. They must make us struggle in order to have the euphoric drug like effect.**

Second, and this is where many people, as they age, miss out or they forget. On that "miss out" or "forget" list is little ole me and so many others, especially movie stars and rich and famous people who we always read about. And what is that second mistake that gets so many of us? It's that we don't pick another mountain to climb once we've successfully climbed our first big money or fame producing mountain – or any other kind of mountain we choose to climb.

We make the huge "depression causing" mistake of thinking…"Ah ha! I've now arrived. I am successful now. I've got it made now." I did what I set out to do (and that goal can be anything from remodeling your home to finishing your degree, or to making a fortune, or retiring). Now you may start thinking it's the time to sit back and relax and sit around my beautiful swimming pool and drink mai tais and truly enjoy life.

Big mistake – huge mistake!

And in our very wealthy society (where almost nobody starves to death), this kind of thinking hits more people than the rich and famous. Any of us can get trapped into the "one hit wonder" mentality and start **resting** on our riches…or resting too long after achieving any goal we set. And it's not about making more money, as most people would think. Sure, that's a nice side benefit, but the real lifesaver is all about

---

**CNN's doctor Fanjay Gupta recently quoted a diet study that showed people who set much higher goals [than people who set more conservative goals] experienced greater weight loss even though they fell short of their higher goals.*

keeping a person turned on about life and living. You've just got to push yourself to new horizons – those new horizons will in turn stimulate your mind which will give you more bodily energy and ultimately so much more life satisfaction.

Look around you and see how easy life is for most people – especially if you compare our lifestyles to the average person of 150 years ago. We don't even have to work hard to make a meal for ourselves. All we do is travel to the store to buy it and throw it on the stove. Or look at what little effort it takes us to go to and from work or any other place in our cars. Things are too easy.

But, at the same time, so many movies and TV shows makes a person (especially the young minds) think that great achievements (whether in sports or financial or any super success) come quite quickly and easily. Nothing could be further from the truth.

We all need a mountain to climb and it's got to be a **steep, tough climb** – not a stroll to the top of a hill. AND – this is a critical part of the whole second key – as soon as we make it to the top, we've got to find another mountain. If we don't, it's so easy to start feeling unfulfilled, which can easily lead to feeling sorry for yourself and onto full-blown depression.

GREAT STRUGGLE PRODUCES
GREAT SATISFACTION

Let me ask you this simple question. What do you think of those guys who risk their lives – put themselves through incredibly excruciating pain – almost freeze to death, and intermittently spend hours and hours of mind-numbing boredom? I'm talking about those guys who attempt to climb Mt. Everest or K-2. Most people think these guys are absolutely crazy. At least I have.

But why do they do it?

I think they know something that most of us don't know – or we may have known it at one time and forgot it. And that simply is this. **Great and long lasting satisfaction and fulfillment comes from achieving something that is very, very difficult and something that pushes us to do more than we think we can do – something that challenges us to really stretch ourselves to the limit.**

As noted above, our free enterprise society systematically goes about making things easier and easier. And we all buy into that and think that is what we want and that will make our lives better and happier, and we'll be more content and satisfied.

Look at how easy life is – we have totally packaged and pre-prepared food, complete with a "don't even move your big butt drive-up window" to "eat that fattening stuff that took absolutely no energy on our part to prepare." Oh, excuse me. I was wrong. You did have to reach out of your car window and take hold of that so-called food which is mainly hollow calories.

Look at all that we have — cars that take us everywhere without a struggle on our part, that keep warm when it's cold outside and cool when it's hot outside. We don't have to wash our own clothes, clean our own house, or do our own taxes, if that's what we choose and we have the money to pay someone else to do it. I could go on and on, but I know you know what I'm talking about.

Life, for many people in America, is a life of pleasure and ease, and we have too much. Paraphrasing the book *Flow*, by Mihaly Csikszentmihalyi, "Every modern nation builds more and more shortcuts to pleasure: TV, drugs, shopping, and spectator sports. And pleasure does not bring long lasting satisfaction – it should be just the dessert, not the main course that it has become in the U.S."

No wonder the first bout of depression hits people now

at an average age of 14.5 versus the average age of 29.9 that it did 40-years ago. If we want to flourish, mentally and physically, and prosper in our society today, and most importantly derive deep satisfaction and contentment, we've got to be proactive and take the right actions. Those actions have to be something that is extremely difficult – specifically, we've got to struggle and struggle, and push ourselves to the limit.

I'm like most people when I see a person risk their life and put themselves through hell to climb some huge clump of dirt and rock just because it's the biggest mound on the earth. Yes, they're crazy. But I think they're crazy like a fox.

They've figured out their life needed a huge challenge. Not just for fun or the challenge of it, but for the huge reward. The life fulfilling reward of long lasting satisfaction that they inevitably receive from rising to the challenge. No, I'm not saying we all need to go out and climb Everest. What I am saying is that most of us need bigger and bigger – and tougher and tougher goals!

Only you can decide what that goal or challenge should be for yourself. But it does need to be big enough and tough enough that it makes you work your mind and/or your body to the limit. Tough enough to give your life meaning, some depth, and maybe give something back to the world while you're at it.

And remember, if it's a lofty or tough goal, it will stimulate and create more actual mental energy in your mind and then physical energy in your body. And on top of that, look at what a human can accomplish. And so many of our seemingly selfish goals not only accrue to our benefit, but they lift the entire human condition, even though they seem selfish at first.

For example, take the self-absorbed scientist who spends his whole life in a seemingly selfish activity of studying the sex life of some obscure bug in Africa because he wants to become famous and he then may consequently discover a new cure for Alzheimer's Disease – which will benefit him, but it also benefits the world.

In my own life I set goals to make money by buying "beat up" properties, improving them, and selling them for a profit – thereby making a fortune. I was first trying to serve myself by reaching my goals, but at the same time I benefited other people by fixing up those properties.

Since 1998, I've carried around in my daily planner a full-length photograph (taken from an article in Men's Health Magazine) of a man named Harry Scott. Understand, I've never met this guy. I don't even know where he lives. Harry obviously worked very hard on his health and body over the years because in that photo (see in photo section) he looks like a perfect 10 at the age of 30. However, Harry was an unbelievable 65 years of age. Anyone looking at that photo, like myself, would be absolutely shocked when they read that he was 65. I'm sure he paid a price for his perfect body goal – but at the same time, I'm just as sure that he received great satisfaction for achieving a really tough goal. And I need to add this very important thought. I seriously doubt he even knew that his seemingly selfish tough goal, that stretched him to the limit, would be of great benefit to the world.

And I do think that Harry's goal is of great benefit to the world. It certainly was with my world. Because that photograph of Harry Scott has been an inspiration and a motivation to me for all these years and, no doubt, to others like myself. It pushed me to take care of myself and let me know that even at age 65 and beyond, you can look and feel like you did when you were young.

My only point is this — You should know when you really push yourself that there will be huge rewards, and great satisfaction. *BUT*, and this is important, what you may not know, or even ever see, is your great effort and dedication, even though it seems selfish at the time, will almost for sure change the world for the better.

(If you would like the latest science-backed information on health and longevity, please email me at moh@reincome.com)

GREAT GOALS

I really don't think it matters what your goal is as long as it's a positive one. It could be anything from improving your own or someone else's health, wealth, or mental abilities, to growing a better strain of vegetables, or feeding a thousand hungry people, or teaching them to feed themselves. There's almost as many great goals as there are potentially great people in the world.

YOUNG AND OLD ALIKE NEED GOALS

Goals push and pull you to be a better you, and as a bonus they get some marvelous things done that can change the world – all while spinning off a byproduct that the world of medicine calls an anti-depressant. Wow! That's a lot of powerful reasons and rewards* to keep setting and going after your goals.

It doesn't matter so much what your goals are – they should be whatever you choose. The key thing is that you set them and you go after them, and that they are not easily accomplished.

In my opinion, the premier goal setter of all time, who has been a great example and inspiration in my life, is Paul J. Meyer of Waco, Texas. Even now, at the age of 77, he is still setting new challenges for himself. I called Paul the other

---

* *Be sure to read more in this chapter about reasons and rewards under the section entitled, BIG BRAIN BOOSTERS.*

day at his second home in the Cayman Islands. His wonderful wife, Jane, answered the phone saying, "Paul is not home, he's at the gym working out." I called him to thank him for the four DVD's and two booklets he had authored and sent me on every subject from being smart with your money to self-talk, self-affirmation, and self-suggestion – and another one called *The Awesome Power of Affirmations*. Paul never stops putting out great stuff to help other people's lives.

What an inspiration he has been. What a life he is living. He packs so much** in and he's not stopping or, from my eyes, even slowing down. I think he'll live to be 120.

We desperately need to teach our children and young people as we preach to ourselves to choose the most challenging roads. Not just for the prize at the end of the road, but for the feeling of flow and fulfillment along the way. To quote again the author of *Authentic Happiness*:

> "Pleasure is a powerful source of motivation, but it does not produce change; it is a conservative source that makes us want to satisfy existing needs, achieve comfort and relaxation… enjoyment (gratification) on the other hand is not always pleasant, and it can be utterly stressful at times.
>
> A mountain climber may be close to freezing, utterly exhausted, in danger of falling into a bottomless crevasse,

---

**Paul not only set a world record for sit-ups when he was a young man, but his successes and accomplishments would fill up many volumes. He founded SMI (Success Motivational Institute, Inc.) which is world-wide now and doing millions of dollars of business and helping millions of people with goal-setting and learning from his methods of self-talk and self-affirmation. He has donated more than $43 million to religious and charitable causes. He started so many other successful companies I couldn't count them. He owns many, many millions of dollars worth of income producing properties (it was from my first book that I got to know Paul), and so many other ventures, I lost count. He has a wonderful family who he has involved in some of his businesses and helped them start other businesses for their own. (But maybe his biggest accomplishment of all time is he beat me in tennis one single time – if you ever meet him, don't ask him how many times I beat him.)*

yet he wouldn't want to be anywhere else. Sipping a cocktail under a palm tree at the edge of the turquoise ocean is nice, but it just doesn't compare to the exhilaration he feels on that freezing ridge."

Life is all about the "mind road" we choose and setting a goal is the beginning of sending yourself down a particular road.

CHOOSING THE RIGHT "MIND ROAD"

Personally, I have found that if I stop and deliberately choose a different "mind road" I can many times quickly turn things around.

The unique thing about the human mind is its ability to pick and choose what it wants to think about and what it wants to dwell upon. You can choose which mental road you WANT to go down. If, for example, I'm laying in bed and I start fretting and worrying about a particular deal I'm working on that has problems, I stop myself and put my mind on another road. Usually I pick a tennis road. I begin playing a game of tennis in my mind, or practice a particular shot that needs work. This thought process and changing my mind road works almost every time – and I know it can work for you.

Our thoughts are linked together. In fact, that is how our memory works. Consider your favorite music CD. You know every song in the order that it appears on that CD. You might not be able to tell me right now what the order is, but as one song gets close to its end, your mind will automatically tell you what the next song is going to be. Since the mind has the ability to stay on one road for some time and link thoughts when you find yourself on the wrong mental road, stop and get off it. Get on the mind road that is courage building. That is a mind road that is positive, that will take you places that are good for you.

We do in fact control the mental road that we go down. And I don't care if you have recently gone through a divorce, the death of a loved one, a business failure, a heart attack, a cancer operation, or are several million in debt. Or all of the above! Though you may be feeling miserable, you have to realize that you can get off that road. You can choose which road your mind will take.

I'm not saying it's easy to change your "mind road" and stay on the road. What I'm talking about is a lot like meditation where if your mind takes you off the "mind road" you want to be on and starts going down another road, what you need to do, just as in meditation, is gently remind yourself to get back on the right road and continue down that road that you choose.

If you change your "mind road" and refocus on your written "goal road," you'll see your energy automatically return. A depressed person gets so self-absorbed and spends an excessive amount of time thinking about **how he feels**. Again, that's a bad "mind road" to stay on. I know, because I've been there many times. But you really can quickly take a detour and get back on the "mind road" you want to be on and the one that is so very good for you, if you return to your "written goal" road.

That's why goals, even the ones you kind of force on yourself, are so very important. They drive your life – at least they can if you let them – and provide you with so much more energy.

But you've got to let those goals work for you. And as I've stated earlier, the starting point has to be for you to capture those goals on paper or on your computer. There really is a magic to writing a goal down.

I don't exactly know why or how – I just know that it does. My own personal and financial results prove that to me and if you don't believe me, just try it. Write down a goal for yourself, right now. Just about anything will do – even a simple thing like…today I'm going to call three old friends and say, "hello, I miss you, and when can we get together?". Put a time limit on that goal. Get serious about it! You will see how (1) it will create brain energy that can quickly become physical energy, and (2) it can literally get your body out of bed, off the couch, or out the door with less conscious effort and with a good attitude in your mind, and so much faster than if your wife, mother, partner, or drill sergeant was yelling at you.

Or how about this for proof of an idea creating actual physical energy – Try it! That is, if you have kids, walk into a room where they're watching television (the great energy draining machine) and ask the questions, "Hey kids, who would like to go out to the airport and jump on a plane and fly to Hawaii, or Disneyworld, or Europe (depending on their age), and see how fast you can create energy in those kids that were sitting with hardly any energy before.

THE WORLD WILL STEP ASIDE
FOR THE PERSON WHO KNOWS
WHERE HE/SHE IS GOING

Years ago I remember reading something that **said it all** about goal setting. The story was about the then young tennis champion, Tracy Austin, who had a plaque on her bedroom wall that states, *THE WORLD WILL STEP ASIDE FOR THE PERSON WHO KNOWS WHERE HE/SHE IS GOING*. Tracy Austin obviously followed this philosophy to get to the top of the tennis world. And she did it while still a teenager at only age 16. Tracy currently is an announcer for TV's USA network channel.

MAKE YOUR DEADLINE A DEAD LINE

If you know where you're going, you also know that the setting of time limits is crucial, and if you're really smart, you'll make sure that those time limits are really time deadlines and you'll treat them as real deadlines.

Originally a deadline was a line drawn within or around a prison that meant just what it sounds like: cross the line and they shot you dead. Failing to set and meet deadlines or objectives you want to reach can kill us off too!

When we finally let go of fear, we see and act at levels above and beyond what we have imagined possible. It is then and only then that we begin to discover our real selves and take advantage of our full potential.

THE JIMMY SHEA STORY

Jimmy Shea, Olympic Gold Medalist of 2002, knows all about goal setting. When he was young he set a goal to "do well" when he went to perform in the world cup. (As you may recall, he got the gold medal later in a new Olympic event called the Skeleton.) Jimmy returned from the world cup where he in fact "did very well" and promptly told his grandfather. His grandfather said that's great, but why didn't you go to **win**, rather than go just to "do well"? That comment by his grandfather was something that Jimmy never forgot, and it was the turning point of his career and he never went to an event again without a specific goal – and that specific goal was winning. (Jimmy did go on to win the world cup and the previously mentioned Olympic gold medal.)

Jimmy's story now is all about his goals in real estate. As I sat with him recently over lunch, he told me about some of those goals. But more importantly, he told me of all the time he spent writing in his journal, recording what he wanted to do, and making notes of how he did relative to his goals.

When Jimmy Shea decided to win his first World Cup (and he is the only American ever to have done that in his sport), he wrote that down as a goal. He then made a checklist of everything he needed to do each day and how much time he needed to spend on each item. Then he would check off each of those items as he did them.

He also told me that many times when he was out and about or doing other things, like hanging out, the thought would pop into his head, "Hey, I'll bet Willy Snyder (his biggest competition) is working out right now." That thought would energize Jimmy's mind to the point that he would go back to the gym and work out some more.

And you know what? Jimmy probably knew there was a good chance ole Willy Snyder wasn't anywhere near the gym, but Jimmy created that myth in his mind to push himself. We all should understand and know that the truth many times doesn't really matter, because the actual reality of what we believe is not as important as the fact that we believe it. **Remember this – a total myth can drive our lives and make us better. Whether the myth is true or not, is inconsequential.**

Jimmy Shea built a myth about his biggest competition and Jimmy bought into that myth to the degree it pushed him to win an Olympic gold medal. But never forget this fact – it all started with a thought that turned into a goal that produced energy. At first the goal was, "I want to do well" – then it specifically turned to, "I am going to win" – and lastly, it changed to the driving force of, "I'm going to win the gold medal".

The future for Jimmy Shea? Just keep a look out for another real estate fortune to be made.

TRY THE IGDS PHILOSOPHY

You tell me where you want to go socially, professionally, personally, or financially and I can tell you how to get there. I can even guarantee that you'll make it. If you begin today to use Tracy Austin's philosophy combined with the IGDS philosophy, your success, financial or any success, is virtually guaranteed. What is IGDS? It is accepting the truth that "I'm Going to Die Someday." You see, all of us are going to die someday. That's a fact we cannot change. The older we get the more we seem to accept that fact. So why not really live life now? Why not really go for it? Why not? What have you got to lose? Just imagine what you have to gain as you begin moving toward the fulfillment of your potential: you will begin to really live, not just exist.

I want you to keep in mind the philosophy of IGDS: I am Going to Die Someday – so I might as well go for it now! Think, "My life is now in each moment. I'll fill my moments with good things."

As you think about what you want to accomplish, I believe what matters most is that you and I become the best possible human that we can and do something great with our lives. I am totally convinced that **YOU** – and that means everyone – have the power to be great. You are totally unique and you are unique for a reason: to do something that nobody else in the world has done. Money or wealth is only a means to an end. If your goal is financial freedom, that goal can buy you the opportunity to discover and exploit your uniqueness and that of your children, parents, and friends. Here is the icing on top of the cake: if you let the IGDS philosophy dominate your thoughts, you'll have an exhilarating time pursuing your financial goals. Or any goal that you have set for yourself.

FOOLISH FEARS TENSE YOU UP

People fear failure, which makes them timid and self-conscious. They are terrified of making fools of themselves. And that's where the philosophy of IGDS can really help: it doesn't matter if you make a fool of yourself for a moment or even a whole day. We all do foolish things, but that doesn't make us permanent fools. We just did something dumb and we probably learned from it. Think about that right now. I mean, really think.

So what if you do something dumb? The fact is that the more you pursue life with great vigor, without fearing failure, the more relaxed you will become and the fewer failures you will have because you have in your mind the fact that IGDS.

HOW A THIRTY-FOUR-YEAR-OLD GETS A QUICK $6,000

Take the thirty-four-year-old man who desperately needs some quick cash. He reluctantly calls the local bank for a $6,000 signature loan. He's never met the banker and is not exactly sure how to ask for a loan or what interest rates he will be charged because he has never done this bold a thing before. But with the IGDS philosophy, he blunders ahead. The phone rings. The banker answers and Mr. Thirty-four-year-old asks for a $6000 signature loan at 1 % over prime rate. The banker laughs and asks if he is serious, telling him they don't make signature loans in this market and certainly not at that rate. A major failure, right? Maybe it is a failure, but it is not major. A serious setback? Not really. It just doesn't matter. It is merely a temporary setback if Mr. Thirty-four-year-old doesn't give up. Sure he got turned down, but it just doesn't matter.

In fact, now is the time to get the banker to help. Though Mr. Thirty-four-year-old was turned down, how about referrals? "Mr. Banker," he might have asked, "what other banks could I go to? Who specifically should I ask for? Can I use your name as a referral? What interest rate would be reasonable to ask for? Please help me. I need your help. How can I improve my approach?",

The banker is now somewhat on the defensive. He is like an employer who has fired somebody, which is a difficult thing to do. The person being fired, if he or she is smart, will ask for favors at that point because most employers will do just about anything to save their own guilty conscience on the spot.

Some people would look at this call to the banker as a failure because they didn't get the loan on the first bumbling try. Many would feel bad that they were rejected. But so what; who got hurt? It just doesn't matter-at least if the lesson is learned and applied later. Wisdom comes from experience. Skill comes from practice, and it is a skill that you are developing as you pursue the IGDS notion. You become wise and courageous.

GO AHEAD, OVERSTUFF YOUR LIFE

Those people who decide to live by the philosophy of IGDS and overstuff their lives with experiences are the ones for whom the world will step aside. Remember: it is not what happens in life, but how you **react** to it. If you expect some setbacks in your life, you'll digest them more easily when they come and they'll hardly slow you down. You might get turned down by ten bankers in a row, or you might get jilted, or you might face a divorce, a bankruptcy, a drawn-out lawsuit, or the untimely death of a loved one. Whatever the external circumstances are, almost everyone has gone through tough times. And I mean tough. If you learn from those experiences and figure out what those so-called disasters are teaching you, life becomes more meaningful. The emotionally strong, the real winners in life, are those who accept the fact that they can't control all external circumstances but know through experience that they can control how they react to circumstances.

STARTING WITH A NEGATIVE NET WORTH

In my late twenties I started to realize that our least-complicated problems are financial, a truth that most people fail to recognize.

I decided to do something about my financial condition, which at the time was a pathetic net worth of approximately $7,000. That was the good news. The bad news was that the sum had brackets on both sides of it: ($7,000). I didn't know it then, but my decision to make a million dollars by age thirty put me almost halfway there.

YOUR CURRENT DOMINANT THOUGHT

If you know precisely where you want to go financially, and start moving forward (even though you may not know exactly how to get there and will make mistakes along the way), you will come so close to your target or goal that it may scare you. Research has proven over and over that a person moves consistently toward his or her **current dominant thoughts.** It's all about what you think most of the time – the key is making sure that you take the time to carefully craft, and set with timeframes, what you want to achieve. Then that will become your current dominant thought and over time, will move you toward your goal. That's why fat people get fatter and rich people get richer. It all about what they're thinking.

MY TWENTY-FOUR-HOUR INNER COACH

When I decided that the nice, round number of one million dollars was what it would take to retire at age thirty, my inner coach said, "Okay, if that is what you want, that is what I'll help you work on." And work on it we did – coach and I. (All of us have an inner coach – my name for the subconscious mind – which, given a well thought out serious goal or objective, can do wonders without you hardly knowing what that work beneath the surface of your conscious mind is.)

I didn't realize that he was working on it full time, around the clock. He never stopped. I had some doubts in the back of my mind, but coach didn't have any, not knowing the meaning of the words doubt or escape. He wouldn't let me watch football on TV all weekend. He would make me get out of bed early. He was coaching my thinking about ways to make money almost all the time. He really did believe me. Just by making that decision I had unleashed a twenty-four-hour partner who was relentless in helping me achieve my stated goal.

As I started heading toward that goal, I had many detractors who said that I was crazy and headed for failure. As I became more sure of what I wanted, many of these naysayers stood back and watched my smoke. Small newspaper stories began to report my successes. I was labeled everything from a genius to considered just plain lucky. But only I knew about the great power of my inner coach and what "we" could do.

IMAGINATION CAN TRICK YOUR CENTRAL NERVOUS SYSTEM

Inner coaching plus imagination can help you reach your objectives, which science and various experiments have indicated the truth of that statement. The central nervous system cannot tell the difference between reality and fantasy, and that has huge implications for any person who wants to change or improve their skills and self-confidence. This means you can trick your central nervous system into believing that you are doing things like giving speeches, making presentations for bankers, investors, etc., which in actual fact you are only doing in your mind. Vivid imagining can help you reach your objectives. As far as the control center of your body is aware, you are actually doing what you are imagining.

23% IMPROVEMENT WITHOUT EVER TOUCHING A BASKETBALL

The experiment that demonstrated so powerfully this point involved three groups of students who were each given a basketball and told to shoot free-throw shots. Each group shot for the hoop and the percentage of successful throws was tallied. Each group was asked to do something different before repeating this exercise twenty days later: the first group, the control group, was told to go home and forget about it until they were to return. The second group was told to practice shooting the ball every day. The third group was told to spend twenty minutes every day imagining themselves standing at the free-throw line and shooting the basket.

When the control group shot again, their percentage of increase in accuracy was zero, just as would be expected. The second group, which had practiced for twenty minutes each day, improved their accuracy by 24%. The third group, which had visualized themselves shooting successful baskets, improved their accuracy by 23% without ever having touched a ball in the intervening time.

The implication of what this type of visualizing can do for life is nothing short of phenomenal. You can basically trick your body into believing you are actually doing whatever it is you are visualizing, whether it's giving a speech or performance, playing a game of tennis or golf, or making a sales pitch to potential investors or would-be-clients. By setting your mind on an objective and then visualizing it will make your goal easier to achieve.*

---

* *This is possibly the reason that the "inner coach" concept works so very well. You set a goal, write it down, put a time limit on it, and get excited about it – and what you are really doing is programming your inner coach or subconscious mind, and once you do this, even if you falter a bit or get down, your "inner coach" keeps on going. That coach is going to make you succeed and reach your goal no matter what. In fact, maybe even in spite of you.*

If you spend enough time internalizing your ideas, they become a part of you and will come to pass. In fact, that is what genius is all about. Genius is the ability to clearly visualize the objectives.

HEAD BATTLES

Most battles are fought in our minds. If you want to achieve more than the average person, the battles are tougher. If you are striving for anything out of the ordinary, the average person will never understand what you are up to. And that will make you question yourself. So your head battle will continue for a while. You will wonder whether you're doing the "right" or "best" thing. You will also question whether the achievement of your goal is really worth all that effort, and energy, and sacrifice you're putting into it. You will constantly be asking yourself: Should I invest my savings? What will people say if I fail? Should I pursue this new business full-time? What if I run out of cash and lose everything? What if there is another depression? Am I being fair to my kids? Will my wife (or my husband) leave me if I don't do well? Who am I to think that I can succeed where others have failed? Nobody in my family has ever done anything like this before. What if I get   sick? How am I going to live without any salary when the money stops coming in? And on, and on, and on. Courage takes firmness of spirit.

It takes a lot of courage to fight those mental battles to achieve your immediate or long-range goals to become totally financially free. Or for any goal or goals you set for yourself. Obviously it can be done because so many people have done it. And so many people have made it by starting at the bottom without any handouts or big advantage.

And the climb to the top began with a simple thought or idea that created excitement and energy inside that person's head and that led to a goal, then a plan that was carried out with some of that brain energy for a life changing sense of fulfillment because of the results that you received.

It all starts inside your head.

BIG BRAIN BOOSTER

THE SIMPLE TRICK THAT KEEPS YOU ON TRACK

We all know it's easy to set goals. But we also know it's hard to stick with them even with the twenty-four hour help of your inner coach. Everyone knows that. After all, who hasn't set a goal or goals for themselves – started working toward them with great enthusiasm, only to find themselves saying it's not worth it – and then quietly beat themselves up in their mind over another failed endeavor.

We've all been told we should write down our goals, and many people do. And yet, even then, most people seem to fail. Obviously, we know that just having the intention and the thought, and then the goal, is not enough to guarantee that we will always stay on track. So what is the trick that pushes people to stick with their goal, stay on track, and succeed?

Well, here's that secret Big Brain Booster that will help you stick with your goals and give you extra mind motivation – and believe me, it sure works. Here it is – try it and you'll see that it works virtually every time.

Take time to write down all of the benefits that sticking with your goals will give you as a person.

And, if you think of more benefits as you go, add them to your list. But there are some other things that go along with making your list that are critical.

Let me first tell you how this lesson of writing down the benefits was forcefully put into my mind. I've been reading a fantastic book called *Beyond The 120-Year Diet*, by Dr. Roy

Walford, leading expert on longevity in the country. As I read the book and saw how difficult some of the calorie restrictions and other parts of the diet were, I began writing down various benefits (I labeled those benefits my **B-RAM List**, which stands for *Benefits, Rewards, and Motivation*), which really says it all and better than just the word benefits) that would flow to me. Suddenly, it struck me as I added to that list that this was the very key to keeping me on track. That is, any time I got discouraged, got weak, or got diverted, I looked at this list and it remotivated me and reminded me of why I set the goal in the first place. This part of the formula is critical.

As my very bright Vice President, Marina Miles, said to me just the other day, "You know, many times I forget why I set a goal in the first place. Which, I might add, is one of the reasons it's so easy to give up a goal when the price seems to be high. Heavens, if we forget why we even set the goal in the first place, even for a fleeting moment, how can we ever expect to stick with it." But if the list of benefits (or can I now call it **B-RAM List?**) is in our face every day, reminding us why we set the goal, then it's so much harder to give up on that goal.

That list can turn out to be our own best coach. The list is kind of yelling at you to do what you know you should, like so many of our high school coaches or gym teachers did to us to get us to do more when we were young. Especially, at those certain times in our weak moments.

Quick example: Say you set a goal to work out five days a week – you're up at 6:00 a.m. and you're working out. The first few days – wow, it's working. You feel good. You've set a goal, written it down, made up your mind to stick with it, and maybe you've even run a few of the benefits through your mind. Yes, you've decided it's all worth it.

But watch out! It's now day four, and as you wake with a few sore muscles and a few cobwebs in your head, you slowly role over and squint at the brightly lit alarm that reads an ugly 6:00 a.m. Ugh! "Hey, if I just miss one day, no big deal." At that point, you're mind doesn't even think about the benefits that you've briefly thought through back on the day that you set the goal.

Let's stop right here! What if you had taken time to meticulously think through all the benefits and then list them, and I mean in **big bold print** on paper, completely enclosed in plastic or laminated, and you place that list on your bedside cabinet, or maybe even better, on the ceiling.* So, immediately when you had those thoughts (missing just one day won't be the end of the world thoughts) there is a high probability that you will respond to that list of reasons why you set the goal in the first place, and those reasons can and will (most of the time) push your mind, then your body, into action.

So, I hope I've made my point – here's what you absolutely need to do:

1. Well thought-out goals must be written down; BUT
2. The trick, the secret, the thing that keeps you on track, the real motivation for you to stick with those goals is to know the benefits that are going to flow to you for all your efforts.

THEREFORE
1. Be sure you write down your **B-RAM List**; AND
2. Make sure you put that list in a place where you can see it easily and often. (See my **B-RAM List** on Addendum C that keeps me on track and motivated with the 120-Year Diet goal – Remember, it's just for me but I give it to you as an example.)

---

* *It's an excellent idea to make several copies of the benefit list and put that list in various places in your home, car, and workplace. For those of you who are into having exact schedules and routines, looking at this benefit list as a part of your daily routine can be extremely motivational and beneficial.*

Here is a summary of what I've been trying to impart to you to be the most help I can be:

- Know that goals, ones that are real to you and well thought-out, literally create energy in your mind and body.
- Know this – If you know what your dreams are and where you want to go in your life, and turn those dreams into a goal, and add a plan, your inner coach or subconscious will likely get you there even though you get discouraged from time to time.

Here are the steps to take:

1. Set a goal with forethought.
2. Write it down – record it in a permanent place – journal or computer.
3. Think about your goals – internalize them – imbed them in your brain.
4. Set time limits and deadlines on them.
5. Make that all important record of your **B-RAM List** that will flow to you – these are the reasons you are doing all of this (post it – look at it often).
6. Create a checklist of all the little steps that must be done along the way day-by-day.
7. Celebrate even small progress as you go.
8. Don't forget to return to step one, no matter how great your achievements were.

Remember, when you get to the top of the mountain you set for yourself, that's only the top of one mountain. You have to see and climb your next mountain – it will keep you out of the valley of discouragement and depression. Then your contributions and celebrations can be endless.

PLANS AND GOALS

_____

_____

_____

_____

_____

_____

_____

_____

_____

_____

_____

_____

_____

_____

_____

_____

_____

_____

_____

_____

_____

_____

_____

_____

_____

PLANS AND GOALS

CHAPTER 10
TWO HUNDRED THOUSAND DOLLARS WORTH OF ADVICE

HOW TO QUICKLY DETERMINE A PROPERTY'S VALUE

Remember Deil Gustafson (Chapter 7), how he found an apartment building, bought it entirely with borrowed funds, and put $200,000 in his pocket? Now the important question: Would Deil Gustafson have found the 160-unit townhouse development that he purchased for $1.1 million and taken out a loan for $1.3 million, if he had not been hunting? Of course not. Even if his luck had been phenomenal and he had come across that investment, if he had not been looking and hunting and comparing, he would not have *recognized* Nicolette Village as the remarkable bargain that it was. Opportunity would have knocked, but he would not have answered.

MAKE YOUR OWN LUCK

Countless times people have told me they wish they were as lucky as I was to find the super bargains I have found. Most of these people have not spent even one hour hunting for and comparing apartments, office buildings, stores, and other real estate investments. In fact, I can safely say that not one of these people, had they been offered any one of the super bargains I have bought, would have recognized it as being a bargain. The cause for this bargain blindness is that they have not spent the time shopping and comparing to have the knowledge it takes to recognize super deals. No, it doesn't take a lot of brains, but it does take experience and some knowledge. The knowledge can be acquired by any person with average intelligence. It doesn't have to come through formal education or even from books. (Books will save a lot of time, however.)

This knowledge can be acquired easily, but it will take time. You need to spend time shopping. You need to spend time comparing twelve-unit apartments with twenty-unit apartments, twenty-unit apartments with twenty-five-unit apartments, apartments on the east side with those on the west side, the north with the south, the good areas of town with the less desirable, and different apartments within each section of town. In other words, start acquiring and accumulating data and information about all sizes and types of apartments* throughout your city, and you will begin to understand what makes up value. If you compare at least one hundred different investments, you cannot help becoming an expert in determining value.

Then, when you come across an apartment complex like Mr. Gustafson did, you will quickly recognize it as a bargain. You will be so excited and anxious that you will not be able to sleep until you can present the offer. You will be eager to tell people about it, but you won't. You'll be afraid they will take advantage of the situation before you can. This would probably be a needless fear because most people would not have the knowledge or foresight to see it as a bargain. Still, to be on the safe side, don't tell anyone until the deal is sewn up.

---

* There are many other types of income property, such as offices, stores, warehouses, shopping centers, and medical buildings, all of which can be excellent investments, but in the beginning steps of your program, it is highly advisable to stay with residential dwellings which can cover everything from single-family houses to a several-hundred-unit apartment complex.

Is all this work and effort really worth it? Let me ask it another way: Would you hunt, shop, and compare values in real estate investments if I paid you $100,000 for six months, or $200,000 for a year? Sure you would. And so would every other person in his or her right mind. But, you say, that's a sure thing. Well, that is exactly what you will be getting if you push yourself to do it on your own, if you work as hard as I would have you work for me in that six-month or twelve-month period.

GETTING STARTED

The biggest problem with most of us is how to get started. Vernon Howard tells about a man who is successful in many fields and who has the Midas touch that turns everything he touches to gold. Howard claims it's not the genius-like mind or the inside tips a person may receive or even a favorable nod from the goddess of fate. In an article entitled "$50,000 Worth of Advice," Vernon Howard says it is *making the decision*. Quoting from the article, Mr. Howard is telling how Arnold F. put it:

> Pardon me for saying so, but some of you have splitting headaches right now from trying to decide between Roquefort and French dressing on your dinner salad. Yet you call yourselves men of decision.
>
> Some of you are deciding yourself right out of everything you want. The plain fact is, you don't have the nerve to step right up and take what you want. You have the inner conviction that you maybe *could* achieve ten times as much. But you won't make up your mind to once-and-for-all go ahead.
>
> You rationalize by saying you'll wait until conditions are brighter.
>
> Or you think you'd better think it over awhile longer.
>
> Or you don't think it's been done before.
>
> Or you say you'd better check with someone.
>
> Or you're not sure you can follow through.

Or you just don't know.

Some of you folks out there have more alibis than a kid caught in the cookie jar.

Maybe you are asking, "But isn't it intelligent to wait until I know exactly how things are going to turn out?"

The answer is, if you have to know exactly where you are going you will never go anywhere. That's the big problem. You want so desperately to be secure and to be protected that you're scared to step off into the adventure of the unknown. Go ahead if you want; be what you *call* secure. But don't ever expect to advance beyond the petty positions you now occupy. I'm not being insulting; you know I'm telling you the truth.

Personally, I rather enjoy the idea of not knowing exactly where I am going — that gives me the opportunity for investigation which can lead to improvement. Ladies and gentlemen, if you insist upon safety at every step you might as well close your doors and turn in your business licenses; you have no business owning one anyway.

Indecision is the mark of a fearful mind.

(*Success Through the Magic of Personal Power*, Vernon Howard [West Nyack, N.Y.: Parker Publishing Company, 1961].)

You must learn first of all that you must make a decision to get started. You must make a decision without all the facts, figures, and data to tell you exactly where you are going. Why? Because it would take more than a lifetime to gather all the data needed to weigh all the variables and possibilities that could happen along the way. There is no practical way to pinpoint accurately the final destination.

It seems to me that we have erred in our colleges and universities. We have placed so much stress on the importance of the technical aspects of business that somewhere, somehow, we have lost the total perspective. The emphasis is on how important it is to make finite forecasts, come up with sophisticated computer models, stress the need for complex calculations of risk versus reward, that we never get around to (or at best postpone ad infinitum) making definitive decisions, decisions we will stick by, decisions we will make work!

If you really want to make the $200,000 promised in this chapter heading, then take this advice: Make the decision to get started now. After the decision is made, the first step in earning that amount of money in a one-year period is one that is so simple that it sounds like a first grade reader. It is Hunt, Hunt, Hunt; Look, Look, Look; and Compare, Compare, Compare. There are no substitutes.

YOUR FORTUNE IS IN YOUR OWN BACKYARD

Now the logical questions: Where should you hunt? What should you look for? What should you compare?

The best answer to the first question is the oft told story of Ali Hafed who lived in ancient India. Ali Hafed was a wealthy man and very contented. He owned a large farm with orchards, green fields, and many gardens. One day a Buddhist priest visited Ali Hafed and told him an inspiring story about how the world was created. During that time, many precious metals and gems, including diamonds, were made.

The priest told Ali Hafed of the great worth of the diamond, even if the diamond was small in size. As he heard the story, Ali Hafed became discontented because although he possessed many riches and worldly possessions, he didn't have any diamonds. When he went to bed that night, he was a poor man because he was totally discontented.

The next morning he sought out the priest and asked where he could find these gems called diamonds. After receiving the directions, which were somewhat nebulous, Ali Hafed sold his farm, put his family in the charge of neighbors, and started his search for the diamonds with the money he had from the sale of his farm.

His search took him to Kenya, to Palestine, Europe, and Spain. In Spain, Ali Hafed, a poor, broken, disappointed, discontented man in rags, could bear the pain of his fruitless search no longer. He threw himself into the incoming tide and ended his life.

Back in India on the farm that Ali Hafed had sold, the new owner, while giving his camels a drink from the shallow stream, noticed a glitter in the bed of the stream. From the water he pulled a black stone that reflected the light with great intensity and displayed all of the colors of the rainbow. He took the stone to his home and placed it on the mantle.

Later, the same Buddhist priest came to visit this man in the former Ali Hafed home. He saw the stone and its bright glitter and asked if Ali Hafed had returned. He recognized the stone as a diamond. When he learned that the stone had been found in Ali Hafed's own back yard, he and the new owner rushed out and found literally handfuls of the beautiful stones. It is said that this was the discovery of the diamond mine of Golconda, supposedly the most magnificent and largest diamond mine ever discovered in the world.

The point is: begin your search in your own back yard. Start hunting for properties in the town or city in which you live. Whether it is 500 people, 500,000, or larger, you will find your acres of diamonds in your own back yard.

ARE REAL ESTATE AGENTS REALLY WORTH THAT FAT COMMISSION

First of all let me say I've never been an agent or a broker and never wanted to. Second, there's of lot a poor, lazy, and basically worthless real estate agents out there. But – guess what? – I think real estate agents are worth their weight in gold. The good ones are that is. Some good (no, not good - great) real estate agents out their have made me millions and millions, and I would **not** have made many of those millions of dollars without their highly competent and energized help.

I never mind paying a fat commission if the agent has done their job. Oh sure, sometimes I negotiate their commission, especially if I just can't quite get close enough to the buyer or seller's price…and most good agents will be flexible with their commissions to save the deal.

So I recommend that you save yourself tons (or should I say thousands) of dollars worth of time and let that broker or agent find the sellers and buyers and keep the negotiations moving to the point of consummation. You'll be glad and richer when you do it.

In today's computerized and internet-ized world, good agents can show you a lot of deals and do it so very quickly by giving you access to their internet accessed websites for you to do some easy shopping. Plus, you can use the Internet to quickly find a goldmine of properties. Just go to *Google* or *Ask Jeeves*, or any other large search engine, and type in any of the following word, or any other words that would bring up the type of properties you're looking for:

- Apartments for sale listings
- Office buildings for sale listings
- Retail buildings for sale listings
- Triple net building listings
- 1031 exchanges

In any one of these searches, and many other sites, you'll be able to type in your city and a price range that fits your investment strategy.

You can even go to www.realtor.com, which will show you a huge number of properties in every city.

So, to enhance and aid in your hunt, you should enlist the help of real estate agents in your city. Get to know the good ones. Ask friends for referrals of the brokers and agents of real estate who really know income properties. Don't stop with one or two; get to know dozens. Tell them the types of properties you are looking for. Let them know that you will look at properties at any time, that you are a serious buyer. When they call, be sure you go. Keep notes and glean all you can from the visit.

Use your local newspapers. Study the income property columns and the listings of single-family units for sale. You will need to check dozens and dozens of properties before you will have the knowledge to recognize a true bargain. Before you have seen dozens and are in a position to judge for yourself, don't take the word of the agent or an owner as to whether a particular property is a bargain or not. Remember that his interest is different than yours, because he will benefit from the sale, whether he is the owner or the agent.

ADVERTISING PAYS BIG DIVIDENDS ($5 AD PRODUCES $45,000 PROFIT)

Second, use the newspaper to place your own advertisements. Start with simple advertisements, such as "Private party wants to buy older income property regardless of condition." Then just add your telephone number and your email address. At first, check out all leads you receive, even the obviously overpriced ones. As you do this, you will add to your warehouse of knowledge about properties. From such an advertisement as this, I purchased my first property, a twelve-unit, sixty-year-old building. I didn't have the courage to buy it on my own so I asked a friend to be a partner on that first deal. (He was a friend of mine from college by the name of Steve Blaser and he already owned about twenty units elsewhere in the city.) I made a shaky, low offer of $85,000 with only $4,600 down on a thirty-year, 6 percent contract. Much to our surprise, the owner accepted the offer without a single change. In fact, he accepted so readily and so willingly that we figured something must be wrong; we almost backed out of the deal. That would have been a big mistake. After some minor fix up and rent raises, the cash flow every year exceeded the original down payment. In fact, the cash flow was more than $5,000. (I bought out the partner a short time after the purchase.)

Three years later, with both forced inflation and natural inflation, the building was valued at more than $45,000 over the original purchase price. That little advertisement cost less than $5. Be sure to use this method in your hunt for real estate. Simple advertising can be worth a fortune – use it as much as you can.

Before I wrote my first book, the original *How To Wake Up The Financial Genius Inside You*, I quite by chance saw a full-page ad in the newspaper written by a Joe Karbo entitled "The Lazy Man's Way To Riches." Having always had an interest in the huge power of advertising, I read the ad.

My first impression as I read it was very negative inasmuch as I knew, or thought I knew, that there was not a "lazy way" to riches. In my experience it took a lot of hard work. However, the ad was so very well written, Karbo's words pulled me through the entire full-page ad. What got my attention even more was when I learned that six out of the ten stockbrokers in my office at the time had responded to the ad by sending in money to buy the book Joe Karbo was offering in the ad.

A week later, I was stunned again when I read in the well respected financial magazine, *Forbes*, that this new comer, Joe Karbo, had reportedly sold a shocking $750,000 worth of books in a matter of weeks, and that his total expenses for the ads, including the cost of the book, was only $250,000. That, I thought, was truly the awesome power of mass media advertising.

I NEVER FORGOT THAT REAL LIFE EXAMPLE.

Later, when I wrote my own book, I got to know Joe Karbo quite well and wrote my own ad using some of Joe's techniques and had tremendous success myself. (Later, when Joe died, I was honored to be able to say a few words at his funeral.) If you are interested in the entire Joe Karbo story and the way I approached the market and the marketing strategy ads that I used to market the original *Financial Genius* book and other financial products and seminars, email me at moh@reincome.com.

TAX RECORDS: NEGOTIATE WITHOUT COMPETITION

Another way to speed up the process and make your hunt more efficient is to use the city and county tax records to find out who owns what property. The people at your city or county building will show you the records with the names and addresses of property owners. If you have a computer, you'll find most of what you're looking for on the Internet.

This source can be a most effective tool. Drive through the areas that have the size and type of buildings that would make the best investment for you. Say, for example, that you are looking for twenty units, about fifty years old. Drive around the area with those buildings in it. Write down the address of the building, plus a brief description of the property. When you have a list of fifteen to twenty, go to the records and get the names and addresses (some counties will give the information over the phone). From this point it is a matter of asking. Ask if they would like to sell. If the answer is yes, you begin to negotiate, and the beauty of this kind of negotiation is that you most likely are the only potential buyer and, hence, you have no competition as you are trying to elicit the best price from the seller. (See Chapters 11 and 12.)

ASK AND IT SHALL BE GIVEN YOU

Lastly, the thing that will probably be of greatest assistance to you is your tongue. Ask people who own a particular property. Ask people for referrals. Build a list of the names of those who own good income property. Talk to people who know people who own good income property. Most importantly, when you meet these people, *ask* if they would sell the property to you. The Bible states, "Ask, and it shall be given you." (Matthew 7:7.) Believe me, it works! Asking that simple question — would you consider selling your property? — has made hundreds of thousands of dollars for me. But you have to *ask*. Without asking, they will never answer, and you will never know if you passed up a bargain.

PUSH YOURSELF – SET YOUR OWN DEADLINES

Answer this question. If the U.S. Government did not have the deadline of April 15th, when would you get your taxes done? I thought so – "Never" was probably your answer. It would probably be mine also. (Yes, I know you can push it now till July 15th or October 15th with extensions like I do almost every year.)

There is a huge lesson in that one word called "deadline."

Twice in the last twelve months I was pushed to the last day, in the eleventh hour, to name three properties for an IRS designated 1031 Exchange to defer hundreds of thousands of dollars of tax that I would ordinarily have to pay. (As you may know, when you sell investment property you can defer the tax by taking advantage of the IRS's 1031 rule. But you have only 45 days, and believe me that means only 45 days – and not a second more – to identify, in writing, three potential properties that you are going to trade into.)

Now here's the good news! In both cases that IRS imposed deadline forced me to do some hard hunting, and do it quickly...and BINGO, I came up with two great properties in both cases that added a couple million to my net worth – not to mention some very handsome cash flow.

But here is the most important part of the story.

I most likely wouldn't have found those properties if I hadn't had the IRS with a tax gun to my head called a deadline. (I guess this may be one of the only times you will read where I have actually thought the IRS did me a favor.)

So the real trick – and this is not easy, especially when you get a bit financially comfortable – is to set your own deadline.

What you really need to do is put a financial gun to your own head, which I know is hard. If you can do that the benefits you will receive will absolutely blow your financial net worth over the top!

Plus – and this is huge – it will build your self-confidence to a whole new level, because you will trust yourself when you set benchmarks, goals, and deadlines for yourself.

So now that you might be starting to push yourself and set some deadlines, what are some of the ingredients you should be looking for in a deal?

INGREDIENTS FOR A BARGAIN

The second question — what to look for — can be summarized in six short statements:*

1. Property that is undervalued.
2. Property that has potential for upgrading.
3. Property where rents are too low.
4. Property where expenses are too high.
5. Property where basic use can be changed (from apartments to offices, for instance).

---

* *Since first writing this book I've learned through experience that probably the biggest factor to look for is a motivated seller. A person who wants to sell (for whatever reason) so bad they can taste it.*

6. Property that takes little cash to purchase.

A combination of these six basics is desirable. The more of the six you have, the better off you are. Naturally. If you look hard, you can find deals with several of these ingredients. Remember, bargains are seldom advertised as bargains. You must learn to recognize them. I have found many bargains where the property needed upgrading, the rents were too low, expenses way too high, and little cash was needed. When you find bargains that are bargains from more than one of the basics, you have a good chance of upgrading them to a point where you can completely finance yourself out of the deal. This, of course, gives you all your money back, so you can do the same thing to another property. To do this, one must hunt. When you find such a property, you must recognize the potential it has and how to make the most out of that potential.

To the last question — what to compare — I would add, why compare. Here is a list of those things that you should compare.

1. Building Cost Per Unit. Know and understand fully the building costs per square foot in your area so that when looking at a building, old or new, you have a point of reference to compare the building you are looking at with what it would cost today. Ask builders, appraisers, loan officers, and Realtors for the square foot cost. Get opinions from all so that you are sure that your figures are accurate.

2. Use Simple Formulas To Quickly Know A Property's Real Value. In addition to asking questions and finding out as much as you can about the building costs in your area, let me give you some quick measurements to evaluate each property you look at.

What you need is a few "rules of thumb" to quickly see if a property really has potential.

Most sophisticated investors use the traditional "cap rate" as their first and quick test to see if a property measures up. If the cap rate is high enough for them, they then move on to the next level.

Cap rates are really very simple. A cap rate is simply the Net Operating Income (NOI) divided by the cost of the property. (NOI being all the income, less operating expenses such as utilities, management fees, taxes, insurance, etc. – but not the mortgage payment.) Let me give you a simple example:

If the NOI is $25,000 and the asking price of the property is $275,000, you simply determine the cap rate by dividing the asking price of the property into the NOI ($25,000 ÷ $275,000), which gives you a 9.09 cap rate.

This cap rate represents a 9.09 percent cash return on the price you paid for the property, assuming you paid cash for the property. What a cap rate is showing you, as its name implies, is what your cash return is on invested capital.

It should be noted that if you are going to put a mortgage on the property you are buying with a 9.09 cap rate, and that mortgage has a substantially lower interest rate than the cap rate, then your overall return will be higher than the 9.09 percent, provided the length of the loan is long enough and the interest rate is low enough.

Cap rates are great, but they don't tell the whole story. They just tell the cash return part of the story. Remember, in addition to the cash flow you also have returns coming to you in the form of equity buildup, mortgage pay down, increases in value from inflation, and the added returns from tax advantages. (See Chapter 17 on tax benefits.)

But a quick look at the cap rate is a great place to start. If the property has a very low cap rate, you might not want to even consider it.

Mark O. Haroldsen on the *Today Show* with Tom Brokaw shortly after his first book was published years ago.

Larry Rosenberg, my first Real Estate Mentor and Friend, who gave his time so generously (See Chapter 1).

The *Grand Master* of "How To Real Estate," Bill Nickerson, pictured here with Mark O. Haroldsen (See Chapter 3).

Mark O. Haroldsen with Paul J. Meyer at Paul's Cayman Island home.

Shown here are members of the
Kauai Condo Development Team –
Left to Right: Chris Spencer, Mark O. Haroldsen, George Winquist,
Marina Miles, Kevin Horn, Steve Blaser, and Ben Olsen.
Inset: Hannah Sirois and Mark O. Haroldsen (As mentioned in the
Pre-Foreword).

2002 Olympic Gold Medalist, Jimmy Shea, with Kimberly and Mark
(See Chapter 9 and Addendum B).

Mark E. Haroldsen standing in front of shipping containers on the 3.27 acre property (See Chapter 6).

Article about **Harry Scott,** age 65, from the June 1998 issue of *Men's Health Magazine* (see Chapter 9 – *SETTING GOALS AND THE ENERGY THEY CREATE*).

Mark O. Haroldsen pictured here with Solidarity Leader of the revolution in Poland, Lech Walesa – Left to Right: Interpreter, Camille Haroldsen, Mark O. Haroldsen, Danielle Haroldsen, Mark E. Haroldsen, Lech Walesa. (See Chapter 9)

This photograph was taken during an electrifying discussion between Mark O. Haroldsen and Mikhail Gorbachev, pictured here with Gorbachev's interpreter and Mark's two sons, Mark E. Haroldsen and David Haroldsen (See Chapter 9).

This photograph was taken shortly before Mark O. Haroldsen had the rare privilege of introducing His Holiness, the Dalai Lama, at a fundraiser for Tibetan Refugees. (See Chapter 9)

Mark O. Haroldsen with the winners of awards at the Annual Granite Education Foundation – one of Mark's favorite charities (See Chapter 9).

My First Real Estate Deal – The 12-Unit Oaks Apartment Building in downtown Salt Lake (See Chapter 10).

Typical "dirt-bag" property, after fix-up – one of Mark's early deals that he Found, Financed, Fixed, and quickly Flipped.

This is the building that Dell Loy Hansen bought, in conjunction with Mark O. Haroldsen and a few other partners, that pays an automatic monthly return of $6,720. Inset: Dell Loy and Lynette Hansen (See Pre-Foreword).

This is the Denny's building with a long-term triple net lease (See Chapter 10). It requires very little management.

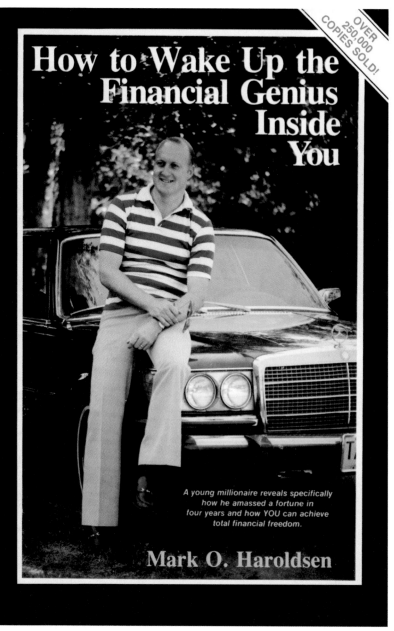

The Original *How to Wake Up The Financial Genius Inside You* . . . has sold over **2,000,000** copies to date!

How to Achieve Total Financial Freedom

Millionaires Are Not 100 Times Smarter Than You, They Just Know The Wealth Formula.

"... more than 250,000 people have discovered that my formula will provide the road map that can lead to total financial freedom ..."

Mark O. Haroldsen spent 4 years perfecting a "wealth formula" and became a millionaire in the process.

We've never met and probably never will, but I think we share a common interest. That interest is in achieving complete and total financial freedom.

Because of this common interest, I think we can be of great help to each other. You see, a little over twelve months ago my net worth reached the magic million dollar mark, and it only took me 48 months to achieve that.

That might not impress you, but if you had seen me just a few years ago, you might wonder how I did it. I lived in Denver then, in a cramped, tumbled down house at 2545 South High Street. My wife was expecting our second child and we were so broke we had to borrow $150.00 from a relative just to buy food and pay the rent.

By the way, I know I didn't make a million dollars because of my superior intellect — I barely got through Ames High School (Ames, Iowa) with a C average. I did a little better later on but I soon realized that a salaried job was not the way to become financially free. If you'll stop and think, you'll realize that millionaires do not work 10, 20, or 50 times harder or longer than you.

Now, how can we help each other? I am willing to share everything I have learned and know that would help and guide you to achieve your own financial freedom and independence. But the only way I would ever give you my secrets, methods and formulas is if I benefit also.

You will find when you reach your ultimate financial goals, you really don't want to stop there but you are motivated to go on and make more.

It seems that most people who are charging for financial advice have studied how to "do it" but have never actually "done it" themselves.

You will find as you read my formulas, that since I have actually achieved total financial freedom myself, that you will receive from me more than just the motivation to achieve your own financial independence, but a workable step by step plan to actually do it.

You may have seen part of my formulas described in many publications, such as *National Business*, and the *Wall Street Journal*. This work is entitled **How to Wake Up The Financial Genius Inside You.** The various formulas contained in the volume will show you exactly how you can do each of the following.

- buy income properties for as little as $100 down.
- begin without any cash.
- put $10,000 cash and more in your pocket each time you buy (without selling property)
- compound your assets at 100% yearly.
- legally avoid paying federal or state income taxes.
- buy bargains at one-half the market value.

If you apply these formulas and methods you will find in a very short time, you will be able to spend three weeks out of every month doing anything you care to do.

I think, at that time, you will find as I have, that spending several weeks on the beaches of Hawaii, or on the ski slopes of Colorado, or just sightseeing in Europe, or any other place in the world, you begin to understand what real freedom is all about.

Most people think that it would be impossible to do some of the things listed above. For example, to buy a property, and at the same time put $10,000 (or more) cash in your pocket without selling the property, or to buy a property with little or no cash down. Believe me, it is possible and fairly simple. This is exactly how most wealthy people actually do make 10, 20, or 50 times more money than you do.

These formulas of mine do not have to be used with income properties only. They actually can be applied to virtually any asset.

While I was struggling on making my first million, I often thought how nice it would be to have the personal advice and counsel from someone like Howard Hughes or J. Paul Getty.

What would I have been willing to pay for this service? I can tell you one thing for sure, it would have been a lot more than the $10.00 that I'm going to ask you to invest in your financial future.

What will this $10.00 actually do for you? It will give you a complete step-by-step plan that you can follow to become totally and completely financially independent.

Please try to understand my dilemma. I'm not a New York advertising agency, with all their professional skill and manpower to write a powerful and persuasive ad to convince you that I can make you financially independent. I am just somebody who has actually "done it", and can really show you how to "do it".

What would you do, if you were in my shoes. You have in excess of $1,000,000 net worth, you have a desire to share your formula with others, because you not only have a simple, honest and workable method whereby others too can enjoy the riches of this land, but you also want to benefit and make money from sharing this information, so you can continue to grow financially.

I think you might do what I'm doing — that is to write a simple open letter to the type of people who share similar goals as mine asking them to try the formulas for themselves, to see if they work as well as the claims described. Because, I know, as you would know if you were in my shoes, that if I can just convince you to test my formulas and methods, you will see for yourself that they will work as easily for you as they did for me.

It's really quite frustrating to have something so valuable as I know I have, but lack the skill to convince people to try it for them-

selves. I hope by my simple, direct approach, I can convince you to try my formulas.

It seems the majority of the people in our rich country lose, not because they lack intelligence, or even willpower, but because of procrastination, or lack of action — please don't be like the masses. Make a decision while you have this paper in your hands. Make a decision now to either act now and send for my material or immediately round file this paper. If your decision is to subscribe, do it now, not later. Otherwise, you may lose, just by default.

To order, simply take any size paper, write the words "Financial Freedom," and send it along with a check for $10.00 to Mark O. Haroldsen, Inc., Dept. TE35, Tudor Mansion Bldg., 4751 South Holladay Blvd., Salt Lake City, Utah 84117.

If you send for my materials now, I will also send you documents that will show you precisely how you can easily borrow from $20,000 to $200,000 at 2% above the prime rate using just your signature as collateral.

Mark O. Haroldsen

P.S. If you are still somewhat skeptical, and believe me, what I started out I certainly was, because of the many people in the world trying to deceive others. I would encourage you to postdate your check by 30 days, and I promise and guarantee that it will not be deposited for at least those 30 days, and if for any reason you do not think that what I have sent you lives up, in every aspect to what I told you in this letter, send the material back, and I will quickly, without question, refund your money and send back your own uncashed check or money order. Also, if you would like to check a few of my references, I have listed some below.

Charles Huber, C.P.A., 1850 Beneficial Life Towers, Salt Lake City, Utah 84111 801-531-8293.

The Salt Lake Chamber of Commerce, 9 East 200 South, Salt Lake City, Utah 84111

© Mark O. Haroldsen, Inc. 1978

This offer has appeared in over ½ billion pages of print since 1976.

This offer has appeared in over 1/2 billion pages of print since 1976.

Famous Olympic Skier Stein Ericksen and wife Francoise with Mark on one of their frequent trips to Hawaii (See Chapter 4).

Double the Mark! Mark Victor Hansen, best selling author of *Chicken Soup for the Soul*, with Mark O. Haroldsen in Salt Lake City.

Mark's first new construction/development project, 68 condominiums, sold out in one week even before ground was broken. It's located on the island of Kaua'i, Hawaii.

Kimberly and Mark enjoying life, biking through the French countryside.

On the other hand, if you know the rents are very low and can easily be increased, or that expenses can be cut, then a cap rate of 5 or 6, or even lower, might quickly be increased to a 10 or 12 or even an 18 percent cap rate after you close on the property and do what needs to be done.

Some people (I've done this many times) do a quick evaluation based on another measurement called "Gross Rent Multiplier" (GRM). It's not nearly as accurate and dependable as the cap rate, but I use it only as a very preliminary test of value.

The GRM is simply figured by multiplying the annual gross rents that a property is generating by a **preset** number. For example: A property that is selling for 6, 7, or 8 times the gross rents will usually get my attention. But remember, that's not net rents, but gross rents (before any expenses). Also remember that the GRM should only be used to make a quick evaluation of the property to determine if you want to look deeper into the numbers. Obviously, if the operating expenses are higher than normal, and you're buying it at 6 times the GRM, you may be paying way too much.

So, if you look at properties first with a quick GRM valuation, then look closer by calculating the cap rate, you should be able to determine what the real cash return on your investment is going to be.

Note: When figuring the cap rate be sure to take a very hard look at the expenses and I don't mean accepting the seller's figures and financials blindly. Use your head, use commonsense, and question everything! It's a very good idea to insist on two or three years of back tax returns on a property, which will almost always show a worst-case scenario.

When it comes to tax time most owners of investment property tend to "expense" everything they possibly can to minimize the tax they owe. Sometimes they go too far and deduct (or expense) non-legitimate items that are personal expenses or other non-deductible expenses. If these expenses are obvious to your eyes as being not connected to the subject property, you would, of course, back out these expenses. A warning, however! Be wary of the seller who tries to convince you to "back out" expenses that are apparently or obviously really legitimate operating expenses of the property.

I've had many sellers try to convince me of that very thing, saying, for example, that the management expenses are way too high because he paid his manager to work on his home or other properties. That may be true, but I'm not easily convinced, and neither should you be. Remember, real values of all income properties are based on their income and expenses – and if the seller "fudges" his figures and convinces you that his expenses are really much lower than shown on his tax return, he can justify a price that may be way too high and financially hurt you. Just be cautious and very skeptical. (See number #3 on Comparing Expenses.)

In the beginning of my real estate investing days, my biggest objective was to increase my net worth. At that time I didn't buy a property just to have a nice comfortable cash flow, I bought to maximize my overall return. I did that by fixing up the property and selling it, taking my profit as a capital gain and not worrying about the cash flow of that particular property – except for how it made a difference on the overall value. In other words, I just wanted to make the most amount of money in the form of a chunk of capital that I could reinvest in another, hopefully larger property.

That's different now inasmuch as today, with a very comfortable net worth, I love to buy triple net leased properties with national tenants or very strong long-term tenants that send me a check each month. My objective is an 8 to 12 percent cash flow return, or what I call a cash-on-cash return. That is, if I have $500,000 into a building that has a Denny's Restaurant in it as a tenant, then I would expect to receive anywhere from $40,000 to $60,000 per year, paid monthly.

I was recently asked by some beginning investors, "What is the best way to go about making your fortune?" These investors were also very interested in receiving <u>passive</u> <u>income</u> – two of my favorite words. I told them in order to get passive income in any significant amount you need to start by making deals that will give you a large gain, usually a capital gain. Then you need to move that gain into bigger and bigger properties until you have a large enough chunk of capital to put into a property that will give you enough cash flow to make a difference – and of course, that amount is different for everybody.

3. Compare Expenses. See what the rule of thumb in your city is and create your own formula for total expenses and the percentage of gross income. For example, I use a rough rule of thumb for expenses of around 30 percent of the gross annual income, assuming the tenants pay the utilities. (Of course, this will vary by area according to how expensive the utilities are.) If the utilities are paid by the owner, I use a 40 percent rule of thumb of the gross income for total expenses. Example: if I look at a building where my value formula of either gross or net compared favorably to other buildings in that neighborhood and where expenses were say $48,000 with a gross annual income of $80,000, it would immediately attract my attention. The reason, of course, is that it would be showing expenses of 60 percent of gross income. I would look closer to see why expenses are so high. If I found, for example, that the manager was being paid an exorbitant salary (I had one building where this was the situation), I would move quickly. Assuming that all other items were in line, I would make an offer, knowing that I could cut the expense figure from 60 percent to 30 or 40 percent (30% being $24,000 to 40% being $32,000).

In today's financial market, the type and cost of financing are usually critical parts of the expenses and you will want to compare the figures of similar buildings. There are a lot of fancy formulas when it comes to financing a project, but I like to keep it simple. The one I use applies to the entire picture, not just to the financing part of the expense. It is simply: What is the total yearly return percentage-wise of my cash down payment? As I compare all the aspects of a particular building with other buildings in the area, I place even more importance to my own requirements — to the total return I must receive from a building. The total return is cash flow plus equity buildup plus inflation plus tax advantages. This total must add up to a minimum of 30 percent per year; ideally, it will be a much higher percentage.

4. Compare Prices. Check what both the asking price and the actual prices have been for apartments and other income property of comparable value. This information can be obtained usually from Realtors. Most towns and cities have a multiple listing service that publishes both a record of properties for sale and those that have been sold and the actual selling price.

5. Compare The Condition Of Different Buildings. Look for and avoid buildings that have major problems (that would require high costs to correct), such as major structural damage, total rewiring, or a complete replacement of plumbing fixtures and drainage pipes.

Why compare? So you will learn to recognize a bargain when you come across it. Although it is good to know all the standards of comparison, the quick and almost foolproof method of analysis is to simply figure your anticipated overall return. Overall return can be defined as the total of cash flow, equity buildup, appreciation through inflation, and tax benefits expressed as the annual percent of your total cash down payment. As a rule of thumb, the absolute minimum you accept should be 30 percent. But don't hang everything on this one formula; be sure the quality of the investment is there. In other words, be reasonably certain that the return will be there for a number of years to come. If the building is in good condition, the basics are sound, and if your projections have been conservative for your city, rest assured that the quality of the return is there.

To make the advice worth $200,000, you must recognize that there are two types of bargains. First, there is the obvious type; the super low price versus current market prices. Amazing as it sounds, two identical buildings, side by side, often sell for drastically different prices, prices that vary 10 percent, 20 percent, or even 50 percent. So, for you to find a super deal, you must spend sufficient time hunting. You must look for those things mentioned above that make a bargain. Have a point of reference and compare values quickly. Then when you come across such a deal, you will recognize it and move quickly to make that deal yours.

The second type of bargain is the potential bargain or the sleeper. This type of investment has been around awhile, but no one has recognized the potential that you will be able to see in the building. The sleeper needs some new ingredient or a new combination of ingredients. The sleeper needs something creative to add value. Don't let the word creative scare you away, if you don't consider yourself creative. The type of creativity needed in real estate can be learned. Creative financing for example (discussed in Chapter 15) is easily learned and quickly imitated.

The types of creativity that make potential bargains into real bargains are simple remodeling, a cosmetic-type building face lift, cleaning, painting, fixing up, carpeting, and basically making the building a place in which people want to live; change of use to higher, better, and more productive use;

and better management techniques that lower the costs of running the building and consequently increase the value.

Is it really worth it? Well, you answer it. Say you spent one or even two years doing nothing but hunting, looking and comparing. At the end of the second year, you came across that super bargain and bought it. Through your efforts and accumulated knowledge you were as fortunate as Deil Gustafson and you put $200,000 in your pocket. What would your answer to the question be?

NOTES AND THOUGHTS

_____

_____

_____

_____

_____

_____

_____

_____

_____

_____

_____

_____

_____

_____

CHAPTER 11
SET THE STAGE FOR MORE THAN $800 AN HOUR

Your bargaining time, as you will learn in the next chapter, can be worth several hundred or more dollars an hour. Before your time can be worth that, before you can actually collect that much an hour, you must take the pains to set the stage to achieve those results.

The old times in real estate used to say there are three and only three rules for a successful real estate deal. They are (1) location, (2) location, and (3) location.

To this I say horse feathers, horse feathers, and horse feathers. At one time this was possibly the law that led to success. But in today's market of high financing costs and mobile population, the rules have changed.

KEY TO GOOD DEALS — TERMS

Today's rules would be terms, terms, terms. In order to get those terms in the way you would like them, in the way that will benefit you most in the short run and the long run, you must take the time to pre-assess the situation. You will need to find out the seller's situation, so you will know how and where to bargain the hardest. Ask a lot of questions and listen carefully to the answers. If you are dealing directly with the seller, ask him the questions. If you are dealing through a broker or agent, ask the same questions and listen carefully to the answers you get through the broker. His answer will be what the seller is saying.

WHY IS THE OWNER SELLING?

What questions should you ask? Number one, find out exactly, and I mean *exactly,* why he is selling; be sure to listen carefully to his answer. He may say he is selling because he needs the cash. This indicates that on the surface at least he needs a lot of cash down or he might want to be completely cashed out. Don't be satisfied with that answer alone. Ask what he intends to do with the cash. In my experience, what the seller is really saying is that he wants to sell and take his gain because he knows he has one, possibly a big one. He is also concerned that the profit might not remain so he wants to cash in and be safe.

If you ask exactly what he is going to do with the cash, in most cases you will find that he intends to put it in an interest-bearing account, usually a savings and loan or a bank. At that point tell him that you understand his situation and that you think you can help. You can help by giving him a higher interest rate than he could earn from a bank or savings and loan. Next, ask specifically what rate he can achieve from a savings and loan or a bank. Point out that you can increase that by one or two percentage points. Then proceed to explain that by accepting a small down payment he can, by carrying the balance on a contract or a first mortgage basis, better his position by a substantial amount. Point out that his financial security is even better because he has a specific piece of collateral to guarantee that his position is safe. In most instances, this argument is convincing and everybody is better off.

BUY AT 20 PERCENT BELOW MARKET

By probing deeper, you will find out what the seller really wants. Then you are in an excellent position to do some hard-nose bargaining. When you finish bargaining and end up with a property at 20 percent less than its true value, with an interest rate 2 percent below market, you will agree that the terms are far more important than the location.

If, in asking why the owner is selling, you find that he needs the cash for a specific investment and that nothing but a large amount of cash will do, continue to pursue the questioning until you are satisfied that this is the real reason. If you find that, in fact, the seller does need all of his money in cash, this could be time-saving and beneficial information when you begin bargaining. (Chapter 15 on creative financing will show you how to structure an offer to meet the needs of this seller and give him the bulk of his cash on the deal.)

BAD TENANTS CAN MEAN A BARGAIN FOR YOU

Think of questions that will give you an indication of how, from a management standpoint, the property is being handled. What you are trying to find out is whether the seller is fed up and wants to sell the property because of bad tenants and management problems. (This is the largest single reason for people leaving the most lucrative business in the world.) However, very rarely, when this is the reason, will the seller actually tell you his motivation for liquidating the property. If this is his reason for selling, there are several routes you may wish to take on proposing a deal. You must know with certainty his real motivations for wanting to sell.

In your questioning, find out what his tax situation is, not only on the property being sold, but his personal situation and the approximate tax bracket he is in. An offer to a seller who has a large profit and is in a high income-tax bracket would be much different than to someone in an average tax bracket, selling at a loss. Think through the tax problems of the seller, then make your offer so he will be in the best possible position.

CAREFULLY PLAN YOUR QUESTIONS

Take time to figure out exactly how to ask these questions so that they are discreet, and so you will receive answers. Don't approach the questions with reluctance or from a negative standpoint; you probably won't get answers. Don't be like the securities salesman I knew in Denver, Colorado, who used to call people and say, "You wouldn't want to buy XYZ stock, would you?" After a short pause, he would almost always say, "Well, I really didn't think so, but I just thought I'd call and check. Nice talking to you. Goodbye." Plan your questions so they are positive and so you will receive answers to them.

If, for example, after probing, you found your stage was set as follows: The seller has large capital gains (long-term basis); has owned the property for six years (tax basis as far as sheltering other income has all been used); and is a person in a high percent tax bracket with little other shelter; then the bargaining point and the structure of an offer would be drastically different than to a seller who has a small gain; has only owned the property for 6 months so still has a lot of tax shelter left; and is in a low percent tax bracket. You must take the time to see the seller's position and what he really wants to accomplish. If you don't, you will be twisting the seller's arm as you bargain, and you may find out that you are twisting the wrong arm.

Take the time to check expenses, including taxes, and scheduled rent and rent-rolls before you actually submit the offer. In some cases this is not necessary, as you should make your offer "subject to" the verification of expenses and gross receipts and acceptance of same within a specified time (usually forty-eight hours) after acceptance of the offer by the seller. But by checking all expenses beforehand — especially where the expenses or gross rents seem out of line and are the basis of your interest in the property — you would be better able to negotiate and understand where to bargain hard. Taking time to do all this before the offer is presented will give you a great advantage over other competitive buyers. If you know rents are 30 percent to 40 percent low and costs can be cut by 10 percent or 20 percent, you may well jump at the seller's first price, recognizing it as a low price. I have been able to do this while my competition was trying to get an even lower price out of the seller. Knowledge of the seller's position usually makes the difference when it comes to the actual bargaining. And that difference can be worth thousands of dollars, so be sure you ask lots of questions.

NOTES AND THOUGHTS

_____

_____

_____

_____

_____

_____

_____

_____

_____

_____

_____

_____

_____

_____

_____

_____

NOTES AND THOUGHTS

_____

_____

_____

_____

_____

_____

_____

_____

_____

_____

_____

_____

_____

_____

_____

_____

_____

_____

_____

_____

_____

_____

_____

_____

CHAPTER 12
BE A POKER PLAYER
WHEN YOU BARGAIN

A few years ago, a twelve-year-old, 100-unit apartment building was brought to my attention. After some checking, I found that the building had not been shopped — the real estate community did not know that it was for sale. I found out from the agent who brought it to my attention that I could only get more details on the building by making a special trip to the sellers in New Jersey.

KEEP ALL YOUR POKER CARDS
WELL HIDDEN

Having business in Washington, D.C., I decided to go on to New Jersey, especially since I had learned I would be the only one dealing on this property. After spending a morning in their office going over the books and records of the property, I sat down with the sellers to discuss price and terms. They were eager to have me make the first suggestion as to the price I would be willing to pay. They were, in effect, asking to see one of the cards in my hand. The poker game had started. I countered that since it was their building for sale, they needed to indicate a selling price before I ventured further. We played verbal poker for a few minutes longer before they mentioned the price of $1 million. I told them that sounded quite high, so I would have to study the figures carefully before I could talk price at all.

Four months later, after spending about 180 hours in bargaining, we agreed on a deal at $850,000, $150,000 less than the seller's beginning price. A cursory calculation of the number of hours and the amount of money saved by bargaining, showed that the rewards for the time spent figured out to $833 an hour. Of course, this beginning price of $1 million and the ensuing drop to $850,000 would be meaningless if the price had been jacked up by $150,000 to begin with and the seller expected to drop by that amount. In this case, however, even the $1 million was a fairly good price. Remember this, $833 per hour for a top-notch negotiator can be on the low side – even though it's hard mental work and takes time and can be a real cat-and-mouse game – but what's at stake is measured in the thousands and even tens of thousands of dollars, and is really worth the extra time and effort.

By spending long hours bargaining and using logic and persuasive argument, the $150,000 saved turned an average deal into a super deal. Incidentally, the sellers in this case were certainly not dummies. They have thousands of properties throughout the United States. I did have the advantage of dealing in my own back yard and knowing the market I was dealing in. Also, I knew that I was the only potential buyer, so I didn't need to be concerned about someone moving in with a higher price. Even if you have competition on a deal, you want to bargain, but you won't always be in a position to hold out for the absolute bottom dollar. Many sellers try to use a potential buyer against another. Don't be bluffed.

BEGIN PLAYING WITH A LOW
BID AND A STRAIGHT FACE

When you start bargaining on a property, look at it as if you were playing poker. In other words, *don't* show your hand to anyone, especially the real estate broker or agent. If you do, your hand will be shown to the seller and the bargaining will be over. If you are trying to buy a property listed at $150,000 for $130,000, begin by bluffing. Begin with an initial offer of say $120,000 to $125,000, maybe even lower depending on the circumstances. (If the property is a bargain at the asking price, don't try to chisel.)

In several instances, I have made offers at a low price to bluff the seller and have had the offers accepted without a counter offer, much to my amazement and delight. When giving an offer to the sales agent or directly to the seller, don't ever show your cards by indicating that you know this is a low offer, that you expect a counter, or if the seller doesn't like the offer, maybe you can work something out. I heard one buyer say to the agent, "Gee, if I could get it at this low price, I would be tickled to death." That is tantamount to laying all your cards face up on the table as the betting begins, so everyone in the game can see exactly what your strengths and weaknesses are.

If you make statements like that to the agent, you can be sure they will be repeated to the seller, inducing him to make a counter offer at exactly what you planned on, or higher. However, if you make such an offer and send the agent along with the idea that that is your best shot, either it will be accepted (which, of course, is rare) or more likely (if your agent knows what he is doing), you will get a reasonable counter, probably very close to your targeted price of $130,000.

Since you will be speaking to the agent or seller when presenting the offer, take time to think through exactly what you are going to say and how you are going to say it. Otherwise, you may tip your hand and indicate what your feelings are. By the same token, listen carefully and ask probing questions to indicate the seller's feelings, attitude, and whether he will bend more. Entertain the idea of another counter to his counter.

MOVE FAST ONLY IF
YOU HAVE TO

As in poker, don't get over-anxious, unless you know that you are dealing on a super bargain and that there is another offer coming in. In cases like this, you may want to move ahead quickly, give up that bit of bargaining, and ensure that you have a deal. I had a case on a downtown Salt Lake property on which I was contemplating making an offer. I was waiting because it seemed to be the best thing to avoid letting the seller think I was too anxious.

The building was run down, had a lot of problems, and few people were interested in purchasing it. In fact, there had been absolutely no offers made on the building. (I found that out by asking.) While waiting for a respectable period of time to pass, I found that another offer was going to be presented. I quickly put my offer together and it was presented at the same time as the competing offer. The two offers were not even close. The other offer was trying to steal the building and was thousands of dollars away from my price which was also quite low. After the other offer was eliminated, the "poker game" the seller and I played for the next three weeks was indeed quite a game. He made a counter offer to my offer; I countered his counter; he countered my counter; then I countered his counter again; and on and on we went. In fact, this game went on all the way down to the day before closing. We were still debating, kicking back and forth who was going to pay the two-point loan fee for refinancing the property. (I finally won and he paid it.) What was all this poker playing worth?

Well, as it turned out, I saved 10 percent from starting at a low price. Not only that, but the terms of the deal were in my favor because of the long period of well-planned bargaining.

The only reason I could continue to bargain so hard and long on an already low-priced property was that the other offer had been completely eliminated. I knew that no other offers were being made on the property. In fact, I checked daily with the agent to make sure that he knew of no other offers coming on the property. Had I heard of any such offers, I probably would have curtailed my bargaining and quickly come to an agreement with the seller.

Whether a real estate agent is involved or not, your approach to bargaining should be essentially the same. The only difference when using an agent is that you are selling and working on him rather than on the seller himself. Remember, no matter how good a friend or close associate he is, don't show him all your cards.

The seller was obviously a so called "motivated seller" and that is the kind of sell you should always be looking for. The more motivated the better the deal you are going to come up with. You see motivated sellers will many times make "big concessions" that under "normal" circumstances they wouldn't dream of — so be sure to seek those kinds of sellers. Your checkbook will thank you.

YOUR FIRST DEAL WILL BE THE TOUGHEST

Your first purchase, if you haven't already made it, is the toughest, mainly because, if you are at all like me, you will be extremely nervous and over-anxious to get on with your acquisitions so you can reach your goal. Remember, just like an over-anxious basketball player or other athlete, it is easier to make mistakes when you are in that frame of mind. Be cautious on the first deal. Look at it from all sides. Weigh it carefully. Don't move hastily, at least on the first one. If an agent is involved, he will, no doubt, bluff you into thinking that another offer is about to come in on the property. Think carefully of questions you can ask him to smoke out the truth regarding any other offers. In any case, don't let this rush you unduly to make too high an offer.

Unless you have made dozens of inquiries and inspections, as well as figuring many times the overall return on the investment, you may find yourself owning a property that was far from a bargain and that in no way fits into your investment program. This type of investment will not lead you to your goal. In fact, it will discourage you from continuing in your pursuit of a million dollars, or whatever your goal is.

Although William Nickerson is talking about bargaining, purchasing of small properties (in this case, a single family home), his suggested method of bargaining is excellent. (These are market prices of many years ago, but his strategy is timeless.) He states:

HOW TO BUY PROPERTY

Buyers and sellers who dislike bargaining may establish a firm figure and state, "That's my price. Take it or leave it."

When they do this in real-estate transactions they are usually left with no deal or a poorer deal than they could realize by tactful negotiation. After a certain amount of dickering, the average seller, especially if his place has been on the market for several months, will accept an offer 25 percent under his original asking price, although he would refuse so low an initial offer. A competent Realtor often convinces the seller to set a price near market value; so the broker's listing may already be considerably lower than the seller's initial asking price. Subtracting 25 percent from the asking price is of course no final gauge of value, since the knowing seller prices high to begin with. But we can use the resulting figure as a guide after checking other value factors. Discounting the listed price of $11,500 by 25 percent gives us $8,625 as an approximate target.

Before making an offer it is well to fix in mind the lowest price the seller might accept, then also set the top price you will pay, so that you are not apt to be swayed by subsequent sales pressure. In this case, discounting our target figure by about 5 percent to $8,200 would represent a bargain. Increasing the $8,625 about 5 percent to $9,000, the figure we arrived at when making our appraisal, would give us a good buy. To the target price about 10 percent might be added, making $9,500 our top price. If the offer is too low, the seller might shy off completely and refuse to negotiate without a higher starting offer. If the offer is too high, negotiations will be difficult to complete within the boundaries set. The first offer should probably be about 10 percent less than the $8,625 we aim for, rounded to $7,750.

HOW TO NEGOTIATE A BARGAIN

Make mental and written notes of defects, but don't point them all out to the Realtor as you go over a property. The agent can be better conditioned to negotiating a low price if the worst defects are enumerated as a prelude to giving an offer. You can be sure the salesman will repeat your knocks and add his own to pull the seller down. We tell Mr. Bokay the building is closer to forty years old than to the twenty he mentioned, since the inspection cards show it was built in 1926. We were looking for a place that needed fixing, but this is rougher than we had anticipated. The foundation looks bad, the way the porch is sagging. The place is badly in need of paint. To make it look decent some of the electrical and plumbing fixtures and all the furniture should be replaced. Instead of being worth the $10,000 the Realtor mentioned, the actual gross rents of $90 a month show that from an income standpoint, the place is worth only a base valuation of $9,000. And that figure should be discounted considerably to take care of the painting and other much needed expenditures.

Mr. Bokay expostulates, "Although I mentioned $10,000, that is pretty close to rock bottom. The owner is asking $11,500. The house is now renting for $90, it is true, but should rent for more even in its present condition. It might rent for as high as $200 if you fix it up. Besides, there is the full basement which could be converted into a new flat, and the two rentals could turn the building into a gold mine."

We say that if we were selling we would expect to sell on the basis of the actual income, and that when we consider buying we apply the same yardstick. Any additional income that could be obtained would be eaten up by the cost of painting and remodeling, so all we can go on is what the building is actually taking in now. If the place can't be bought on that basis, we might as well forget it and look at something else.

Mr. Bokay tries to pin us down on how much we would pay. We say the place is probably worth a top price of $7,000, taking into account all the money that has to be spent on it. The agent repeats that he doesn't think he can get the owner below $10,000, but he finally agrees to write up our offer for $7,750. (*How I Turned $1,000 into Five Million in Real Estate—in My Spare Time,* pp. 74-76.)

DIFFERENT APPEALS FOR DIFFERENT DEALS

Variations should be used to this basic bargaining method. By knowing why the seller is selling and what he wants in addition to the position he is presently in, you may not want to bargain for a low price at all. For example, the situation of a person who is desperate for cash is drastically different than the seller who is in a high tax bracket and doesn't need cash. In the first case, a very low all cash offer using Nickerson's suggested method of bargaining would be the best route to go. In addition, where he is desperate, you would want to put a short-term fuse on it; that is, to close the deal as soon as possible.

In the second case, you may want to offer more than the property is actually worth to get attractive terms, and make a low down payment, possibly 5 percent or even lower. (You might need to show the seller you are a strong buyer so he will not risk getting the property back since he would be carrying the financing on the balance.) Or you may possibly be going for an extremely low interest rate of 3 percent to 4 percent. (Yes, I know the going rate is now higher than this, but with enough negotiation and persuasion on your part and the fact that you're offering him more than the property is worth, you just may be able to talk your way into rates as low as these.) The seller would benefit by this higher price. (See Chapter 15 on creative financing.) By paying more than the property is worth, but getting it with a low down and low interest, your cash flow could be very high. Consider this type of offer if the seller is only concerned with his price.

Remember to listen carefully to the seller. Discover his wants and needs first. Then frame your offer and plan your bargaining around the knowledge you have acquired. By doing this, a high percentage of your offers will be accepted and you will move more rapidly toward your million-dollar goal.

HOW TO WRITE AN OFFER
WITHOUT RISKING A CENT

The purchase terms are not the only thing you should concern yourself with when negotiating for a favorable deal. There are technicalities you should become familiar with. First of all, become intimately acquainted with the earnest money offer or deposit receipt, as it is called in some states. Study and know all about it. Ask Realtors to explain the different sections in it. Seek help from a competent real estate attorney, if at all possible.

It is a good idea to use an attorney at closing time, if you have not been through this process many times before. This could save you a great deal of money. I always make it a practice to put in plenty of "subject to's." These little additions in the earnest money offer give me a great amount of flexibility and have saved me from losing my earnest money if I didn't go through with the deal. These clauses are for your protection so that if things are not as represented, you have an escape hatch. The ones I usually use are; "This offer is subject to the buyer inspecting and accepting the financial records and data of the seller within forty-eight hours after acceptance of offer." "This offer is subject to a complete inspection and acceptance by the buyer of the property within forty-eight hours of seller's acceptance of offer." Another good "subject to" offer is; "This offer is subject to the approval of my partner within ten days, or twenty days, or more if you think the seller will agree." In essence, you can end up with a free option on just about any kind of property and the longer you stretch it the more valuable the option is. The "subject to" line is pretty much up to you as to what you want to make the offer contingent upon. So just use your head here. It is also a good idea to put in the clause, "The seller warrants that all appliances, electrical fixtures, and plumbing, heating and air-conditioning devices to be operative at time of closing." If the property on inspection does not measure up to what you expected, you can easily back out of the deal without losing a cent.

A LITTLE TRICK THAT WILL
CUT YOUR DOWN PAYMENT

One other technicality that can assist the buyer and make it easier from a cash standpoint to purchase any property is the date on which the sale is closed. If the rents are collected on the first of the month, always try to close as soon after the first as possible, say on the fifth or so. This will make it so you, as the buyer, will not have to put up near as much down payment as was stated in the offer. That is, all the rents will be prorated. Since they will have been collected (the seller does this, insuring you from problems in hard-to-collect rent), the pro-ration works in your favor. If you close on the fifth, the seller's portion of those prorated rents would be five days. Your portion, as the buyer, would be twenty-five days.

For example, if the gross rents were $3,000, the pro-ration would work out to $500 for the seller, $2,500 for the buyer. The $2,500 would be deducted from your cash down payment which would in effect reduce your total investment in that particular property. Of course, if you are selling a property, you want to do it the other way around; that is, close toward the end of the month if the rents are collected on the first.

Bargaining, dickering, and fussing over seemingly small technicalities such as the closing date can often make you literally thousands of dollars. It can also be extremely challenging, entertaining, and a lot of fun. As Conrad Hilton said, "I have played variations on that scene [the scene was bargaining] throughout my whole life, often with bigger chips, often over longer periods of time. But the rules are always the same and I have never lost the thrill of the game." *(Be My Guest,* p. 56.)

PLANS AND GOALS

_____

_____

_____

_____

_____

_____

_____

_____

PLANS AND GOALS

_____

_____

_____

_____

_____

_____

_____

_____

_____

_____

_____

_____

_____

_____

_____

_____

_____

_____

_____

_____

_____

_____

_____

CHAPTER 13
NINE NEGOTIATING HINTS FOR HIGH RETURN ON INVESTMENTS

Make a 100% return on your money (starting with $1000) for just ten years and you'll be a millionaire. That's easy to say, and mathematically sound, but how do you make a 100%? It's really quite simple. You can wait for inflation to do the job, or you can create the inflation yourself by fixing up yuks. But there's another way, which may be the cleanest way of all – by negotiating.

Assume, for example, you are able to buy an asset for 5% less than its real market value because of your negotiating skills, then, within a year, you are able to negotiate a sale for 5% above the fair market value. The bottom line of those negotiations is that you made yourself a full 100% return on your investment by negotiating well. The key is skillful negotiations, and the skillfulness is developed through study, practice, and effort.

JAW, JAW ALONE CAN MAKE YOU 150%
Winston Churchill said, "Jaw, Jaw is better than War, War!" And I say that Jaw, Jaw can make you rich, rich. If you use the right negotiating words and actions, you can make a 150% return on your investment just from your talk (See Example 2, Table 1).

When I made an offer on a large student-housing complex, I knew I was making a very low offer. When the seller started shuttling my negotiator back and forth in his corporate jet, I was certain that the seller was motivated. By long and careful negotiations (Jaw, Jaw), I finally ended up buying the building for $500,000 less than the current market value.

Negotiating is both a science and an art. It can be subtle or blunt. Sometimes you should use a hardheaded frontal attack and other times you need to take your time and stroke the seller or buyer. If you are good, (and a good part of being good is learned), you can make yourself wealthy using just your mind and your mouth.

BRAIN IN GEAR BEFORE ENGAGING MOUTH

Before the tongue starts to wag, the brain needs to work and work hard. You must be a very aware person and plan your strategy carefully. You need to be aware of what the other party wants. To persuade people, show them the value of what you are selling in terms of meeting their needs and desires. *Successful* negotiation comes *from figuring out what the other person wants and showing him* or *her a way to get it.* You get what you want, too.

HIDDEN AGENDAS

The problem is that most people won't tell you what they want. Don't get me wrong. They think they are telling you what they want, and a lot of words will come out of their mouth, but most of the time they don't know what they want. The typical seller or buyer throws up a smokescreen without even knowing he is doing it. Therefore, you must develop an awareness not only to 'what he is saying but, more important, to what he is not saying. You must read between the lines and be aware of a person's entire situation. You must guess the hidden agenda.

By careful observation and the right kind of questions, a good negotiator knows within minutes what method will be most effective for negotiating the best possible deal.

AN ALERT BROKER, AN UNFORGETTABLE LESSON

When I was training to be a stockbroker, I spent a day with an institutional broker who was a master negotiator. While walking out of the bank after meeting with a bank trust officer for thirty or forty minutes, this seasoned broker turned to me and said, "It's very helpful to now know that they are buying stock through Merrill Lynch and E. F. Hutton and also to know that they just bought 50,000 shares of General Electric. And it's too bad that he is being audited personally by the IRS. By the way, did you notice that he is a real tennis nut? And I'm pretty sure he has major problems with his wife right now."

I looked at him in total disbelief and said, "How in the world do you know all that? I didn't hear him say one word about any of those things."

He proceeded to give me a lesson on awareness—one I have never forgotten. While we were sitting there, his eyes were scanning the bank officer's entire office, including his desk top, on which rested stacks of papers that were topped by confirmation slips of the 50,000 shares of General Electric that he had bought. Also on the desk was correspondence from the brokerage firms of Merrill Lynch and E. F. Hutton. I had not even seen the small tennis trophy on the credenza behind the broker. My friend, whose eyes and mind were alert, had picked up the marital problems from the man's facial expression when he asked how his kids were doing.

THE MIND IS QUICKER THAN THE TONGUE

By keeping your mind very alert and questioning yourself throughout a conversation, you can learn five times more than someone who is not actively trying to be aware. Remember that the mind can think much faster than you can talk. This gives you time to listen to what the person is saying and to formulate many questions about what you should look for, observe, and be aware of.

NINE NEGOTIATING HINTS

The following nine negotiating hints have been proven to work on thousand-dollar deals and multimillion-dollar deals alike. Try them and you'll see for yourself. Remember: saving just 5% on each end of a deal can make you 100% on your money!

1. LABOR UNIONS MAKE A TON OF DOUGH WITH THIS ONE: THE LIST TECHNIQUE
    People who want to do things fast, the efficient people, use lists. These lists are prioritized. Being clear about your priorities is essential in negotiating skillfully.

    It works for kids. Your junior-high daughter asks if she can sleep over at her friend's house and you say, "No."

    "Well, how about if my friend sleeps over here?" Your answer is still no.

    "Can I then at least go out shopping with her tonight? We'll be back early." No.

    "Can she at least come over and watch TV? There's a good movie on and it'll be over by eleven o'clock."

    "Well" (pause), "okay," you reluctantly respond.

    Bingo, she has won: score, daughter 1, father O. She had a list for you, and by design or by just feminine intuition from her list of four, she got you to give in on possibly the only item she really wanted. The first three were just a smokescreen to make it seem that she was giving in on the bulk of requests. Number four was the true objective in the first place.

    1. Sleep at friend's house

2. Friend sleeps at her house
3. Go shopping at the mall
4. Watch movie till eleven P.M.

Your daughter would possibly have liked items one, two, or three, but she probably knew there was no way you would give in, so perhaps she wasn't planning on them. But she surrendered on each of the first three, building you up for the kill, number four. If you had given her a negative response on number four, she would have had lots of ammo to shoot you down.

"Dad, give me a break – you won't let me sleep at Cindy's house or let her sleep here and we can't even go to the mall for a few minutes. So at least let us watch the movie tonight. She'll go home right after the movies. Dad, really-let us have at least a little fun!"

What a setup. It is quite obvious what's happening when you think of it in its entirety. But it works every single day and in every single city and in every single home.

Copy Kids and Unions

Maybe kids don't consciously plan out this kind of strategy beforehand, but you better believe the subconscious is working overtime so they can reach their objective. And we as adults should get our minds working the same way on our deals.

The use of lists when dealing with business propositions, or when buying an income property or any business asset, really does work because people respond to what seems to be fair. Sometimes you need to point out to the other party all of the concessions you are making on your long list of demands.

Unions in America have been using the list technique for years, and have been negotiating the socks off otherwise astute corporations. They offer management a long list of items that they say they need. Most of the items won't be critical ones. On these they will make many concessions, building up credits, establishing themselves as friendly and flexible. But toward the end of the list lies their real objective, and it is usually money. They will concede on how many tables should be in the coffee-break room, but they will hold firm on the $2.50 hourly wage increase.

First Item on the List: Make a List

Let's say you are trying to buy an appreciating asset. The first thing you should do is to sit down and make a list of your objectives, demands, and things you would like to have. Put the items that are most important to you toward the end of the list and the least-important items (ones that are, however, important to some people) toward the beginning. For example:

1. The price you want.
2. The roof to be repaired by the seller before closing.
3. A new carpet to be installed in the back rooms by the seller.
4. The dilapidated building in the back of the property to be torn down.
5. The date you want possession of the asset.
6. How much cash you are willing to put down (if you are buying).
7. What interest rates you will pay or receive.

On the above list, the price appears first because in buying most assets it is not usually a critical item. But the amount of cash down and the interest rate paid or received can be very critical, so negotiate hardest on these items. If, however, you are paying all cash for an asset, then price would probably be put toward the end of the list because it would be more important, possibly your key negotiating objective.

Carefully Compromise

Assume this is not a cash transaction and that the seller is willing to carry some of the financing (whether it is an income property or a business or some other kind of appreciating asset). After terminating negotiations on the possession date, you should gradually concede on other initial demands until you get your cash down, or the desired interest rate: things that are essential to your profiting on the deal. It is in negotiating these later points that your earlier concessions can be used to get your terms. (I point out that I have compromised on the other items—one, two, three, four, and so on, whatever they are-so in fairness if the other party really wants to sell – or buy, whichever the case may be – he or she surely needs to do a little compromising too, and should meet me halfway.) And this, of course, is what I specifically point out to him.

Practice this skill. Learn to compromise on the unessential in order to give clout to your firmness on down payment and interest rates, which are critical for profit. You can add to your list as many possible points to be considered for compromise as you need to show yourself reasonable in the negotiating process, just as the unions do.

Union Demand Lists: A Pattern

Remember the typical union demand lists and how they load the top of them with washroom and coffee break items and leave the request for a $2.50 raise at the bottom. It works for them, it works for the wealthy, who have been doing it for years, and it will work for you. So do it next time you buy an appreciating asset you want. Take the time to make a good-sized demand list. Take the time to study it and have enough verbal ammo to discuss each item. Don't compromise and surrender the top items on the list too fast or it will be obvious that they really don't matter to you.

Parade Your Particular Concessions

Lastly, be sure to point out each of your compromises, making sure the seller or buyer sees that you are trying to satisfy both his needs and yours. Say to him, "Look, I'm trying to make this deal work. Sure I'm looking out for myself, but I've given or compromised on some of these items. If you want to sell (or buy), then you have to do the same and meet me halfway."

2.   WIN-WIN

"If you can show me how to win and how to win big, I will give you just about anything you want." Isn't this the key to most of our negotiating today? Isn't this what a good salesman does when he or she tries to sell you something? He tries to show you that what you are buying can help you just as much as the sale will help him. I'm sure that you would pay me a hundred thousand dollars tomorrow if I could show you how to make two hundred thousand that same day. That is the essence of win-win in negotiating.

Insane Deal Creates Two Winners

Darreld Martin must not read the papers. Doesn't he know that there is no money available for investments? Doesn't he know that there aren't any deals out there anymore? Besides, if he wins on this deal, won't that make John Hagman, the seller, a loser?

Here's the story. Mr. John Hagman had a nice apartment building in a good location, with excellent tenants, and he had a respectable cash flow. But John had just retired and decided to cash in on his investment. He wanted to travel and see the world.

So he put the property up for sale, and bingo, to John's delight it sold and sold fast. The buyer of John's property is convinced that John has lost all his marbles, but is he ever glad!

The buyer, Darreld Martin, knows that John is not permanently insane, but that he was a motivated seller. It was an insane deal for sure, but nobody was really crazy because both parties came out the winner.

Creative Financing

The real key to this great transaction was a bit of creative financing. That creative financing allowed Mr. Martin to buy Mr. Hagman's property without a single cent of his own cash. And when the deal closed, Darreld Martin (remember, he is the buyer) actually put several *thousand* dollars' cash in his pocket.

That's what creative financing is all about. Most people don't understand such crazy deals, but they are really quite simple – you just need to follow the right steps.

How was Hagman able to come out so well, too? He agreed to "subordinate his interest," thus allowing Martin to put a new first mortgage on the property (this gave the seller cash, with Hagman carrying a low-interest second mortgage, and allowed the buyer to get some cash from the first mortgage, too. Pretty slick). When all the dust settled, both Martin and Hagman had cash in their pockets.

Hagman is now enjoying his cash in Europe and Martin is ready to buy another property with his.

Does Someone Have to Lose?

Most people are convinced that when one person profits from a deal another person automatically has to lose. This IS not true. Business deals are not sports. There need not always be a winner and a loser. Business is contribution and productivity. It's the process of providing goods and services to people. It's helping people. It's fulfilling needs. And if you can figure out what people really want, or what they think they want, our economy will reward you in proportion to your contribution.

Figure Others' Wants

The trouble is that most people don't stop to figure out what others want. They just start talking or arguing, mistakenly thinking that is negotiating. It is said of Napoleon that he won his battles in his tent before ever taking the field. A good negotiator does the same thing. He thinks through the entire negotiating process before he begins negotiating. As he thinks, he writes down those things that will help him.

If you are smart, you will think through the negotiating process beforehand. You will put on your list an item that will help the other party win. You want to tell him that, right up front, so you'll put it at the top of the list. What does the other person need? What does he want? I mean, what does he *really* want and need? You show him how he can win, especially in the first or second step, and you will both win.

Turn Out the Lights But Don't Go to Sleep

A sixty-two-year-old New York man wants to sell his business (or an apartment building). He wants all cash because he has worked hard and finally wants to enjoy the fruits of his efforts. He is asking $175,000 for his appreciating assets, which he has owned for seventeen years. The asset is now free and clear of any mortgage or bank loan.

You want the asset. It is a good one and meets all your needs. But for the $175,000 cash he wants, no way. Even if you had that kind of cash, you wouldn't put it all on this one deal. And the fact is, you don't happen to have $175,000 lying around. So what do you do about it? Try turning out the lights, but don't go to sleep. It's time to think.

Think about the seller and get to know him in your mind. He's worked hard. He's done well and wants to take it easy now. That's reasonable. How can you help him reach his goals and turn the deal into a win-win situation?

The first question that you will probably want to ask is: What is he going to do with the cash that he will receive? The second question: Does he really need all of the $175,000 right now? Why not find out by talking directly to him or through a middleman, broker, or agent? Let's say you find out that he has planned a worldwide one-year trip, then he plans to retire in Phoenix. In a year, after the trip, he'll have the cost of moving from New York to Phoenix, where in the warmth of the Arizona sun he will live off the interest from the balance of the $175,000.

THEREFORE HE DOESN'T NEED ALL CASH

Through reason and research you have discovered that he really doesn't need all that cash up front. Now it is fairly easy to structure a win-win deal by giving the seller enough cash down to cover his two big expenses: First, his world trip and second, his move from New York to Phoenix. Then the balance of what you owe him can be paid over a number of years, so that he has enough to live on and so that the monthly payments you need to make can be covered by the income you'll receive from his own asset that you bought. You could even offer to find several condos in the Phoenix area from which he could pick during his one-year trip. On his arrival, all he would have to do is fly to Phoenix and be chauffeured around by you to see the properties that you tied up for him by the wise use of the "subject-to" clause.

You have solved three big problems for the seller. Number 1, he sells what he wants and he does it now; Number 2, he gets the cash he needs plus income to live on later; and, Number 3, you have helped him and given him red-carpet service (which we all love) by doing a lot of his legwork in a new town to find a place where he can live. Best of all, by doing this you probably will get exactly what you want. It could turn out to be a real win-win situation — two winners and no losers. Ten or fifteen years from now you may sell it exactly as he did to someone exactly like you for another win-win negotiated deal.

3. NEGOTIATIONS – LOGIC MIXED WITH PRE-THINKING

Thinking pays *big, but pre-thinking* pays *bigger.* The trouble with thinking is that it's hard – most people would rather take it easy. But if you do the thinking *before* you negotiate, you won't be trapped when someone asks you a tough question. You will have a good answer because you have pre-thought the conversation. You will have thought through the situation and know all the questions and answers before they ever come up. In fact, if you spend enough time thinking ahead before your negotiating sessions, you'll end up asking most of the questions during the sessions, which will give you the upper hand.

I've seen people get trapped at the closing table because they were not prepared. I saw a seller put in a penalty clause for late payment right on the spot, even though the parties hadn't previously agreed to such a clause. The fellow merely asked the buyer if he was going to be on time with all his payments.

The buyer said, "Yes, of course." "Then," replied the seller, "I am sure you won't mind my putting this penalty clause in here for any late payments."

"Ahhhhh," said the buyer, "I suppose not." The buyer was not at all pleased with the deal, but he was trapped because he hadn't pre-thought the situation. He lacked the right words to counter the seller's query. He lacked confidence to make a stand because of the temporary confusion in his mind as to just exactly what to say. So he took the easy course. He created no waves. He said to himself, "Well, it's no big deal anyway and I probably won't ever be late."

As a matter of fact, it could be a very big deal. If the buyer had thought it out in advance, he never would have been trapped. In a crunch he should have had a few standard "buy-some-time" phrases in mind to throw out to stop the flow of events for a while. Keep in mind phrases such as the following, to be used for "stall time." While you are at it, take time to develop your own standard phrases for awkward situations.

- "Wait a minute-let's discuss (or talk about, or think about, or explore) that comment." Then quickly go through his or her proposal in your mind and ask questions. Questioning is not only a great way to buy time, it is also an excellent and effective negotiating technique because it puts the other person on the defensive. But don't overuse it or be too demanding. Don't make the other person feel as though he were on the witness stand.

- A catch-all question the buyer can throw back at the seller is, "Now let me think – was that clause something that we agreed to in our preliminary agreement?" Then reach for the agreement and start looking for the clause (which of course you know isn't there). As you look, you have time to think of something to say that is polite and yet shows that you are taking a firm stand against the addition of this or any other clause that might come up. After looking for a few minutes, you say, "No, it's not here. We didn't agree to that, so it wouldn't be fair to put it in right now. Don't worry, I won't be late with my payments in any case."

- "I'll need time to run that idea (or question or new part of the contract or deal) past my partner (attorney, CPA, financial adviser, wife, girlfriend, or banker)."
- "I really don't have time to discuss (or talk about or think about) it right now. Let's meet tomorrow at my office."
- "I'm not sure I understand what you're saying. Back up and start over."

To win at negotiating you need logic on your side. Logic is expressed by words, and without the proper words in your mind, you will lose, so be prepared. Refer to the key phrases above and be familiar with them. Have them ready in your mind so you can win at negotiating through pre-thinking and logic.

4.   TANGIER RUG LESSON

Many years ago I sponsored a special investors' seminar in Spain, and while there we took the hydrofoil across the Straits of Gibraltar to Africa and toured the city of Tangier.

The tour was arranged ahead of time, and the talkative guides took us through the narrow, winding back streets, through the open markets with their pungent odors. Then, after half an hour's stop at the Kasbah, we finally ended up at a rug merchant's large second-floor shop.

It was there in the next hour or so that some shrewd negotiating took place. We were hot and tired, sitting comfortably on mounds of beautiful Oriental rugs. Our gracious host began telling the group about the uniqueness of his rugs. Then his troupe of articulate salespeople proceeded to sell their captive audience on the quality of the merchandise. They explained the custom of haggling over price. They would be offended if we were to accept their first price without some sporty bargaining. The price on one rug was $4500. Priming the crowd in a jovial joking mood, the merchant asked for someone to make him an offer. He wanted an offer, no matter how ridiculous. Well, someone in the crowd humored him with an offer of $500. And from that point the haggling, or negotiating, started in earnest. After a few minutes I couldn't even hear what was going on because the salespeople had divided the group into smaller groups and were noisily haggling away.

I found out later that the $4500 rug had gone for $1200. The buyer had been assured that its value was over $2000. He received the written appraisal stating that fact. A couple of months later he had the rug appraised in the States and found out that its true market value was $600.

The Oldest Gimmick in the Book

It's one of the oldest gimmicks in the book—starting with a very high price to give the illusion of a bargain when the price is cut dramatically. Thousands of stores use this technique every single day of the year. And you know what? It keeps working and working. We all love to buy something on sale. If we see on the ticket that it has been marked down from $180 to $99, we feel that we are getting a terrific deal. A lot can be learned from this if you just think about it for a while. *Whether* you are *buying or selling, start the bargaining process with a price substantially different from your target price.*

When I bought the student-housing complex mentioned earlier, the seller was asking $3.4 million for it. Although he was willing to carry the financing, he wanted 11 % interest. My target price was $2.5 million with 7% financing, so my beginning offers on the property were $2.1 million on the price and a ridiculously low 4%. By starting much lower than the two targets I had for interest rate and price, I was able to give and take and finally ended up on target.

If you *are selling* an asset, *price it high enough* so you can *reduce your* price *substantially* to *give the illusion* that *it's a real bargain for the buyer.*

This is elementary, but it is so elementary that many people today don't think that this technique will work when selling investment items. Consequently they miss out on maximizing their profits. They are too proud to haggle!

5.   BONUS FROM BLUFFING
Some years ago I walked into an Audi dealership to look at their cars. I wanted to buy a new car and saw a beautiful red Audi LS 100. After checking it out thoroughly, I sat down with the salesman and a friend of mine who had come along to shop with me. I started the negotiating process by making a ridiculously low offer, to which the salesman made a counteroffer. I bumped my offer up a little bit and he came down a little bit. He finally came down to where we were just a few hundred dollars apart, and finally he announced that this was as low as he could go, whereupon I announced that my price was as high as I could go.

I was bluffing, but he didn't know that. He was bluffing also, only I didn't know that for sure. But he had more to lose than I did, so my friend and I got up, thanked him for his time, and told him how sorry I was I couldn't get the car, because I really wanted it, but that I had given him my top price. As we walked toward the door I said to my friend, "Don't look back! Just keep walking and see if he does anything." Well, we got to the door and nothing happened. We stepped outside and the door closed behind us. I turned to my friend and said, "Well, I guess we lost! I really thought 'd stop us."

I was just about ready to turn around and go back, because I had decided I was going to buy the car. You see, I knew I could walk *out* of the showroom just to see if he would stop me. If he didn't, I could always go back in and tell him I had changed my mind. I could then pay the full price that he was asking. Before I had a chance to turn around, I heard the door open and the voice of the salesman saying, "Wait a minute! Listen, you guys, it's past closing time and I haven't had a sale today. Let's go ahead and write it up. I'll agree to your price." I went ahead and bought the car, and saved over $300. This is not a lot of money, but it does make the point. Besides, my effort to save that $300 was minimal.

Heads I Win, Tails I Win

People bluff at poker all the time. The problem is that in poker, if you bluff and someone calls your bluff, you lose. In negotiating to buy or sell appreciating assets, there is a big bonus. If you bluff and win, you win. If you bluff and lose, you still can win. If the car salesman had called my bluff and hadn't called me back, I still wouldn't have lost anything because I still would have ended up buying what I wanted to buy.

The key to bluffing is that you absolutely cannot show one single, solitary crack or let it be known that you are bluffing. Like a good actor, you have to play the part to the hilt, not falling out of character even for a moment.

I Even Fooled My Comptroller

Some time ago I needed to borrow $100,000 to renovate a project I was working on. So I asked my comptroller to apply for a $100,000 loan at one percentage point over prime rate. He returned to the office the next day and told me he had met with the bank, and the bank was willing to lend the money but they insisted on my signing personally rather than just as a corporate officer. I told my comptroller that there was no way I would sign my name personally. We had dealt with the bank long enough that they should accept my signature as a corporate officer only. There was no need for me to obligate myself personally. My comptroller was quite put out with me. He said, "Mark, you know that we need the money." But even at that point I resisted telling him that I was bluffing.

He left the office convinced that the bank would not grant the loan unless I signed. He returned later with a surprised look on his face. "I can't believe they accepted the papers without your signing personally. I'm shocked." Only then did I tell him that I had been bluffing and that I would have signed if they had pushed it any further than they did.

Many times in the bluffing process you have to have a tremendous amount of patience. If you have bluffed before, your opponent will suspect that you are doing it again and will try to out bluff you by telling you he won't accept whatever you have offered. And he will want to wait a day or two to see if you "change your mind." It is here that your patience is important. You need to outwait him. The younger, the more inexperienced a person is, the less patient he is.

Take for example the young man who goes to a used-car dealer to buy a car. He finds one that he falls in love with. Inevitably the salesman will tell him that someone was in earlier looking at the car, and, "if you want this car, young man, you'd better buy it now because he's coming back and will probably take it." Anybody who has gone looking for a used car has heard that line many times. Here you need to use patience. The car will wait. There is a 90% chance (or more) that the salesman is bluffing. If you don't believe me, go out and make a survey: when you hear that statement, wait a week, then go back to see if the same car is still there. The problem with many people is they fear losing what they think is the best deal of their life. First of all, it probably isn't the best deal of their life, and secondly, they probably won't even lose it.

The big bonus in bluffing comes when you make a ridiculously low offer on an asset-a total bluff-and to your surprise someone accepts it without any changes or compromises. You were bluffing but they didn't know it. Perhaps the person was a very highly motivated seller who grabbed the only offer. So you won and you won big. Granted, this doesn't happen every day, but if you are in the marketplace, making lots of offers, it will happen enough times to make people think you are a genius and call you lucky and enough times to make you wealthy.

6.   WEAR THE SON-OF-A-GUN DOWN

Jake Ebach, who lives in the Midwest, needed a substantial loan for a project he was working on. Mr. Ebach presented his loan request to four different banks. Each bank turned him down. Not a man to give up easily, Jake tried again. But even the second approach met with the same response. Still determined to get the needed money, he approached each of the banks again. Finally, in round three, Jake scored a knockout.

Jake Ebach didn't keep going back with the same questions. Each time he went into a bank he was prepared with new proposals, new ways of meeting the objections they had for turning down prior requests. He was building a case and presenting it to the bank to prove that he wouldn't fail with his project. Let's face it. Any banker has to sit up and take notice when somebody is that persistent. I am sure the banker projected Jake's persistence into the project and reasoned that if he used that same persistence in making his project go, the possibility of failure was slim. Therefore he was a good loan risk.

As pointed out at the beginning of this chapter, there are many ways to negotiate. This is just one. The persistence approach. Asking over and over again. Showing the party with whom you are negotiating that you won't give up no matter what.

7. DIPLOMACY: BE MR. NICE GUY

Think for a minute who in the entire world is your best friend, the person you would do anything for. If you were very well off and had more money than you knew what to do with, and had an appreciating asset to sell cheap, and ten people wanted to buy it, how long would it take you to decide to sell it to your friend?

People say that it isn't what you know but who you know. The statement is partly true because most of us would rather do business with people we know, especially our good friends. Friends can be made quickly by diplomatic people, ones who know how to say the right thing at the right time, and who know when to keep their mouth shut if tempted to say the wrong thing.

I am not talking about flattery, which almost everyone can see right through. But a diplomatic, aware person can quickly identify those traits that are admirable in the person he is talking to. After recognizing what interests the other person, compliment or makes positive statements about those items. Honest statements about real traits enhance self-image and signal others that you are telling the truth.

The same technique must be applied when you are trying to buy an office building. It makes no sense to put the seller on the defensive by making comments about how poorly the building is being managed, a direct reflection on the owner. Even if the building has been beaten up badly and indicates poor management, a much more diplomatic way to say this would be something like, "You know, it's really a shame what some tenants do to beat up a building. Look what they've done with the copy machine; they just about destroyed the wall behind it." You have made your point and you haven't offended the seller.

Of course, what you say is only a part of diplomacy. What you do is critical. Doing special things can draw attention to you in a positive way. Years ago, I was trying to rent a million names from the American Express list and I needed the list in a hurry, faster than the normal procedure would get me the list. In desperation, I finally sent a dozen roses to one of the key women in their New York office. Well, this woman hadn't received very many roses, at least in the course of business, and so my gesture stood out and made a difference. The service that we received from that point on was phenomenal. I am sure that she hasn't forgotten it to this day, even though I haven't had contact with her for years.

All of us like people to pay attention to us, and the more sincere it is the more we like it. If you want to negotiate and win, be a real diplomat. Cater to the needs of the buyer or seller. Become their friend. Make yourself so valuable through word and deed that they will do almost anything for you. If they really like you, they are more apt to do business with you.

8.   BUFFER ZONE

"You tell the seller that his price is so far out of line that it even fails to qualify as a joke. The guy must be nuts if he thinks I'm dumb enough not to see the problem he has. No wonder he wants to sell.

"Okay," says the agent. "I'm meeting with the seller this afternoon and I'll tell him."

When he meets the seller, the agent says, "Listen, I talked to the buyer this morning and he thinks we just may have a deal – a few changes will have to be made. He's a little concerned about some of the problems, but I'm sure we can work something out."

The buyer was obviously quite emotional, but the agent took the emotion out of the buyer's words and no doubt moved the parties closer toward a deal. Had the agent quoted the buyer, the seller no doubt would have responded with similar words, thus killing any hopes of consummating a deal.

Using a middleman can do wonders for your wealth. Many people are always trying to save money, and I understand that, but the right middleman (or woman) can pay for himself many times over. He acts as a buffer zone to cushion abrasive words, actions, and emotions because he is in a position to be more objective.

True, he has a commission to earn, but many times without his skill and persistence, the deal wouldn't go through at all. That commission, which so many people begrudge him, motivates him to keep pushing the parties together. Oh yes, there may be a lot of lazy, uninformed, and greedy agents who don't want to earn what they get, but *good* middlemen are worth their weight in gold.

- They supply education and information. All you have to do is ask, then listen.
- They supply excellent contacts with the right people at the right time.
- Commissioned agents don't lose you anything until the job is completely done.
- They save you a bundle of your precious time.
- They help you and the other party to overcome inertia.
- They keep tempers and emotions in proper perspective so the deal can continue toward a settlement.

I think middleman negotiating is great, but there are some do's and don'ts.

- Do use the best in town. Ask around (they're usually the busiest).
- Do, when possible, use one who specializes in whatever you're dealing in.
- Do use your own employees, friends, associates, rather than negotiating directly.
- Don't tell agents all that you're thinking (for example, what your highest price is).
- Don't accept the agent's word as to whether the deal is good or not good (remember, he or she stands to make money from it).

A good middleman can save a deal that might otherwise have been lost. So use these people and their skills.

9.   INTIMIDATION / VICTIMIZATION

You walk into your office on Monday morning and find out you didn't get the raise you'd planned on for over a year. You are naturally upset; you feel like a victim. After all, you really deserved the raise. But now the tables start to turn as you avoid talking to your boss. When you can't avoid him any longer, you give him the silent treatment. You pout, you sulk, and you act mad. Remember, you are fully justified. Now who is the victim? The boss is now feeling guilty. He probably knew you deserved the raise. Even if no one received a raise because of poor profits, he still feels the pressure. The silence is getting to him. You are intimidating him. You are controlling him by your actions. You are victimizing him by playing as if you were the victim.

This manipulation occurs daily in business, in politics, and in families (especially between husband and wife), and it works. Those who use it are dealing on a childish level. And when they get caught and the intimidation doesn't work, they have to dig deeper and try harder to act as if they were the victim.

Don't act *the victim in business.* You can win through intimidation—and many people do—but you may end up without any friends, or worse. To intimidate someone is literally to make him or her timid, and it does work, but it really doesn't show your courage. People do give in to the pressure that is put upon them. If you've ever been pushed into buying or selling against your will or judgment, then you know the negative feelings you harbored toward the offending party. If you want to use this method of negotiating, you should at least understand the price you may have to pay.

It is important however to recognize when someone is trying to intimidate you, because your early recognition of their attempt can totally thwart it. Thwarting intimidators builds up your courage.

Below is a list of things people say and do in an attempt to intimidate you:

- Give you the silent treatment, pout, cry, or sulk;
- Act put-out or mad ('cause you "done them wrong");
- Tell you they are losing money at the price they are buying or selling;
- Give you money or gifts to make you feel obligated;
- Do favors for you to make you feel obligated;
- Drop names: people, places, prestigious brand names, etc.

The last two Items can be very effective intimidators, but if you use them, use them sparingly.

NOTES AND THOUGHTS

NOTES AND THOUGHTS

CHAPTER 14

MOTIVATED SELLERS WILL LINE YOUR POCKETS WITH CASH

THE SUPER KEY TO SUCCESS

Analyzing my own successes and the successes of others shows conclusively that finding and dealing with motivated sellers will make you rich in the shortest amount of time. Someone who is super motivated to sell something suffers from a sort of temporary insanity. If, for some reason, he or she is "down" on a property or asset, reason seems to fly out the window and emotion takes over. Stop and think of your own actions. Have you ever owned a car that you became totally disenchanted with – the water pump goes out one week, three weeks later it's the distributor or the battery? There's a dent in the side, and then the speedometer cable goes, or one of the headlights, so you finally reach a point at which you are totally fed up. You think, "What a piece of junk! I've got to get rid of this garbage heap. It's falling apart. What I need is a new car." The instant you think these thoughts you cease to be objective. Your emotions say the old car is nearly worthless. You unknowingly have just set the perfect stage for someone to make a quick and easy profit, even if it's only a few hundred dollars. And so you say, "So, what's a few hundred dollars?" But the same thing happens with hundred-thousand-dollar and million-dollar properties.

2-1/2 % DOWN: WHAT A DUMB OFFER

Many years ago I decided to buy a new home. I found the ideal home, complete with tennis courts, swimming pool, and almost three acres in a beautifully wooded area. I bought it and moved in. So there I sat with two homes. I paid $260,000 for the new home and I was trying to sell the old one, which cost $55,000, for $100,000. I was making payments on both, $1,550 a month on the new home and $550 on the old one. For a month, nothing happened. I hadn't received a single offer on the property that I was trying to sell. Two months. Then three months. Nothing. During the fourth month some kids broke in and did several hundred dollars' worth of damage. I fixed the damage only to have the FOR SALE sign stolen about every other week. As the summer grew hotter, the lawn started to burn up and I had to make many trips to the property to water it.

Well, I was rapidly becoming a motivated seller. I was sick and tired of the property. I just wanted to get rid of it. Finally, in the seventh month a young man made me the following offer: $2500 down. Remember, the price was $100,000, so his down payment was only 2_ %. He did offer me full purchase price, but his monthly payment to me would be only $450 whereas mine was $550 a month. He wanted me to "carry it" on a so-called wraparound whereby I would be putting out $100 each month to make up the difference between his payment and what I owed the bank. What a ridiculous, dumb offer! But I was dumber than he was. I took it. Why did I take it? Because I was a motivated seller.

WHEN ARE PEOPLE TRANSFORMED INTO MOTIVATED SELLERS?

Do you think that I would have taken that same offer within two or three weeks of listing the property for sale? Of course I wouldn't have. What about after two or three months? Probably not. When did I become a motivated seller? I can't really pinpoint the exact moment I was transformed into a motivated seller, but I was transformed by the time the low offer was made.

It was a great experience because it taught me what a motivated seller thinks about when he has a property that he is emotionally down on. Oh, I could afford the payments on both houses, but I didn't like making both. I started to project in my mind that this could go on forever. Knowing that it was costing me $6600 a year, I became very concerned. I had projected far into the future what it was costing me. I thought I would continue to have the problems of vandalism, dying lawns, and other nuisances. I thought I was pouring money down a rat hole. I worried that the economy was getting worse and might collapse. I was motivated to sell. With these worries and negative thoughts rumbling around in my head, his offer looked good. It was a way to get out of my problem right now.

I look back and see I should have waited. At the time it seemed like a good enough deal. Consequently, someone else got a super deal – and I learned what motivated sellers think about.

If you are in the right place at the right time, you can take advantage of the eagerness of motivated sellers and pick up $50,000 to $100,000 in one fell swoop. With that kind of money on the line, it is well worth your time to scout out the motivated seller.

A BEGINNER MAKES $100,000 ON HIS FIRST DEAL. WHY? YOU GUESSED IT. A MOTIVATED SELLER!

Dick Hamilton, of Indianapolis, didn't know much about buying properties, but he did know about the motivated seller from reading just one book. He says in his case ignorance was bliss. He could really see that some people are at times extremely motivated to sell their property, so he went about to capitalize on that understanding. Even though Dick didn't fully understand the mechanics of buying, selling, or managing property, he forged ahead.

When Dick Hamilton found an eighty-year-old gentleman who owned a forty-eight-unit apartment building that had thirty-two vacancies, he knew he had found a motivated seller. Besides that, the man lived in Florida and had hired a local company to manage his property. (Obviously they weren't managing the property very well with thirty-two vacancies.) Knowing the man had headaches with the property and wanted to get rid of it, Dick offered $100,000 total price on the property, which was worth $200,000.

That's right, he offered half of the true value of the property. He told the seller he would give him $50,000 at the time of closing and that the balance of $50,000 would be paid over a five-year period with a 10% interest rate on a ten-year amortization, which worked out to be an average payment of $833 a month, with a balloon payment after the fifth year. (Amortization is spreading payments out to keep them and interest rates lower each month. That is, over ten (or thirty) years, even though you have agreed to make the balloon payment in five years. The balloon payment is a lump sum that pays off the balance owed.)

CRAZY OFFER PRODUCES A MIRACLE

With a crazy offer like that, Dick didn't expect the seller to accept it. He thought the offer would be rejected and at very best he would have to make a counteroffer. But, miracle of miracles, it was accepted exactly as written. Dick couldn't believe it. It seemed too good to be true. But it was. Even though Dick didn't know much about property management, you can believe he learned fast. In a short time he had the vacancies reduced to zero.

Recently he refinanced the property with a new first government loan for $138,500. So not only did he make a $100,000 paper profit, he turned $38,500 of it into cash and still owns the property, currently appraised at $225,000.

You will be interested to know that he didn't even have the $50,000 that he offered as a down payment. But he quickly got it. How? He simply put a second mortgage on his own residence and got the money from a bank.

I know that many people are reluctant to encumber the very home in which they live. But if you knew that you were buying an asset that was worth $200,000, and your purchase price was only $100,000, it isn't a question of courage to acquire such a super bargain asset. This deal worked because of a motivated seller, a seller so motivated that he would sell his property for half price, a hundred thousand dollars less than it was really worth. That's motivated.

NOT A UNICORN

You might be thinking this story is unusual and that Dick Hamilton was very lucky. But it's not that unusual. Most of the properties I have bought have been purchased from motivated sellers. Many of those purchases have also been "yuk" properties (ones that were rundown and visually undesirable), which has given me a double chance of winning. Years ago, when I first started, I found and negotiated with dozens of motivated sellers on small properties, picking up profits of $5000 and $10,000 per property. I was flabbergasted when I found a motivated seller on a larger property. On paper it looked as if I could make $50,000 on one single deal. I found it hard to believe, but it was true. In fact, I have since found that there are motivated sellers at all levels, from the $10,000 properties to the multimillion-dollar ones. The same applies for all types of businesses.

SOME CAUTIONS

Be sure you know the price you are getting is truly a bargain price. Some people pretend to be motivated sellers when, in fact, the bargain come-on is a gimmick to get the buyer's attention. Be skeptical when listening to reasons sellers give for selling. Truly motivated sellers don't usually announce that they are motivated. The circumstances generally tell the full story, and the seller tries not to appear to be overeager.

COMPARISON SHOPPING

There is no substitute for spending time to shop around and comparing one asset with another, or one property with another. If you don't do this, you could be offered a super deal and never recognize it for what it is, or you could end up paying too much for a property or business. If you take the time to shop and compare, you will know value when you see it. That helps you know when a seller is truly motivated or just pretending to be. The hours you spend getting to know prices and values will reward you handsomely.

The first time you ever make $50,000 or $100,000 on one deal, in a matter of months, people who know you will call you lucky. That is what they said about me when I ended up buying a very large property for well under the market price.

A "LUCKY" TWO-MILLION-DOLLAR DEAL

I received a phone call one Friday from an obviously motivated seller in Pennsylvania. The numbers that he gave me over the phone were too good to be true. I asked all the necessary questions and the deal still sounded terrific. In fact, it sounded so good that that very day I put an employee on a plane to Pennsylvania. He called me the next day to tell me the apartment complex was as good as it was represented to be. I was so excited I could hardly sit still, and barely slept that night. The numbers indicated that the property was worth at least $700,000 more than I had to pay for it. As a matter of fact, I sold it one year and one month later for more than $2 million cash in my pocket over what I paid for it.

Sound unbelievable? Well, it may sound that way but that is exactly what happened. Who in their right mind would sell a property that is worth so much more than the purchase price? The answer is a super-motivated seller. In fact, there were three motivated sellers. Here is what happened.

The court forced a man into a very illiquid cash position because of his divorce. That man lost the property to the court. The court was now the motivated seller. It had a property that it didn't want, and had to dispose of it. The court, like most government bodies, really didn't know what it was doing.

The court sold the property to an individual investor who had figured what it was really worth, but was trying to finance the property so he wouldn't have to put a single penny of his own money into it. He had given the court a $50,000 deposit to show his good intentions. At the last moment the finance company which had agreed to finance the deal found out that the buyer had no money of his own in the deal, so they quickly withdrew their commitment to finance, leaving the investor in a very bad position. When he called me, he was about to lose $50,000 because he only had three days to come up with financing for the property, and he knew he couldn't get it.

Realizing what the property was worth, I moved fast, so fast I even shocked myself. But I knew that I would be missing out on an easy automatic profit of $700,000 if I didn't come up with the financing, so I was prepared to move heaven and earth to get the money. And after all that, people called me lucky! But anyone can be "lucky" if he or she goes out and takes the time to compare properties to hunt, to find, and to negotiate with motivated sellers.

That is exactly what I did to be sure that the property was worth at least $700,000 more than the asking price. Then with great persistence I was able to come up with the money within three days.

You have heard of people lifting automobiles off trapped children. Well, we also have Superman strength to accomplish nonphysical tasks. If you are sufficiently motivated, if you know for a fact that you can make a small or large fortune in a very short period of time, then you can do it.

CLUE YOURSELF TO THE RIGHT ASSETS

You may not be able to come even close to identifying a million-dollar super deal unless you are out there looking for it. If you want to make some huge profits, for heaven's sakes get out of the penny-ante stuff. With the same effort, energy, and time spent looking for super-motivated sellers of dogs and cats, you could look for motivated sellers who own appreciating assets that are worth tens of thousands, or hundreds of thousands, of dollars or even more.

I know a young man who spends countless hours finding motivated sellers of automobiles. He finds them, negotiates an even better price, fixes the cars up, and turns around and sells them, making two or three thousand dollars at the very most on each one. With that same energy the young man could be making hundreds of thousands of dollars each year on larger deals.

MOTIVATED SELLERS:
WHO ARE THEY?

You are no doubt wondering who these motivated sellers are. How can they be identified?

There are many reasons why people are motivated to sell at lower than true value. Here are a few:

- Death
- Divorce
- Relocation
- Getting older
- Seller wants new challenges
- Seller is uninformed
- Seller has a fear of the future
- Seller is tired of managing property
- Problems with tenants or employees
- Physical problems with buildings, plant, equipment
- Market for the product seems to be dropping

FEELINGS OVERRIDE FACTS

You must realize that most of us make the majority of our decisions based on feelings rather than facts. We do listen and digest and react partially because of facts, but under certain circumstances (see the list), feelings tend to override facts. Many people are pushed to the point of saying, "I'm selling it for a much lower price than it is really worth, but I just don't care. I just want out. I want to be done with it!"

ADVANTAGES TO THE BUYER

The list of advantages of buying from motivated sellers include:

- Lower price.
- Possibly no cash outlay now.

- Pay over the long term. (Here you really end up buying the asset with the seller's own cash, which is generated from the asset.)
- All terms-the length of time it takes to payoff the asset, the amount down, the price of the asset, and most important, the interest rate that you will be paying on the balance – are all negotiable.

HOW TO RECOGNIZE THE MOTIVATED SELLER

There are two things that are normally a dead giveaway in identifying a motivated seller. The first one is the seller: what he does, what he says, and how he acts. The second is his property or business and what it looks like.

Does he talk negatively about the asset that he is trying to sell, or make disparaging remarks about the physical aspects, the tenants or employees? If so, then that should raise a red flag in your mind. He might be motivated.

If he talks about how bad the market for his product is or how slowly things are selling, that is a sign. If he is fed up with his business or buildings, or if he is worried about the future, that is a sign of a motivated seller. Or possibly his profit margins are starting to narrow. It is a sign if he talks about recession or depression. If he doesn't talk about any of the above items, ask questions to pull it out of him: "What do you think is going to happen to the economy?", you might ask. Or: "Isn't it a shame the way profit margins are being squeezed now?" Or: "Boy, the cost of property taxes and operating expenses are just about more than anybody can take these days!" Asking these Questions and then listening carefully to the answers can give you a clue to his or her level of motivation. Be sure to listen hard to his answers.

After looking at him, look at the property or the company he owns. What does it look like? Is it run-down; is it in bad need of repairs? Are there lots of vacancies? Are there problems with the employees? Many of these things are very obvious; they just take time to observe. Is the business run in a neat, organized way? Or are there papers strewn every which way in a disorganized mess? Again, you can probe if he or she doesn't volunteer the information. Ask questions such as, "It's really a shame that they don't build buildings like they used to." Here you are attacking the building, not the owner personally, so he won't get defensive. Or the old catch-all statement, "You just can't get good help these days, can you?" Or: "Don't you find it hard to find good, stable, hardworking employees?" Again listen to his answers.

HOW TO SMOKE OUT A
MOTIVATED SELLER

Finding a motivated seller is not as difficult as you think, but you really do have to make it happen. *You* can't *sit home and expect deals* to come *looking* for you. You need to be out in the marketplace, asking Questions, asking for referrals, telling people what you are doing and asking them to spread the word. There might be a perfect purchase for you out there somewhere, with a motivated seller who would love to sell at exactly your price and terms, but if you never meet the seller you will never make the deal.

Fortunately there are some methods that help you dig up motivated sellers with relatively little time expenditure on your part.

THE SHOTGUN METHOD

The shotgun method is quite simple in concept but it does take some work. The results, however, can be phenomenal, because you can reach so many people in a relatively short period of time. A twenty-gauge shotgun has the ability to bring down a bird more easily than a rifle because of the hundreds of BBs that are released. It only takes one or two for success. Similarly, the shotgun method is a matter of numbers. Send out enough offers and you're bound to win.

The shotgun approach can be used when you are buying or selling any type of asset. When most people apply for a job or a loan, they approach just one bank or employer, fill out an application, and then wait to find out the results. At the end of the waiting period, which can be five or six weeks, they have to start all over again if they are turned down. If, however, they were smart enough to use a shotgun approach, applying for jobs or loans at six or so places, they might get turned down on two or three, or even five, but are accepted by one and end up a winner – plus having saved all that time and anxiety.

When you look for motivated sellers, why not go with a shotgun approach? For example, if you are looking to buy a small business through a business broker, write the same letter to twenty or thirty brokers at the same time. If you are buying an office building or shopping center or apartment complex in a nearby town, write to *all* the brokers. For that matter, write to all the apartment owners in the town, if it is not too big a town. If you do this, you will save a lot of time, which, of course, is the most precious thing that you and I possess.

If 80% of the business brokers are not interested in you or haven't got what you want to buy, that's okay, because the other 20% will. Ditto for real estate brokers and/or owners of whatever kind of asset you are trying to buy.

The second way to use the shotgun method, a way specifically designed to smoke out the motivated seller, is by sending dozens of letters with an actual written offer for the asset. Since you are looking for the motivated seller, your offer will be very low. For example, you may offer 20% to

30% lower than the asking price for the asset. Your offer of cash out of pocket should also be very low, as well as all the other terms of the offer. In fact, you may wish to offer nothing down at all. *The point is* to *try* to smoke out *the motivated seller.* If you send out one hundred low offers, more than 90% will come back marked not acceptable. (Of course, some of them won't even come back because your offer is so low.) But you are looking for the motivated seller, and since he is not sitting out there with an "M" branded on his forehead, you have to find him through the most effective and efficient way that you can. This way works. I know, because many people have used it successfully. In fact, one major merger firm in New York City uses this as its primary method of soliciting medium and small-sized corporations that need or want to be sold.

REFERRAL METHODS

I rarely go to a movie that hasn't been praised to me. Before I waste my time sitting in a theater, I need to talk to someone who has seen it to get his or her opinion. Word of mouth is the best, the least expensive, and the most powerful advertising that any company can hope to have.

In your quest for financial independence and freedom, a good, well-oiled, well-organized referral system can work wonders and is critical to your success, since your time is so limited. If you tell ten friends that you are looking for a certain type of distressed asset, give them some particulars, and ask them to talk to at least five of their friends, you will have contacted sixty people in short order.

You should also use this technique in trying to sell any of your appreciating assets. In fact, I use this method when trying to find partners for ventures. I alter the method slightly by calling ten friends and asking them for a list of ten people by name and phone number. I specifically ask the question,

"Who do you think the ten most successful, upcoming young people in the city are?"

When I ask specific questions like this I get specific answers. If, on the other hand, I were to call a friend and say, "Listen, do you know some successful people in this town? If you can think of their names why don't you give me a call sometime?", I would get an answer of, "Sure, I'll call you if I can think of somebody. Good-bye." Click. Hang up. And that would be the end of that. My friend would never call. But when I specifically ask for a certain number of friends, (three, five, or ten), using the right words so that it is not a threat to them or to their friendships, then I almost always get results. When I call these people, I use the friend's name as the person who referred me to them. Like magic, I get a warm welcome from these people.

FORECLOSURES

It is safe to say that anyone who has had a property foreclosed qualifies as a motivated seller. An investor who has an understanding of the foreclosure process can often buy real estate far below market prices. Prudent use of investment dollars in this fascinating market can create excellent returns. Though lenders usually foreclose on less than 1 % of their outstanding mortgage loans, the great volume of mortgages makes even this small percentage meaningful.

TYPES OF FORECLOSURES

There are two types of foreclosures in this country: "strict foreclosure" and "foreclosure by sale." Few states presently have strict foreclosure procedures. In those states the borrower loses his or her title to the property unless the lender is paid in full by a court-designated date. The time allowed the borrower is in direct proportion to his or her equity in the property; that is, the fair market value of the property (as determined by one or more court-appointed appraisers) less claims against it, such as mortgages, taxes, and other liens. The more equity in the property the borrower has, the more time the court will give the borrower to payoff the delinquent mortgage.

The most common type of foreclosure is foreclosure by sale. Under this procedure the property is sold to the highest bidder at a court-supervised public auction. The proceeds of the sale are applied to all claims against the property and any funds left over are paid to the borrower.

ONLY ONE BIDDER

Often at public auctions of real estate the only bidder present is a representative of the lender whose mortgage is being foreclosed. The lender's representative bids an amount sufficient to payoff the lender. If there are no other bidders, the lender winds up owning the property. Usually the lender thereafter attempts to sell the property at fair market value.

Let's look at a hypothetical case. Borrower Jones buys a property for $80,000 and pays $60,000 of the purchase price with the proceeds of a mortgage loan from Dollar Bank. Several years later the property is worth $100,000 with a mortgage balance of $50,000. Jones then fails to make payments and Dollar Bank forecloses. Attorney fees, court costs, appraisal fees, accrued interest, and unpaid real estate taxes total $5000. Dollar Bank needs $55,000 in order to avoid a loss.

If the bank were the only bidder at a public auction, it could own a $100,000 property for $55,000. Instances of this sort may be rare but are not unheard of. Jones would lose the property and be paid nothing. An investor could bid $60,000 or $75,000 at such an auction and get a bargain. Jones then might at least realize a few thousand dollars for his equity instead of zero. Even on those occasions where several bidders compete at a public auction, the successful bidder usually makes a very good deal.

AN ATTRACTIVE MARKET

How does the investor involve himself in this active and attractive market? A real estate broker has at his or her fingertips the most efficient sources of information concerning pendency of foreclosure actions. Public auctions of real estate are announced and advertised in designated media with which the broker is familiar. The broker often checks public records to get early leads. He or she keeps in close contact with the attorneys and bankers who are central to this market.

Get to know and develop a rapport with an experienced, well-qualified broker. If the broker is convinced you are serious, you might negotiate an arrangement whereby the broker gathers data for you about foreclosure sales in your area of interest for little or no fee. You could offer to list the properties you acquire through his or her efforts with the broker, for lease or resale at current market prices, so the broker could end up making some good on his arrangement with you. Innovative thinking coupled with prudence can earn rich rewards in this exciting and often overlooked market.

YOU MAKE IT HAPPEN

All the techniques in the world won't help unless you make it happen. There is an amazing synergistic effect once you get started. It may seem slow at first, but once you get moving, things will begin to snowball. Referrals and answers to offers and letters you wrote weeks and months before using the shotgun method will start coming in. You will start building the reputation of a person who is ready, willing, and able to make purchases of the right type and the right price for investment.

AN EXTRA $5,000 A MONTH

Using the techniques above, I bought a small, rundown, two-bedroom house that looked like nobody cared about it – nobody did. The seller wanted out so badly he could taste it (he fit the profile of the ideal motivated seller). After I had bought the property and inspected it more closely, I began to worry that the seller was a little too motivated and that maybe I was too anxious and had paid too much. Fearing I had made a mistake, I worked twice as hard and twice as fast. The first thing I did was make sure that the property didn't look as though the seller was motivated, even though in truth I was. Mainly out of fear-the fear of losing money.

After completing the work, most of which I did myself, I attempted to sell the property, using some of the same techniques that made me buy it. After several false starts, close calls, and a fair amount of worrying, it was finally sold. Looking back over the deal, I saw that I had made a little over $5000. It worked so well that I decided to do it again, and that's exactly what I did. I found that by finding the right seller, one sufficiently motivated, I could make most of my profit just from the negotiating process with the seller. In several subsequent deals, the amount of time, effort, and money that went into improving the property to make it saleable was minimal. I was now doing a deal a month, making $5000 net after costs every month.

As I began to develop my skills in negotiating (see Chapter 13 on Negotiating Hints), I saw that the same process could be used on larger properties and that it was much simpler to do one or two deals a year involving larger properties rather than one small property every month.

I recommend that you start with smaller properties. Do one or two deals in one or two months. That will give you the confidence to recognize the motivated seller and his or her bargain and also teach you some negotiating techniques that will help you when you move to larger properties or similar appreciating assets.

What you *can learn from actually going out and doing is fifteen* or *twenty times more powerful than what* you *can learn from reading this book* or *any book.* Sure, you can learn from this book and others. Go to all the seminars that teach techniques that are pertinent to what you are trying to accomplish. But in the final analysis, your own experience is going to be the very best teacher. The $5,000-a-month trick is a great way to start. Go do it! Be like Napoleon, for whom to think was to act. Without action, the greatest thinking, planning, and conceptualizing in the world yields a big fat zero.

PLANS AND GOALS

_____

_____

_____

_____

_____

_____

_____

_____

_____

CHAPTER 15

CREATIVE FINANCING HELPS YOU BEGIN WITHOUT CASH

You can create miracles. It is amazing the miracles you can create in financing real estate, if you put your mind to it. This is where the brain compounding talked about in Chapter 1 really starts to pay big dividends.

While negotiating terms on a refinance package for the Coventry Hearth (the Coventry Hearth deal is described in Chapter 7), I began to see variations of my initial offer to the seller to refinance this building.

In my first letter to the former owner, I asked him to discount the $24,000 that I owed him by about $4,000. My concession was to pay off the discounted amount immediately instead of in four and a half years when it was actually due. He answered that he wouldn't do that, but with a large payment, he would carry back the balance on a second mortgage basis, allowing me to refinance with a larger first mortgage.

At that point the light bulb flashed on. There was the beautiful answer to my big problem (lack of excess cash to buy more properties) staring me in the face. It had been there all the time, but I hadn't seen it. His letter set off the series of events that would allow me to purchase in excess of $2 million in additional property.

After thinking through the idea to make sure there were no quirks, I wrote to all the people I had bought property from on uniform real-estate contracts or where the seller held the first mortgage himself. I made the same basic proposal to each one. I offered to pay part of the remaining balance owed them, increase the interest rate slightly, and shorten the payment period, thus giving them an incentive to accept the offer. Of course, my request was that they take a second mortgage position and allow me to place a new first mortgage.

The results were astounding. Letters and phone calls came back, agreeing to my terms. In fact, some of the responses were so enthusiastic that the amount of money I raised via this type of creative financing was around $200,000.

Using a couple of my examples, here are the details of how this was done. (Refer back to Chapter 7 for details on the Coventry Hearth package.) In a small outlying community in Salt Lake County, I had a modest income property (a single family unit). I had purchased it approximately fourteen months before. The price and terms were both attractive. I paid $1,000 down on the $8,500 purchase price with the balance of $7,500 on an 8.5 percent uniform real estate contract (land contract). The monthly payments were just under $90.

There was no question that this was an attractive price and a real bargain for me. (But, as you will see later, the method I am describing can be used even if you don't buy at a bargain price.) My letter to the former owner was somewhat as follows:

Mark O. Haroldsen
Salt Lake City, Utah

Mr. & Mrs. L. Somebody
Salt Lake City, Utah

Dear Mr. & Mrs. Somebody:
    In reference to the property located at 2894 South 8900 West which you sold me in 1974, there is a possibility that,

assuming you are interested, I could pay part of the amount owing to you and change the terms so you would be able to receive your money at a much faster rate.

Here is my proposal: I would pay you $1,000, which would leave a balance owing to you of approximately $5,326. That balance would be paid at $109.27 a month thereby cutting the term to five years, a reduction of almost four years and the rate would remain at 8.5 percent.

To make this change possible, you would need to subordinate your interest in the form of a second mortgage. Of course, if you still owe Mr. R.C., this would have to be paid at the same time or before we made our transaction.

If this would be advantageous and desirable to you, please let me know and I will take care of all the details to achieve this change.

Sincerely,
Mark O. Haroldsen

About a week later I received a phone call from the former owner. He was enthusiastic and said he would be glad to change his interest to a second position to receive the extra benefits offered him. I told him I would check on financing and get back to him within a couple of weeks. My next step was to go to a savings and loan association and secure a promise on a first mortgage refinancing.

I had to pay 11.5 percent, an extra high interest rate for that time (the house was in a less than desirable area and was an older house which most institutions do not like to finance). So after paying the $1,000 I had promised him, I put $7,400 in my pocket. (Of course, it went from my pocket into the bank to be used for acquisition of other properties.)

That capital *must* be reinvested or in no time at all you will find yourself swamped with debt and no assets or income from those assets to bail yourself out. Debt is a fantastic instrument if it is used carefully. If not, it is the most devastating of all the financial tools.

After the transaction was completed, my position was this: (1) I had $7,400 capital that I wouldn't have otherwise (it can work as leverage for me to buy a $75,000 property). (2) I had a property that was financed to the hilt and a little beyond. Cash flow wise, the property was slightly negative; that is, there was more cash being paid out each month than coming in. This is a bad situation in some cases, but not so in this particular case. Why? Because by using the $7,400 excess capital wisely, I increased the amount of cash flow over what I had with the former property. In essence, I ended up with a low-cost loan in terms of the cash I had to pull out of my pocket each month to pay for that loan. In addition, I continued to have the appreciation of the property through inflation, and of course, the tax advantage and an attractive equity buildup each year. Although the numbers are going to be different today because of interest rate, the concept is the same and is still working and will work for you.

A YOUNG MAN PUTS $5,000 IN HIS POCKET

Many years ago I was approached by a Realtor who had a similar opportunity to buy a real beat up, dirt-bag house for an extremely low price – only $8,000. (Remember, the concept behind what you're going to read with these low numbers still works – if the numbers bother you, just add a zero.)

He had found a property that was a total disaster. Every window in the entire place was broken and the place was an absolute wreck. The price was ridiculously low, but the terms were wrong. The owner wanted a down payment, and the Realtor didn't have any cash. It seemed unworkable, but it wasn't.

My advice is so simple that it amazes me that more people do not use this easy method, especially in periods of high and tight financing.

Here is what I told him to do and this is exactly what he did. Make a full price offer to the seller with 25 percent cash down, the balance to be carried by the seller on a *second* mortgage, but then the seller must allow the buyer to put *a first* mortgage on it at the time of closing. If the seller still insists on a larger down payment, it still can work.

The Realtor went out and secured a first mortgage to close at the same time he closed on the property.

The amount of the first mortgage was $10,000 (you'll see in a moment why the bank loaned him more on the property than the selling price), $2,000 of which would be paid to the seller at the time of closing. (The total price was $8,000.) This left a balance of $6,000. But most important, this put $8,000 in the Realtor's pocket (but sometimes, as you will note in the next paragraph, the bank doles this money out slowly but eventually the Realtor still had cash in his pocket). He spent approximately $3,000 to fix up the property, but still had $5,000 to purchase other properties. It should be noted that after the house was completed, it sold for more than $20,000. It was this potential end result that convinced the lender to loan $10,000 on an $8,000 purchase. The real trick here is to be able to put forth a convincing argument, complete with a package showing what improvements you are going to be making to the property, and prove your case on paper of what the new value of the property will be when you're finished. Normally, if the bank approves such a loan, the bank will dole out the money in that newly created first mortgage only as progress is made and the bank can verify the progress by inspections. But for you it's still a super success that put cash in your pocket when it was all done. The other key, of course, is convincing the seller to take a second position.

A word of caution: since each such deal creates a negative cash flow in most cases, be careful not to overburden your financial position to the point that you drown. This type of leverage can be a tremendous boon to you and get you on your way in a hurry, but it can also be a millstone around your neck if not used wisely and cautiously.

YOU CAN STILL GET 4 PERCENT MORTGAGE MONEY

Get your nest egg started, whether through savings or through the method just described. Then, another method of creative financing, which can catapult you to even greater levels, is the use of 4 percent money, which you can create.

First of all understand this. If you buy a property and pay only 4 percent instead of, let's say, 7.5 percent on a large mortgage or contract, your cash flow will obviously be much higher. This is because your total payments will be smaller.

> NOTE: I need to say this at this juncture. People ask me all the time if you can still get seller carry-back financing because our interest rates are so much lower than they were 10 or 20 years ago. The answer to that question is, yes you can. In many cases you can get the seller to carry back financing, but it probably is a little more difficult than it was many years ago because the rates were so very high then and money was tighter. With money being more available and rates lower it's more difficult to talk the seller into carry-back financing, but not impossible. Again, remember it's all about the motivation of the seller and what the seller's going to do with the money. If the seller is just going to stick the money in the bank, you can use that time tested argument that you will pay them a better rate in most cases than a bank or savings institution will on their cash.

One hundred thousand dollars ($100,000) borrowed for twenty years at 7.5 percent would make your monthly payment about $805; whereas at 4 percent your payment would only be about $418, almost $387 a month difference.

This $387 a month could allow you to buy the property for a price much higher than the asking price. (Many sellers will jump at a higher price with a lower interest rate.)

In fact, you could easily offer up to $50,000 more for the property and still be ahead. A mortgage for $150,000 at 4 percent for twenty years would make the monthly payments $627, still $178 a month less than the payment for the 7.5 percent rate on the $100,000 mortgage.

In addition, in Chapter 12 you will see how even $178 a month savings would add almost $18,000 value to the building. (If 4 percent seems ridiculously low to the seller, bump it up to 6 or 6.5 percent, whichever is acceptable to him and which makes a good deal for you based on the increased price. Many years ago I made an offer to a super-motivated seller with a 3 percent interest on a $2 million property. He finally accepted a 7 percent compromise as a seller carry-back — originally he had asked for 10 percent to carry it back as the seller.)

To take advantage of the 4 percent formula, here is what you do. Look for large income properties that are owned by older people. Usually this type of property is older. You will be looking for one that is free and clear. The ideal situation is one owned by a person in a high tax bracket, one he has probably owned for a long time, and if he were to sell it outright, the tax consequences would be devastating to him.

When you find the property, here is what you would propose. Offer to buy the building with a low down payment. This would be to the seller's advantage since the tax consequences to him would be minimal. (By selling it with a low down and on a long-term contract or mortgage, he will qualify for an installment sale. Installment sales spread the gain over a number of years and can reduce the total taxes drastically.) Consequently, he only has to show a small portion of his gain each year.

To make the offer even more attractive, offer a price somewhat above his asking price, but rather than pay him the 6 percent to 7 percent interest, offer him a 4 percent rate. Be sure to explain the benefits to him. Basically, the benefits are from a tax point of view. First, he is selling under an installment sale which gives him a big advantage. Second, by selling at a higher price and a lower interest rate, a larger part of the monthly payment will be going to principal than would have been with a market interest rate. So he saves money by paying capital gains tax (usually a much lower rate than ordinary income tax) on a larger principal payment.

This method of creative financing can be used in more situations than the one described above; the seller doesn't have to be an older person with a free and clear property. Sometimes the seller would rather have a higher price with a lower interest rate for tax reasons, even though the underlying mortgage (when he sells on a wraparound mortgage or contract*) is at a much higher rate. Others will accept this type of offer just because they put a premium on selling price only and not on the terms of the deal. So give them their high price with low rate and you can have a much larger cash flow.

A 100 PERCENT FINANCING IDEA THAT'S WORTH A MILLION

In his excellent book, *How Real Estate Fortunes Are Made*, George Bockl explains another creative method of financing. (This old concept can still work today.)

> Here's a little known idea where you can get 100 percent financing when you show the lender how he can earn

---

* *A wraparound contract or mortgage is where a property is sold and the original mortgage or contract is kept intact. Payments are then made to the seller. The seller continues to make payments on the original mortgage or contract.*

17 percent interest while you're paying only 8 percent. Sounds improbable, doesn't it? Well, it isn't when you can find this set of circumstances, and it's not difficult to find, because it's fairly prevalent.

Let's assume you're a competent young man with a good record in property management. You have found an owner of a sixteen-family apartment building who wants to sell it to you for $200,000, subject to a $150,000 mortgage balance at 5 percent. But there is that clause that the lender can terminate the loan upon transfer of title, legal or equitable. It's a deal stopper.

Of course, you can't blame the lender for not being happy with the 5 percent interest, but there is nothing he can do about it as long as the original borrower owns the property. But here's where you can put an innovative leverage idea to work that is favorable to you and the lender.

Find the mortgagee who has the authority to make decisions, show him your managerial credentials, and tell him you are willing to sign a new $200,000 mortgage at 8 percent, if that's the going rate, and cancel the $150,000 mortgage at 5 percent. What that means, you tell him, is that the effective rate of interest for the $50,000 he'll be advancing will be worth 17 percent. You don't need to explain too carefully that getting 8 percent on the $150,000 instead of 5 percent means 3 percent more interest on three times $50,000 plus 8 percent on the additional $50,000 adds up to 17 percent on the new $50,000 advance. The chances are he'll have it computed before you get through explaining it to him.

The only problem you may encounter is that he may not want to stretch his loan $10,000 or $15,000 to reach the $200,000 you request. But if you can convince him of your reliability and of your willingness to ride the loan without cash flow because of your prime goal to have a free and clear property by age sixty, then he would indeed be shortsighted if he turned you down. The chances are that raising the interest and the amount of loan will dry up all of the cash flow.

Your only risk is that you will have given the mortgagee a new idea and he may steer the deal to a friend of his who he may think is a more reliable vehicle for your idea. It's a risk you have to take, but it's not a great one, because most lenders are honorable men. If you convey a sense of integrity, he'll hold on to you because he'll respect you for your innovative idea, and because when he sees 17 percent, he'll act quickly.

Search for these situations. Every city must have hundreds of them. When you find a 2 percent or 3 percent interest spread which will give you an opportunity to leverage innovatively in a tight, high interest money market, move in on it. It's one of those remarkable ideas which enables the seller to sell his property, the lender to increase his interest yield, and you to ride in on a 100 percent financing plan.

Even if you consider yourself an ordinary salesman, if you can pull it off, it will turn you into an extraordinary one. ([Englewood Cliffs, N.J.: Prentice-Hall, Inc., 1972], pp. 202-203.)

As a variation to George Bockl's idea, try adding some second mortgage money. That is, ask the owner to carry some secondary financing. This will put cash in your pocket and make it 100 percent-plus financing. Of course, if you can't find one big deal, you can find two or three smaller ones and continue to find them until you have mortgages in excess of a million dollars.

Then all you need to do is sit back, manage the properties carefully and wait until the mortgages are paid off. If you are thirty years old or thereabouts and are able to sign your name on mortgages of a million dollars or more, and if these are twenty-five-year mortgages, you will retire at the age of fifty-five with over a million dollars worth of property. (This of course is assuming that properties do not depreciate any faster than the rate of inflation during that period of time, which is a very safe bet indeed.)

That is how simple it is for a thirty-year-old to become a millionaire by borrowing a million dollars.

Through the use of this type of creative financing, you can make seemingly unworkable deals into workable deals. You can turn small money-makers into large money-makers. You can put large amounts of cash in your pocket for reinvestment in bigger and even better deals.

The few methods described in this chapter are by no means the limit to creative financing ideas. As you begin to finance your own deals, you will see new and better ways to fit your needs and the particular financial market at the time you buy and sell your properties. But like anything else, to make it work you must begin.

If you are cautious and have had no experience whatever in real estate, start with a small property. If you are not aggressive, would rather not use secondary financing, and you have saved a nest egg, then begin by finding properties you can buy with a low down payment. This makes your capital go further, and in each case you attempt to get the highest possible return on the cash you invest.

Later when you get more confidence, you can always go back to the people you purchased the property from (assuming the owner is carrying the financing) and suggest that they change their first position to a second position, thus allowing you to place a first mortgage on the property.

If you are aggressive, particularly if you have a little experience in real estate, the only things stopping you from making a million dollars are lack of ambition, drive, and the energy to apply the techniques outlined in this and other chapters. Remember what Conrad Hilton's mother told him when he was having a hard time getting started and taking big, aggressive steps, "If you want to launch big ships, you have to go where the water is deep." You can start in either shallow water or deep water, depending on the size of ships you are desirous of launching.

NOTES AND THOUGHTS

CHAPTER 16
FORCED (PLANNED) INFLATION CAN DOUBLE YOUR MONEY EVERY YEAR

When I use the example of one penny doubled every year (see Chapter 1) or compounding at the rate of 100 percent annually, the majority of people do not think it is feasible or practical. I must admit I didn't believe it was possible for the average person when I started acquiring and improving real estate.*

The key to achieving the goal of 100 percent compounded annually lies in improving the real estate. Had I not achieved the 100 percent goal so consistently, I would, even now, find it difficult to believe that it was an achievable goal.

The only reason I say this is because there are so many people who own income properties, apartments, offices, and

---

* *I clearly remember being on Tom Brokaw's morning network television show many years ago, before Brokaw began doing the evening news. On that show Tom also had a Federal Trade Commission attorney who challenged just about every word I said – But what I clearly remember most of all was that attorney challenging my claim that you can compound your money at a one hundred percent rate of return. He just couldn't believe that. He just couldn't think outside the box. He could only grasp the concept of interest rates that he had seen advertised by banks, or lending institutions, or what an average person receives in the stock market. He couldn't grasp the concept of how anyone could receive, with the wise use of leverage, and by applying your own hard work and creativity, one hundred percent or two hundred percent or even higher rates of return.*

rental houses, who have been in the business much longer than I have and still do not believe it is achievable because *they* haven't achieved it. These people are not using their heads to figure out how higher rates can be achieved.

APPLY 100 TIMES FORMULA TO DOUBLE YOUR NET WORTH

If you understand and use the 100-times formula, you can easily double your net worth annually for many years.

<u>100 Times Formula</u>
$1 x 12 months =
$12 x 8.34 gross rent multiplier * =
$100 added value
or

One-dollar increase in rents or one-dollar decrease in expenses per month is worth an average $100 added value to property. (That is on the average. In my experience the range is from $60 to $140 added value.)

What I'm saying is that by using this formula, you will be able to justify an increase in rents of one dollar per apartment for every $10 you spend per apartment on improvements. By doing this, you will add $100 to the value of your investment. If you spend $100 per apartment and raise the rent $10 per month, you have added $1,000 value to the building.

---

* *The use of 8.34 GRM is somewhat arbitrary to make the 100 Times Formula come out in a nice round number and make my point. Obviously, if you use a 6 or 7 times GRM, the number will be much lower – in this case 72 and 84 respectively. Still, if you are leveraged on the property, any of these numbers will put you well on your way to a doubling of a particular property's net value and eventually the doubling of your net worth.*

Now you can see how the $178 a month savings in your monthly payment talked about in Chapter 15 really can add almost $18,000 in value to the building – ($178 x 12 months = $2,136 x GRM formula of 8.34 = $17,814.24).

Now it should be obvious how by the improvements you make to these buildings and subsequent rental increases, you can compound your assets at 100 percent per year.

Remember that with a 10 percent down payment, a 10 percent increase in value of that property equals a 100 percent return on your investment. It's that old thing called leverage that's helping you get the 100 percent return on your investment.

This theory is quite simple and the application is not much more difficult. Let's again use the simple example of buying a $100,000 property with 10 percent down, or $10,000. The balance of $90,000 is owed to either the seller or a financial institution or both. Through the use of forced or planned inflation, you increase the value of the property by 10 percent. The building is now worth $110,000 and the balance owing is $90,000, less principal payments you have made during the year. Your principal payments would approximate $600. (This would vary according to the length and interest on the loan.) The balance owing at the end of one year would be $89,400. Assuming there are ten units in the building, each rented for $225 a month, how can we actually make the building worth 10 percent more?

First, in order for a building to be more valuable, it must have higher revenues. In the case of an apartment building, it would be in the form of rental income. There are many ways to improve the value of a building and the individual apartment units to allow an increase in rents and keep the tenants happy.

The following list is only some of the ways. Any one or a combination of these improvements can be used. In each instance, we will not average more than $500 per apartment and will in effect have doubled our net equity within one year.

1. New carpeting. Assuming these apartments are approximately 550 square feet, we can add brand new high quality nylon carpeting at a total cost of $495 per apartment or $4,950 for the entire building. In order to get a high quality carpet for an average of $7.50 a square yard (it would take sixty-six yards of carpet to do 550 square feet), you must do some shopping. Check all the large carpet outlets telling each your situation, that you have apartments and will need a fairly large amount of new carpeting. Ask them what kind of a deal you can get as far as price. I suggest that you buy nylon carpet with the pad attached — a foam backed carpet you can have laid inexpensively. In fact, an average room of 12 x 16 feet can be laid easily in an hour. All that is needed in addition to the carpet is a good sharp razor and a staple gun. Merely roll out the piece of carpet, cut it to size, and staple it in place using a minimum amount of staples, mainly around the edges, through doorways, and a few in the middle. I stay away from carpets that hide the dirt. Otherwise, tenants can go for weeks, even months, without vacuuming a carpet that hides spills and spots. This makes the carpet wear out much more rapidly as it will have to be shampooed more frequently.

2. Painting Interior. In an apartment 550 square feet, five gallons of good quality paint is sufficient to completely paint the unit. Be sure to get a high quality paint for which you will have to pay, even with a discount, between $18 and $20 a gallon. If you use a low quality paint, you will find that you will spend more for labor because you will have to paint it with two coats, in addition to painting the apartment more often. On a per-apartment basis, you will spend about $100 in material and you should be able to hire an unskilled painter whom you can train for between $10 and $15 an hour, depending on the part of the country in which you live. This cost will run you $160 to $240 in labor for a total of approximately sixteen hours of labor. The total painting bill per apartment will be between $160 and $340 a unit or $3,400 at the most for the entire building.

Add to that figure several hundred dollars, depending on the size of your building, for hallways and common areas.

A word of caution regarding color: Don't try to get too fancy and get into color coordinating the different apartments with the carpets, etc. I did this for a while and found the cost, time and money rising rapidly as we tried to match different colors in apartments we had previously painted. Many hours were spent trying to match wall painting with furniture, carpets, and appliances. Stick with the basic colors, preferably light colors, white, off-white, or beige. You will save a lot of time, money, and headaches.

3. Drapes and curtains. In a 550-square-foot apartment unit, $400 or thereabouts will go a long way to improving the value of the apartment and the building, especially if you shop for bargains. Some of the large, discount chain stores, from time to time, liquidate large quantities of drapes and curtains. When you see such bargains and you think there are any you can use in apartments, be sure to stock up.

4. Furnishing the Apartment. I won't debate the merits of furnished versus unfurnished apartments and the prices you can get from them. But if you do have or are going to buy unfurnished apartments and are looking for an easy way to increase rents by 10 percent don't overlook the possibility of buying a few pieces of furniture. You will be able to increase the rent and make the apartment both acceptable and desirable for the tenant. A good queen-size bed, small love seat, a chair, and two or three beautiful pictures can enhance the worth of an apartment dramatically.

5. Improving the exterior. If the exterior needs to be made more attractive, this is where you should actually start improving. If not, then make the improvements inside that will give you the best chance of increasing the rents with the least amount of difficulty. In most cases, $5,000 spent on the exterior of a ten-unit building will go a long way to improving the value. If it is more than one story high, have a professional bid it and do the job. (Get at least three bids so you know you are getting a good price.)

By using any of these five steps, if you bought the building right, you can probably increase your equity twofold. Remember also that for each dollar in rent increases or expense decreases per month is worth an average increase of $100 in the value of the building.

By using any one or two of the suggested five steps of improving the building's worth, and if we have kept our cost to $5,000 for the whole building's interior, we will discover that we have a dramatic increase in our equity. If we sell the building at the end of one year, the net result would compound our money by 100 percent. We paid $10,000 of our own money and we put in an extra $5,000 to increase the value of the building to $110,000. This is accomplished by estimating before we began that by spending $500 per apartment, we could raise the rent by approximately $10 a month or $100 a month for the entire building which would equal $1,200 increased revenue per year and consequently a 10 percent increase in the overall value of the building.

After selling the building for $110,000 and deducting the mortgage, we have $22,700 left over, $5,000 of which was spent on improvements. So we have compounded our money by 100 percent because we turned $10,000 into $20,000. In this case, we actually did better than 100 percent, because we have not taken into account the cash flow which would have been approximately $1,000 during the first year, nor have we considered the tax benefits that would accrue to you had you bought this particular income property.

Remember, it is not only the *increase in revenue* that makes a property more valuable, but also the *decrease in expense.*

Expenses can be cut in many ways. I have cut expenses by doing everything from adding insulation to cut the heating bill (with fuel costs bound to continue to rise, this will be a big factor in the future), to cutting the garbage bill by reducing the number of pickups. The key here, in my opinion, is to always start with the highest and biggest expenses, because usually that's where you can do the most good by reducing them. Look at every expense with the idea of reducing it. Maintenance can be cut by having the manager do more. Insurance expense can be decreased by shopping harder and asking for a better rate. Management costs can be reduced by finding the right manager for the particular property. The electric bill can be cut by using electric timing switchers to turn off common area lights when not in use. These are just a few areas where you can save a dollar to add a $100 in value. Do some thinking and come up with more cost-cutting methods.

By using this formula, your profits will run wild. You will make more money than you, no doubt, thought possible. If you have the wisdom and self-control to reinvest those profits, you will create assets that will be enjoyed for generations.

Unfortunately, to the uninformed, making a profit, especially a large one, seems to be a bad thing. Even some well-meaning congressmen and senators talk about such things as obscene profits. I say unfortunate because this reflects a misunderstanding of the capitalistic system and why it is, and always will be, the best system in the world.

In the capitalistic system people are rewarded for seeking their own self-interest, but they are only rewarded if, while seeking to do the best for themselves, they also reward others.

John Deere, the man who made America's first steel plow, wanted to benefit himself; he wanted to sell the plow for a profit. It was difficult, at that time, because the superstition was that if you used steel to turn the soil, it would poison the soil. Deere proved otherwise, and made a fortune for himself. But look what the benefits were to mankind.

In modern times, look what has happened to the price of computers, cell phones, and Internet fees. In just a few years, the price has dropped sharply on all of these items. Why? Because people who wanted to make a dollar moved quickly into the market to provide these items at a lower price, so they could sell more units and make more money for themselves.

The capitalistic system parallels the basic nature of man. That is, we try to help ourselves first. If we are smart, we see that by helping others we help ourselves faster. With this sometimes thought-out and sometimes subconscious plan, we proceed to help others with the ultimate goal of helping ourselves. Is this selfish? Possibly so, but is this kind of selfishness bad?

I have purchased income property with the intent of making a big profit. I see that the only way I will be able to do this is by improving the property and consequently improving the living conditions of the residents. When I raise rents, I expect to have a lot of complaints; even though I have improved the property and it is a much nicer place to live. The amazing thing to me is that I expect people to complain, but, for the most part, they don't. In fact, the comments and sometimes even letters from tenants almost make the cash reward secondary. Here is one letter taken from the *Salt Lake News*:

> Dear Sirs:
> I would like to recommend the Coventry Hearth Apart-
> ments, 454 South 5th East, as the most improved housing

accommodations in our area. I lived there almost four years and in all honesty it was the most cockroach and mice-infested place I have ever seen. Most of the tenants were either using drugs or were alcoholics, and prostitution was also quite prominent. There were quite often violent episodes to the point where firearms were used a few times. Also the sewer and drainage facilities were neglected to the point that the smell was quite foul. The police and paramedics were there so often that a person could not keep count.

Mr. Mark O. Haroldsen bought the building and though it cost him a huge sum of money, the Coventry Hearth has new furniture and carpeting, the halls and apartments have been repainted, the sewage and the drains repaired by plumbers, the insects were 95 percent eliminated by exterminators, and the undesirables have moved. They were not evicted and Mr. Haroldsen is not one iota concerned about discrimination. He is a good and patient man who tries to help people.

The main reason the undesirable tenants moved was because there was a different environment for them. They found that Mr. Haroldsen was a man who could not and would not allow himself to be manipulated or used. He was also a good example for us all, in the terms of how responsible people should be and by his personal manners. I strongly think he should win your award because of his achievements.

He has Chicanes, Tonganese and black people who are tenants there, and so far as I have seen no one has problems with their neighbors.

As an afterthought, we are also getting the green lawn into good shape for the simple reason that he makes sure it is watered and taken care of and sections of the lawn have been transplanted. As I mentioned, he has spent a great deal of money to accomplish this and it is not coming out of the taxpayers' pocket – It is coming out of his own.

Take it from one who has lived there for a long time and has seen the big change.

Sincerely,
Roy M. Gallegos

Editor's reply:

We took your advice, Mr. Gallegos, and gave the Coventry Hearth the award. And we are sure that Mr. Haroldsen agrees with us, that you must be a very special tenant to take the time and the energy to point out Mr. Haroldsen's accomplishments. We wish all of you real success in all endeavors.

People are motivated by a lot of different things. To me, there aren't many that are more stimulating than monetary rewards and sincerely expressed appreciation. I have found a great measure of both through my investments in real estate, and I know you can also.

FINDING THE DIAMONDS IN THE ROUGH

Here's how my old friend, real estate investor, author and educator, Wright Thurston, came up with his breakthrough property. It took him from the little leagues to the major leagues.

At the time Wright was a young IBM executive living with his family in Alaska. He had invested in nothing larger than two and three-unit buildings. But it was becoming increasingly clear to him that larger multiple-unit property investments were the way to go in that part of the country.

"We realized," Wright explained, "that because we were living in what was at that time the single most expensive city in the U.S. — Fairbanks, during the Alaskan Pipeline days — that it made more sense to invest in multi-family units than in single-family homes, or even duplexes and triplexes.

"To give you an idea of how expensive things were," he went on, "the cost of the average single-family home back then was in the $140,000 range, and a gallon of two percent milk cost anywhere from $3.50 to $5.00 a gallon. Because of this type of high prices, it was virtually impossible to invest in a single-family home and then rent it out for enough money to cover the mortgage payments. So I had been looking towards making an investment in a multi-family unit property because I realized that the cost per unit would be less, the competition would be less, my time investment could be less because I could delegate some of the management responsibilities to an onsite manager. I could still cover the expenses even if there were a few vacancies — there were all kinds of advantages."

One day, Wright found a classified ad in the local newspaper that appeared to be exactly what he'd been looking for. It said that a 24-unit property was for sale for $325,000. The price seemed incredibly low... that is, until he went with the real estate agent to see it.

"How bad was the property?" asks Wright. "Have you ever been in a building where you didn't want to bump up against anything because you were afraid you'd get something on you? That's how bad it was!"

Wright returned home discouraged to tell his wife, Janett, that the property was a major loser. But Janett reminded him of something — "Is it the worst property in a nice area?" she queried.

"Yes," said Wright.

"And does it have all the right things wrong with it? Couldn't you use your management skills to turn it around?" she pursued.

"Yes," said Wright, bounding for the telephone to call the real estate agent.

As it turned out, the owner was a motivated seller who wasn't involved in the buildings' management; he worked out of state, and hadn't put any money back into maintenance and repairs (obviously). In fact, he owed back taxes and assessments were due. Consequently, his two buildings were real "don't wanters."

The seller was asking $325,000 with a $40,000 down payment. The remaining $285,000 would be satisfied by Wright's assumption of a first mortgage note to an individual at 8-3/4 percent interest, and his signing of a second mortgage note to the seller at 12 percent interest.

Wright agreed to the price and terms, but with two modifications. First, he asked if it would be possible to split the down payment, paying $20,000 at the closing and the remaining $20,000 in 30 days. This would give him a chance to get the money he'd need because he knew there would be a proration of rents and security deposits at the closing, which he could put towards the second $20,000 payment. By scheduling the closing near the first of the month, he would get more prorated rents. The seller agreed.

Second, Wright requested that the seller subordinate his interest in the property so he could use the property as collateral to borrow the funds necessary to fix it up.

Again, the seller agreed on the condition that Wright would not borrow more than $60,000 and that he could hold a note for that amount against Wright's home until Wright could show him receipts proving that all the $60,000 had in fact been put back into the property. Wright said okay, and the sales agreement was written up and signed.

Wright found a banker who was willing to give him $20,000 on a short-term commercial note. He went to the closing as planned with his money in hand and found, to his delight, that he only had to use $12,000 of the $20,000 because of all the prorated rents and security deposits that were credited to him. That left him with $8,000, and meant that he now only had to come up with another $12,000 within 30 days, instead of the full $20,000.

"I met with many rejections", says Wright. "But at one of the last banks left to visit, the banker asked me an interesting question: 'Why should I lend you the money?'"

Wright came up with a good answer: "If you'll give me the loan, I'll take all the rent monies and deposit them in your bank each and every month. That'll be a minimum of $120,000 over the course of a year."

Wright got his loan, pulled off the deal, and spent the next six months fixing up the buildings. "The bottom line," he says, "was that about 18 months after acquiring our first diamond in the rough, I had it reappraised, and whereas I had paid $325,000 for it, an MAI appraiser now valued it at $850,000!"

Demonstrating his ability to make a good deal even better, Wright refinanced the property (after separating from it a 3/4-acre piece of land to one side of the buildings), paid off the two seller-carried mortgages at a discount and walked away with some spending money that was left over. That amount was $268,000.

But the story goes on. The 3/4-acre parcel of commercial property that was separated from the 24-units was appraised for $105,000.

Taking a tally at this point, Wright had $268,000 in his pocket, a $105,000 commercial lot free and clear, and still had over a quarter million dollars worth of equity in the 24-unit property. Add to all that a positive monthly cash flow from the units, and it's not surprising that Wright soon took off his IBM suit and became a real estate investor full-time.

NOTES AND THOUGHTS

_____

_____

_____

_____

_____

NOTES AND THOUGHTS

CHAPTER 17
A TAX TALE
OF TWO FAMILIES

I'd like you to meet Mr. and Mrs. Worker, a nice couple with two young children. Both he and she work and earn $80,000 between them. Their income is augmented by $525 they earn at 5_ percent annual interest on a $10,000 savings account. So their total annual income is $80,525.

Under the current year's rules, the Worker family is entitled to four personal exemptions—$3,100 per individual. (Note: we will be using the rules for the 2004 tax year in this chapter.) The standard deduction for the family for the year is $5,450. (Tax computed on their taxable income is $8,226. However, they also qualify for child tax credit on each of their children for $1,000 each. Therefore, their total tax is $6,226.) For our purposes, we'll assume that the Workers have elected to take the standard deduction instead of itemizing deductions.

That means that Mr. and Mrs. Worker can deduct a family total of $22,100, which makes their taxable income $58,425.

Now, like most Americans, when Mr. and Mrs. Worker collect their paychecks, they can see that the Internal Revenue Service (IRS) beat them to their money and took a tax bite. By the end of the year, they have had $8,000 withheld for taxes, so they receive a refund of $1,774.

Let's meet another couple: Mr. and Mrs. Investor.

Like Mr. and Mrs. Worker, they have two children, their combined salaries total $80,000, they had $8,000 withheld for taxes, and until last year, they had $10,000 in savings. *But they did something last year that made a big difference...*

Realizing that their savings were being eaten up by inflation—and the interest was being taxed as ordinary income— the Investors withdrew their $10,000 in savings late last year and used it to buy a $150,000 apartment building. Their down payment on this building was $15,000. (The seller financed the remaining $135,000 with a mortgage note.)

The property needed quite a bit of equipment (new heaters, air-conditioners, etc.) furnishings, fixtures, and so on to bring it up to the level of its highest potential as a rental income generator. All of this cost the Investors an additional $40,000.

By the time these improvements were put into the "rehabbed" (rehabilitated) property, its new value had climbed to $190,000 (this was a very conservative estimate).

So what did the Investors have? They had a building worth at least $190,000 (probably more).

What had they paid for it? First, there was the $15,000 down payment. Then, there was the $40,000 rehab costs. That comes to a total of $55,000.

Where did they get the $55,000? Remember, they had $10,000 in a savings account, which they used. And they got the other $45,000 into the form of a six-year loan from private sources.

So they really paid only $10,000 of *their own money* for an investment that was now worth at least $190,000.

Of course, they also were responsible to make monthly payments on the $135,000 mortgage and the $45,000 loan, but the rental income the property was generating would pay for these.

Surefire Wealth

That's a Promise.

Who can back up such a promise?

Mark Haroldsen and William Nickerson.

Surefire Wealth

A rare, LIVE Interview with Bill Nickerson and Mark Haroldsen that reveals the fascinating, little known, personal secrets that assured their multi-million dollar real estate fortunes, and how to put their personal Secrets of Success to work in your life, RIGHT NOW!

I could hear the gentle surf just a few feet from Bill's front door. A pristine, private white beach surrounded us on three sides. It was all very serene.

Bill Nickerson had invited me to his magnificent Pacific coast hide-away. We sat together on a huge sofa that stretched across his great room that was lined with floor to ceiling windows, bringing in the wonderful scene around us—up close.

Richard Hamilton was seated across from us with a microphone in hand. He started recording an interview, with these words: *"I'm in the enviable position of being able to interview two men who are probably more influential in the lives of real estate investors across the country than any other two people."*

Ordinary Men—Extraordinary Wealth

Of course that's a pretty bold statement Dick made, but considering the fact that between us, Bill and I have owned over $200 Million worth of real estate—and the fact that our books, together have sold in excess of four million copies—and that between us, we have presented thousands of real estate investment seminars—well, not bad for two ordinary guys who started out small and went BIG!

And we've learned a secret or two along the way. And we share them in this Interview. These secrets have to do with how we live our personal lives—the personal stuff (neither of us shared in our books) that we do each day—the "little things" that *guarantee* our success.

Guaranteed Success

Yeah, you heard right. Bill claims (and I agree) that if you put these same "little things" into your own daily life, and follow the game plan that is laid out in this interview, *you cannot fail.* That is the value we place on what we revealed in this **three-hour Interview.**

And you, a partner, a spouse will want to listen to these CDs over and over again, to ensure all of you keep on the path to success, together—and your children, your grandchildren so they may carry on your legacy and improve their own financial lives.

The late Bill Nickerson (left) is a legend! His huge best-seller, *How I turned $1000 into Five Million in Real Estate—in My Spare Time* inspired two generations. Many millionaires, including me, are indebted to Bill for his brilliant insights. In this photo, I'm presenting Bill with a special *Lifetime Achievement Award* during the 1991 FINANCIAL FREEDOM REPORT Real Estate Investor's Convention in Orlando, Florida ... and he received a standing ovation that went on and on.

The **Four CD** Interview package of Bill and me, that I'm offering you here, is the **only** audio available of William Nickerson that I am aware of. And it is truly a classic!

But YOU be the Judge

Order the complete, uncut interview on 4 Audio CDs, entitled **Ordinary Men—Extraordinary Wealth.** The price is $89.95, including priority shipping and handling—a bargain, considering the one-of-a-kind, *timeless* nature of this unique audio interview.

If you don't agree with me that the advice and wealth-creation insights are invaluable, **even priceless,** to you, then send the CDs back for a full refund. **Ordinary Men—Extraordinary Wealth** is only available through my office. Call 9am to 5pm (Mountain Time) **1-866-286-2912** and place your order by Credit Card. *Or* send a check or money order to the **Nickerson/Haroldsen Interview,** 4505 Wasatch Blvd., Suite 350, Salt Lake City, Utah 84124.

A BIG DIFFERENCE

Because the Investors made this real estate investment, their taxes *and* their overall financial picture are now very different than they would have been had they left their $10,000 in a savings account—as the Workers did.

Let's take a closer look. (See Table II at the end of this chapter) First, you'll notice that not having the 5_ percent interest income from their savings any more lowered their annual personal income to $80,000. Their standard deduction and personal exemptions were $22,000, leaving their taxable income at $57,900.

However, because they have an income property, they add the IRS's *Schedule E* form to their tax computations.

On their Schedule E, they can deduct $8,705 from their taxable income. Where did this $8,705 come from? That's a good question. But just put it on hold for now, and we'll give the answer further on.

As you can see in Table II, when you deduct $8,705 from their personal taxable income of $57,900, that latter figure is reduced to $49,195.

But remember, they had $8,000 withheld from their paychecks. If you subtract the computed tax on $49,195 of $4,617 from the $8,000 withheld, you can see that Mr. and Mrs. Investor have a nice refund of $3,321.

Not bad!

That's $3,321 cash-in-hand to reinvest or do with as they will. (As *Financial Freedom Report* subscribers, they'll probably reinvest it.)

But let's move on to that interesting looking $8,705 that you want to know about. Let's get down to the nitty-gritty.

To find the $8,705, we need to understand the tax benefits that come with the ownership of income property.

Let's take a look at the economics of the property shown in Table III. From actual experience, we can say that a well-managed, recently rehabbed $195,000 rental property can generate a $35,000 annual income. (That figure will vary from one area of the country to another, depending on local rent structures and vacancy factors. But more importantly, it's based upon how well the property is geared for *optimum* rents.)

As Table III shows, from the $35,000, Mr. and Mrs. Investor would deduct $29,000 for interest payments and operating costs. (That $29,000 is comprised of $17,400 to pay the interest figure on the borrowed $45,000 and on the $135,000 mortgage, plus $11,600 for operating expenses including such things as some utilities, painting, and general upkeep.)

Deducting the $29,000 in expenses from the $35,000 rental income leaves a gross profit of $6,000.

From the $6,000, Mr. and Mrs. Investor make $6,000 principal payments on the borrowed $45,000 and the $135,000.

This leaves the Investors at a break-even cash flow situation. (This will change radically for the better in a few years, when the $45,000 loan is paid off.)

Hey, wait a minute! If they didn't lose anything on the property, how can they claim a net loss of $8,705 on Schedule E of their income tax return!

How? Depreciation!

THE DEPRECIATION FACTOR

But, you may ask, how can something depreciate in value when in fact the market value does not decrease by that amount? (Actually, well-managed real estate traditionally *increases* in value over the course of time.)

The answer to this question is one of the beauties of the U.S. tax laws. It's there in black and white.

The whole thing probably started when some business person went to Uncle Sam and said, "Hey, the truck I bought two years ago is wearing out. It's depreciating in value. Can't I claim that as a business expense and deduct the amount from my taxes?"

"Well, okay," said Uncle Sam, and he passed a law making it so.

It seemed to be a good idea to a lot of people, including rental property owners who probably complained to Uncle Sam that their buildings were depreciating from wear and tear. "And what about all that stuff inside?" they asked. "That's depreciating too, you know."

Uncle Sam agreed that all this wear and tear, and all that depreciation, could be classified as a business expense, and he adjusted the tax laws to reflect that decision.

And that is how Mr. and Mrs. Investor's break-even profit situation changed into a handsome tax write-off.

You see, depreciation is an expense that you are allowed to deduct from the income of the building after all other expenses (interest on the mortgage loan, operating expenses, etc.) have been deducted. Often, after depreciation has been deducted, the property will no longer show (for tax purposes only) a profit at all. In fact, it may show a good-sized loss. And unless you're in a high-income category, up to $25,000 of that loss can offset your other regular income, such as wages, salary, interest, and so on.

LET'S GET DOWN TO THE NITTY GRITTY

Briefly, let's review some of our figures. (See Table IV.) We had an annual rental income of $35,000 less interest and operating expenses, leaving a gross profit of $6,000.

Now we feed in a depreciation figure of $14,705, for a net loss of $8,705.

That's where the $8,705 comes from.

But where did the $14,705 depreciation figure come from?

Let's figure the depreciation, starting with the land on which the structure stands.

How do you calculate the depreciation of land? You don't. Land doesn't depreciate. Therefore, owners need to deduct the cost of the land from the purchase price of the property. If this can't otherwise be estimated, a good rule of thumb is that at least 10 percent of the property's purchase price can be attributed to the land it sits on.

For tax purposes, this means that Mr. and Mrs. Investor must deduct 10 percent of the $150,000 purchase price ($15,000) to arrive at the figure that qualifies for depreciation ($135,000).

Since the $135,000 building was purchased and placed in service after 1986, it is depreciated over a 27_-year period, using the MACRS method. After the first year, the building's depreciation amount equals its value divided by 27_. In this case, that figure is $4,909 ($135,000 divided by 27_).

The $40,000 worth of equipment, furnishings, and fixtures that the Investors put into the property is currently considered 7-year property for depreciation purposes. (There may be a few exceptions, but for our purposes let's not confuse the issue, since it wouldn't significantly change our figures anyway.) These items are depreciated using the MACRS 200 percent declining balance method. Using this schedule for the second year of service (remember, the Investors bought the property the year before), these items bring a $9,796 depreciation deduction.

Adding the two depreciation deductions together, we get a total figure of $14,705 that Mr. and Mrs. Investor can deduct for depreciation.

Of course, after the 7-year period, the furniture, furnishings, and equipment they've been depreciating will be fully depreciated, and the Investor's won't be able to take a deduction for them. But they will be able to start depreciating any new items in this category that they purchase.

Their depreciation deduction for the building will last until the end of the 27_-year period. That's a long time!

It's important to note here that if the Investors had not put the $40,000 worth of new equipment, furnishings, and so forth into the building, they would have only had the depreciation write-off for the $135,000 structure and existing contents of the building itself. Under current tax laws, you can't normally factor out from the original purchase price of an existing property the cost of the furnishings, furniture, and equipment. Instead, you have to depreciate these items along with the structure, using the 27_-year MACRS schedule, unless you buy them as new or replacement items after the original purchase, as the Investors did.

A 200 PERCENT INVESTMENT RETURN

Table VI is very interesting. It shows that the total return on Mr. and Mrs. Investor's "out-of-pocket" invested dollar (the $10,000 they took out of savings) is *185 percent!* Compare that to what Mr. and Mrs. Worker's $10,000 brought them, and you'll see there is no comparison at all.

The Investor's return is calculated using an annual property appreciation rate of 6 percent, which is similar to the overall average real estate appreciation rate. Even if the property didn't appreciate at all, the Investors' return on their investment for the year would be a very nice 75 percent.

In fact, even if everything else was taken away, *the tax savings alone* (the difference between their actual refund and the refund they would have got if they had left their $10,000 in a savings account) *gives the Investors a 15 percent return on their money!*

As you can see, starting with the same economic base as Mr. and Mrs. Worker, Mr. and Mrs. Investor found themselves a solid investment with a fantastic return, tremendous tax savings through depreciation, and extra cash…through the ownership of income property.

UNCLE SAM LOVES REAL ESTATE INVESTORS

The tax laws that deal with real estate are always changing. From year to year, rental property owners face new rules of the tax game. Depreciation deductions change. Installment sale rules change. Tax-free exchange rules change. Percentages, limits, and amounts go up and down. Specific tax advantages appear and reappear, changing form constantly…and on, and on, and on.

But one thing *doesn't* change: Uncle Sam loves rental property owners and will always give them some sort of tax break. Why? Because he wants his citizens to have places to live—especially those who may not be able to afford to buy their own homes, or may not want to. (In fact, he offers special tax advantages to those who invest in low-income housing.) The way he can do all this is to offer rental property owners "bonuses" (like depreciation) when it comes time to pay income taxes.

Sure, these tax breaks may be better in some aspects one year than they are the next, or vice versa, but never forget that Uncle Sam will *always* give income property investors good tax reasons to provide rental units to the public.

In today's environment of extremely high taxes, the tax consequences of any investment can be among the most important considerations.

When I bought my first income property, I had in mind making big capital gains. At the end of the first year, I was surprised and delighted by the large gain from several improvements I made, if I had sold the property then. But the real shocker was the added advantage it gave me in the amount of taxes I would *not* have to pay.

My down payment on that building was only $4,600. After improvements (paid out of cash flow) and after subtracting all other deductions from my income that year, Uncle Sam allowed me an additional $8,000 deduction because I owned this particular apartment building.

Believe me, at that point my opinion of old Uncle Sam—about whom I had in the past made disparaging remarks at tax time—drastically changed.

CURRENT TAX LAWS FAVOR
THE AVERAGE INVESTOR

Right now, the tax laws relating to real estate investments are structured to benefit investors in the middle or even lower income categories more than they benefit individuals in the high-income brackets. This is great news for everyday people who are on their way up the ladder of financial success.

Let me explain, using depreciation as the prime example.

For people who own rental real estate, depreciation can create substantial "losses." We've seen that. The IRS considers these real estate investment losses "passive activity losses."

Current tax laws state that you may only deduct up to $25,000 of such passive activity losses that are attributable to rental real estate activities against non-passive income (your salary from work, for instance), and that you must "actively participate" in the ownership and management of that property, as Mr. and Mrs. Investor did. (In their case, they could deduct all of these "losses," since they were under the $25,000 limit.)

But another factor comes into play.

This $25,000 allowance is subject to a "phase-out" for higher income taxpayers. It is reduced by 50 percent of the amount by which your adjusted gross income exceeds $100,000. That means that this benefit completely disappears when your adjusted gross income reaches $150,000. (Your adjusted gross income is basically your total income from wages, salaries, tips, interest, dividends, business income, capital gains, rents, royalties, partnerships, and so on, with a few adjustments, *before* deducting your exemptions and standard or itemized deductions.)

Let's illustrate this.

Suppose your adjusted gross income is $120,000. Because it is over $100,000, you know you're going to lose a portion of the $25,000 allowance. To determine how much, subtract $100,000 from the $120,000. That's $20,000. Now, you have to take 50 percent of that amount, or $10,000, and subtract it from the $25,000 allowance. The resulting figure— $15,000—represents the top limit of the amount of passive activity losses from your rental property investments that you can deduct against your non-passive income.

COMPETENT TAX ADVICE IS CRITICAL

Depreciation is not the only tax break available to those who invest in rental real estate.

Others, such as the tax-free exchange, are right there in the books, and ready to be plucked by savvy investors.

But be careful! The rules and regulations surrounding these tax opportunities tend to be involved and confusing. Plus, as I already mentioned, they seem to be in a constant state of change.

There is a lot of bad advice floating around, given by people who are not informed or up-to-date. They're trying to be helpful, but they usually do more harm than good.

My advice—my *strong* advice—is to seek the help of a competent tax professional before making any moves or binding decisions. Paying for the time of a good accountant or CPA who specializes in this area will be one of your most profitable investments.

Once you know what the tax laws are, and how you can work with them to your best advantage, you'll quickly find that rental real estate investing can be your key to a treasure chest of wealth and satisfaction.

TABLE I

Salary income	$80,000
5_ percent interest on $10,000 savings	$525
Total annual income	$80,525
Personal exemptions at $3,100 each	<$12,400>
Standard deduction for the family	<$9,700>
Taxable income	$58,425
Actual tax computed on $58,425	$8,226
Child tax credit ($1,000 each)	<$2,000>
Net Tax	$6,226
Amount withheld from salary	<$8,000>
Total IRS refund	**$1,774**

TABLE II

Salary income	$80,000
Personal exemptions at $3,100	<$12,400>
Standard deduction for the family	<$9,700>
Taxable income	$57,900
Schedule E deductions (for income property)	<$8,705>
Final taxable income	$49,195
Taxes withheld from salary	$8,000
Less actual computed tax on $49,195	<$4,679>
(Including child tax credit)	
Total IRS refund	**$ 3,321**

TABLE III

Annual income from rents	$35,000
Interest expense on $135,000 mortgage and $45,000 loan for new equipment, furnishings, etc.	$17,400
Building operating expenses	$11,600
Total Expenses	<$29,000>
Gross profit	$6,000
Principal paid on $135K and $45K loans	<$6,000>
Total net profits	**$0**

TABLE IV

Annual income from rents	$35,000
Interest and operating expenses	<$29,000>
Gross profit	$6,000
Depreciation	<$14,705>
Net loss	**<$8,705>**

TABLE V

Property	$150,000
Less 10% factor for land value	<$15,000>
Value of structure and original contents (27-1/2 year depreciation category)	$135,000
Depreciation (MACRS 27.5-year schedule, year 2)	**$4,909**
New equipment, furnishings, and furniture purchased (7-year depreciation category)	$40,000
Depreciation (MACRS 200 percent declining balance method, year 2)	$9,796
Total depreciation write-off	**$14,705**

TABLE VI

For $10,000 "out-of-pocket" costs invested on a property valued at $190,000:

	return	%
Cash flow	$0	0%
6% property appreciation factor ($190,000 x .06)	$11,400	114%
Tax savings ($3,683 less $1,093 they would have received as per Table I)	$2,590	26%
Equity build-up by making loan payments and reducing principal balances	$6,000	60%
Total annual return on $10,000 investment		**200%**

PLANS AND GOALS

_____

_____

_____

_____

_____

_____

_____

_____

_____

_____

_____

_____

_____

_____

_____

_____

_____

_____

_____

_____

_____

_____

_____

_____

PLANS AND GOALS

_____

_____

_____

_____

_____

_____

_____

_____

_____

_____

_____

_____

_____

_____

_____

_____

_____

_____

_____

_____

_____

_____

_____

CHAPTER 18
FOCUS YOUR ENERGY FOR STRENGTH AND PROFIT

The quickest route to any objective, be it monetary or otherwise, is to totally focus the attention on a minimum number of things. Thomas Edison was once asked how he was able to get so much done. He said, "It's very simple. You and I each have eighteen hours a day in which we may do something. You spend that eighteen hours doing a number of unrelated things. I spend it doing just one thing, and some of my work is bound to amount to something."

If Edison had taken the time to do a dozen unrelated things, the 1,093 inventions he patented would probably never have been invented.

SIDELINES TURN TO SLIDELINES

If you truly want to be outstanding in any field, there's one important rule you must observe: you must concentrate your energy and power. Get just one thing in your mind, your heart, and your bloodstream. Put side-blinders on your eyes, like they used to keep on horses to prevent them from being distracted.

With blinders on you'll be able to look straight toward your goal and forget what's happening on the sidelines. It's been said that sidelines are slide lines. You can't serve two masters effectively. Sidelines invariably take one away from his goal. Sidelines divert the attention.

They take away all your focus and instead of doing one thing well you do two things poorly.

That doesn't mean one can't have other interests. It means he can't have interests that divert him from his goals. The minute a second interest begins to compete with your goal is the minute you should drop that second interest.

MESHULAM RIKLIS

Meshulam Riklis is a good example of how we can balance our interests. Riklis is a very successful man, having turned several small companies into the billion-dollar Rapid America Corporation almost on his own. (The corporation is now worth over 2.3 billion.) Through a biographer, we get an understanding of a proper way in which we can share our business focus with other interests:

> "I have been accused of being like a racehorse with blinders," he once told me. "All I see or care about, they said, is the track ahead. Well, that might be a fine quality if I really had it. But the truth is I do get diverted."
>
> I see nothing to regret in being diverted from one's goal — that is, temporarily — if the diversion itself is worthwhile. I saw Rik "get diverted," if that is the proper phrase, during the Israel crisis in June of 1967.
>
> From the moment Nasser massed troops on Israel's borders and blockaded the Gulf of Aqaba, Rik plunged into the job of bringing assistance to the democracy that had for so long been his homeland. He headed a United Jewish Appeal Emergency Drive for funds among merchandisers. He poured his own money into the campaign and helped raise many millions more.
>
> And I saw Rik "get diverted" again when he helped organize a committee whose purpose was to rouse all Americans to strive for security and peace in the Near East. This was not a Jewish committee; its membership was drawn from all faiths. Its aim was to protect *American* rights in the Near East — rights which might be completely lost if the Soviet

Union's influence were permitted unchallenged sway among the Arab nations.

For it was not only disaster to Judaism that Rik foresaw if Israel were destroyed. Israel, an outpost of democracy, was a symbol of freedom. If it were annihilated (and some Arabs were still demanding this in the councils of the United Nations) freedom and democracy through the world would be dealt lethal blows. Rik flung himself into the struggle to avoid the holocaust. "Ask not for whom the bell tolls," he said to those he recruited for his committee. "It tolls for thee." And because he was right he was joined by scores of outstanding citizens representing industry, the professions, the arts.

These manifold activities, however, never interfered with the hours he devoted to business — which is why I say that in his case, as in the cases of many others, a primary requisite for financial success seems to be a dogged, single-minded dedication to one's job. Diversions come, yes; they are part of a man's social responsibility; but they cannot be allowed to interfere with corporate responsibilities. [From Oscar Schisgall, *The Magic of Mergers,* Boston: Little, Brown & Co., 1968, pp. 232-34.]

PASSION AND OBJECTIVE

Even with his diversions, Riklis did not allow himself to become sidetracked from his ultimate objective. He was able to continue to focus his attention on his long-range goals.

Anyone will have a good chance of succeeding if he will concentrate his energies. But, on the other hand, if he divides his time and talents among more than one enterprise or goal, his chances of success diminish rapidly. The man cannot possibly succeed who allows chores, hobbies, politics, art, philanthropy, and other distractions or sidelines to steal attention and energy away from him.

A man's only passion should be his main objective. Once he lets the sidelines become his passion, he's lost, and that's the end of his dream.

THE LAW OF CONCENTRATION
(EVEN EMERSON WARNED OF DISTRACTIONS)

Sterling W. Sill, in his book *How to Personally Profit from the Laws of Success,* explains how the law of concentration works:

"The doctor or lawyer or merchant or prizefighter who specializes is the one who invariably goes places. And yet every day we see persons who cannot resist the lures of the sideshow attractions. They still incline to the thought of cheating this powerful law by having sidelines and outside interests, and by that process they divide their power and subtract greatly from their effectiveness.

"Ralph Waldo Emerson wrote two essays on this subject. One is entitled 'Power' and the other 'Wealth.' The main theme in each is concentration. He said, in effect, 'Stop all miscellaneous activities. Do away with distractions, other duties, property cares, chores, errands, diverting talents, and flatteries — all are distractions which cause oscillations and make a good poise and a straight course impossible.' Distractions always untune us for the main purpose of our lives. Emerson said, 'The one prudence in life is concentration; the one evil is dissipation.'

"As a gardener gets good fruit by severe prunings, thereby forcing the sap into one or two vigorous limbs instead of allowing it to dwindle into a sheath of twigs, so anyone headed for some great accomplishment gets the best results by concentrating his effort in one place.

"A child may be perfectly content with his plaything until he sees something that some other child has. The child usually wants everything he sees and drops one thing after another as new attractions are presented. We are very much like children. We want too many things and are not constant and faithful to any one thing. The Bible says, 'No man can serve two masters.' It doesn't just say that some can't; it says *no* man can. It just can't be done. You can't ride two horses in the same race. The Good Book says, 'Keep your eye single.' That means to keep just one thing in the focus of your vision. 'A double-minded man is unstable in all his ways.'

"The greatest Christian missionary said, 'This one thing I do.' That's why he became the greatest Christian missionary. A great Supreme Court Justice, in trying to indicate the value of concentration and how it had helped him achieve such a high place in the legal world, said, The law is a jealous mistress. It tolerates no competition. The law says to its devotees, "Thou shall have no other gods before me." Success in any field says just about the same thing.'

"Singleness of purpose and an unwearied will give power greater than dynamite. It's a natural principle. We didn't invent the law and we can't do anything about it, but it is the law . . .

"We have only so many hours in a day. If we're trying to do four things instead of one, we can do two hours work on each instead of eight hours on one. But we always have to stop when we change directions. This means the loss of the great power of momentum. It also means we've lost the force and power and enthusiasm that comes from concentration.

" 'Jack of all trades and master of none' describes a human weakness of adults as well as children. We tend to want everything we see. If we take a fire hose and force the water out through the nozzle, we get great power. If we divide it into a spray, it falls softly with no force. The amount of sunlight that falls on the back of our hands is just pleasantly warm; but if we concentrate it through a convex lens and focus it into a pinpoint of light, we can develop enough heat to start a forest fire.

"It is really surprising how many capable men fail because they 'scatter their shot.' Some have sidelines. Others let numerous little cares destroy their success. I know of one potentially capable businessman who tends his own vegetable garden, milks a cow, takes care of his yard, does his own landscaping, paints the house when necessary, and does the plumbing. He runs the errands, does the shopping, carries his shirts to the laundry, and sometimes washes them himself. When his wife needs to go someplace, he does the baby-sitting. Each fall he puts on an apron and helps his wife bottle a winter's supply of fruit. He wipes the dishes and helps care for the children until he probably doesn't know whether he is male or female, businessman or handyman.

"This man thinks he is saving money, but actually he is wasting the most valuable thing in the world — the power of concentrated, one-directional, wholehearted effort. He also neutralizes his mind. He thinks like an errand boy and a babysitter, not like a businessman. His mind is so occupied by this multiplication of little cares that it cannot cope with the important problem of becoming a success. He has even given up the peace and privacy and quiet of his own home by building an apartment in the basement. When the plumbing gets out of order, his renter just calls him; then he takes off his businessman's attitudes and enthusiasms while he becomes a toilet fixer. All of this brings the inevitable result: his wife teaches school to support him.

"This is an extreme case, but there are many people who are continually stumbling over a number of little diversions and spoiling their chances to succeed. They are always starting and stopping, always on the detours or sidelines, always trying to save a few dollars or earn a few in competition with the errand boy, the house painter, and the plumber. The bank president doesn't polish the brass or sweep the floor. If he did, he probably wouldn't be bank president very long. A businessman should learn to think like a businessman. His time is too important to compete with errand boys. He should not spoil a magnificent achievement by turning off the fire of his enthusiasm while he fixes the plumbing."

THE POWER OF CONCENTRATION

If you have an intense, unwavering determination to make your objectives and goals a reality, *nothing* can stop you if you can learn to concentrate your efforts. But that concentration is essential; you must learn to focus your attention on one thing, and keep it focused there, if you hope to succeed.

It's like the magnifying glass that Sterling Sill wrote of. With the glass you can take the gentle rays of the sun and bunch them together until the small shaft of light you've created burns a hole through steel.

When they're not focused, those rays of the sun are harmless. But focused through the glass they can exert tremendous power.

Many people have not set lofty personal goals, financial or otherwise. I have no quarrel with them; they can decide for themselves what they want out of life. Their reward will be in direct proportion to their goals.

But if a person decides to break out of this rut of *averageness,* he can't continue doing what the majority of the people are doing. For example, the average American family watches more than forty hours of television a week. The person who is trying to concentrate his efforts can't do that. He has to forego all that television in favor of his goal.

KARL ELLER

To be a great person — financially, artistically, socially, religiously, politically, or any other way — you must concentrate your efforts and attentions through that tiny magnifying glass. You must resolve not to be sidetracked by the hundreds of diversions that will tempt you — diversions that are sometimes interesting but are nevertheless usually meaningless.

Karl Eller is a good example of what we are talking about. He started out with a small mixed-media business in Arizona. Through a great concentration of power, Eller has built a company worth more than $367,000,000.

Eller's concentration has come much easier because he has believed in what he's doing. Years ago he was willing to bet everything that the billboard business would grow like wildfire. He was somewhat of a pioneer in the field, but he had a vision of what it could become.

He stuck with his objective with the single-mindedness of a doctor performing surgery. Now his company, Combined Communications, has some 35,000 billboards in seventeen Western and Mid-western states. But he didn't stop there. His goal was to build Combined Communications into a billion dollar enterprise by the mid-1980's. He added five VHF and two UHF televisions to his company. Then he added the *Cincinnati Inquirer,* then the *Oakland Tribune.*

Eller increased his company's worth by $141 million in one year! Now he has merged Combined Communications with the Gannett newspaper chain, giving him almost $800 million a year in revenues, very near his billion dollar goal.

Eller was able to expand his company so quickly because he concentrated on a single objective. Most of his employees work long and hard hours, but few can keep up with their boss and his single-minded purpose. He works almost nonstop, and somehow manages to get by on only three hours of sleep a night.

Someone once said that John D. Rockefeller's genius was that he could concentrate all his energy, powers, and attention on one thing for five minutes. That may not sound like a great task, but just try it. In fact, try to concentrate your total mental powers on one thing for even sixty seconds, without allowing your mind to wander down any side tracks.

Not many of us can get by on only three hours of sleep a night. Not many of us have the concentrating power John D. Rockefeller is said to have had. But most of us *can* develop the power to concentrate on a general goal or direction — and by doing that we can become known for something great.

TRY IT FOR ONE YEAR

Give it a try. It's easily worth your time and effort. In fact, I would challenge you to concentrate all your efforts and energies on your goals for just one year. Mark on your calendar right now that for the next 365 days you're going to give single-minded attention to your objective. You'll resist distractions. You'll eliminate sidelines.

Oh, I know it won't be easy. Most of us find it difficult to say no when we're asked to help with some charitable drive — or when we're invited to visit our in-laws on a three-day weekend.

But go after your goal just the same. Try for the next twelve months to eliminate all those things that divert your attention from your objective. Try to have a singleness of purpose.

Then, 365 days from now, look back and see what you've been able to accomplish. I'm convinced that you'll be able to do some great things just in that short period of time. In fact, one year of concentration on your goal will get you so deeply involved with it that nothing thereafter will be able to divert you from what you want to do.

Do you *really* want that goal? Then learn to focus your energy, learn to concentrate, and the goal will become yours.

NOTES AND THOUGHTS

CHAPTER 19
UNLOCKING THE SELLER

We all have a common concern: how to achieve the greatest financial return for the smallest financial outlay.

And in our attempts to find ever-more-profitable deals, we scurry here and there, running from one option to another, always looking for something better. Of course sometimes that's necessary. Sometimes we have to really hustle to get the kind of deal we want. (The willingness to go through the hassle involved in hustling sometimes makes the difference between the poor and the rich investor!)

But as we scurry about we too often miss the source of good deals that pays off more consistently than all the others. What is that source? The seller!

As I travel around making my own deals and hearing about others at seminars, this idea is supported time after time. Let me tell you of one experience I heard about.

A young man and his wife approached me and told me of their *first* investment purchase in real estate. It was a fantastic success — and the reason why was that they let the seller help them!

This couple bought an old hotel that was in pretty dilapidated condition, with the idea of converting it to an apartment building. With a lot of elbow grease and sweat, along with about $4,000 cash, they drastically changed the value of this property. Here are the numbers:

They purchased the building for $50,000 with $5,000 down, leaving a balance of $45,000. The balance was paid on an eight percent contract over twenty-five years, which made their monthly payment $347.32. By adding over 400 hours of long, hard work, they were able to convert this beat-up hotel into a respectable apartment building.

After completing their eighteen-month project, they figured the building was now worth $170,000. How did they know that? Because that's exactly what they sold it for! In fact, they not only sold it for $170,000, but they were able to sell it with a $50,000 down payment.

So not only did they have all their cash back, plus a hefty cash profit in their pocket ($41,000 to be more precise) but they had a very nice income for the next twenty-five years, because the balance of $120,000 was drawing an interest of nine and-a-half percent. They were then receiving $1,048.44 a month for this piece of paper. So they were able to spend, save, or invest $702.12 ($1,048.44 minus $347.32) every month for twenty-five years ($701.12 x 25 years = total of $210,336.00). All they have to do is deposit the incoming check from the buyer and write a check to the person they bought the property from.

So you see, they were not only receiving nine and-a-half percent on their $75,000 equity ($120,000 less $45,000), but they were also making one and-a-half percentage points on the $45,000 since they were receiving nine and-a-half percent on the whole balance, and only had to pay eight percent on the $45,000 they owed to the person they bought the hotel from.

What does this story tell us about working with the seller?

First of all, more than anything else the key to buying bargains today is expressed in those two words: The Seller. The seller can be the key to bargain financing, bargain prices, and bargain terms. Always, always, always look to the seller first, for all of the above three. Later on, you can try for a super leverage deal by talking the seller into subordinating his position behind another, larger first mortgage. Again, the seller is the key. If you have financed with a bank, there's very little likelihood of super leverage.

Because of their initial approach with the seller, this young couple was able to go from being in the property business to being in the finance business. Because banks have been so ridiculously tight with loaning money on old, fix-up type properties, enterprising people like you and me need to get into the financing business.

How can such financing work? If this couple had done nothing more than turn around and sell the property the very next day for the same price, they could have made money by charging a higher interest rate. (They could have made $16,875 in twenty-five years by selling the property for the same price, but with a nine and-a-half percent interest rate.) But they were even wiser than that. They put in "sweat equity" as well as some cash equity to improve the property drastically.

Then when it was time to sell, they again acted wisely. If they had insisted on someone refinancing it, they might still be holding the property, looking for a bank to refinance it. But by taking back the paper (selling the property on a contract and in essence lending the buyer some of the financing) themselves, they not only have a sizable and continuing income for the next twenty-five years, but they were able to sell the property quickly.

So there is benefit in selling smartly, as well as in working smartly with the seller when you buy. Take some time to study the amortization schedules, which really should be your financial bible, so you can structure deals both on the "buy" side and the "sell" side. If you do, you'll move yourself more quickly along the road to financial freedom.

Looking back at my best deals, I must admit that my time was most profitably spent studying the amortization book to see what my payment would be with various lengths of time and amounts of money. (If you don't have an amortization book or calculator that can run the numbers, or a computer to access to the appropriate websites by now, you should get hooked up.) Your time both as a buyer and a seller can be well spent studying what you can learn from these sources.

PLANS AND GOALS

_____

_____

_____

_____

_____

_____

_____

_____

_____

_____

_____

_____

_____

_____

_____

_____

_____

CHAPTER 20
HOW TO RAISE $200,000 IN TWENTY-FOUR HOURS

Years ago when in the growing stages of my real estate acquisitions, I came across a super deal in a residential home. It was a magnificent four-story home built high in the mountains among the pines. It was built to look like a castle with an interior floor plan and design to fit a king. It had five fireplaces, several bathrooms, a fantastic den and library, and was designed with all the extras and luxuries one would want in a home. It was to be sold at a foreclosure auction at the county court house at noon. I found out about it three days before the auction was to take place.

I desperately tried to raise what cash I thought it would take to purchase the home. (At foreclosed property auctions, they generally require a cashier's check for most, if not the entire, price bid.) I was able to borrow $50,000. It was extremely difficult to do because I had not laid enough groundwork prior to this because I had no way of knowing that I would need that amount of cash so quickly.

I went to the auction and found to my surprise that there was only one other person bidding on the property. To make a long story short, the other person outbid me and picked up the property for $60,000 which was only a fraction of what the property was really worth. It is obvious from this story and many others I could tell, the value of putting your hands quickly on large amounts of cash.

In addition, you should take note of the fact that only two people showed up for the auction. If I had been the only person who showed up for the auction, I could have bought the property for $1 over the mortgage.

Literally dozens, maybe hundreds of super bargains are available every day in your town or city. Two ingredients are necessary to take advantage of them, and both can easily be available to you. First, you obviously need to know about such bargains and deals. This will come as you make more contacts, and keep up contacts with people in the real estate business. You might think that Realtors would scoop up these super bargains before they show them to you; in most cases, that is a needless worry. The second ingredient you must have in many cases to take advantage of these bargains is fast and liquid cash.

Many people have had such opportunities presented to them where quick cash was necessary. Most were unable to take advantage of the opportunity because of a lack of cash. A simple process is available where you will be able to generate quick cash within twenty-four hours. It is a many-stepped procedure, it will take time to lay the groundwork, but it is easily executed.

For lack of a better name, I call it the "banking round robin." Go to several banks in your area, preferably in the same day or within a two-day period. The number of banks you contact is up to you and depends on the amount of money you feel you might need. I keep accounts in a minimum of ten banks, from each of which at this point in time I am able to borrow $20,000 on my signature. Take with you to each of these banks a statement of your net worth.

Armed with the ammunition of your financial statement, approach the commercial loan department and tell them that you need a $1,000 signature loan for thirty days. Of course, depending on the amount of your statement, the $1,000 request may be much higher on your initial visit to the bank. As a rough rule of thumb, many banks will lend up to ten percent of your total net worth on an unsecured signature loan.

Repeat this process at as many banks as necessary for your needs. Using a round figure of ten banks, at the end of this first step you will have borrowed a total of $10,000 — $1,000 from each bank.

It is usually suggested, if not required, that you set up a checking account at each bank from which you receive a loan. In most cases, I do this before I request the loan: I can then tell the bank that I am one of their customers. When setting up a checking account, request the unnumbered checks. This way the account will not cost you anything to set the account up other than a nominal monthly charge for carrying the checking account.

With the $10,000 you have generated from these loans, if you do not have immediate use for the cash, I would suggest that you deposit it in another bank in an interest-bearing account, if possible.

Thirty days later, when the notes become due, be sure they are paid on the thirtieth day not the thirty-first day. If you request and bargain for a good interest rate, you should not have to pay more than two or three percentage points above the prime lending rate. (To find the prime-lending rate, call any stock brokerage firm, preferably a member of the New York Stock Exchange, or go online and do a search for "prime rate".)

Wait approximately sixty to ninety days. Go back to each of the banks from which you borrowed an initial $1,000. This time request a larger amount, depending on what you think the banks will loan – maybe $2,000 to $5,000. They may only lend you another $1,000 at this time, depending on your financial statement. Request a longer payback period this time — a ninety-day note instead of thirty days. If each bank approves a $5,000 loan, you would be able to raise $50,000 in the second step.

The "banking round robin" concept is nothing more than continuing this step-by-step process. Each time you go to the bank, ask for a larger amount and a longer payback period. What you are doing, of course, is establishing good credit by repetition. That is, you always pay back the money when it is due, and by being prompt combined with the number of loans you've made and paid, you will have established a good credit rating and relationship with the institutions.

Of course, the amount that the bank will lend you will vary depending on the size of your assets, which are probably a lot more than you realize.

A variation to this method, and I should point out that there are many variations you could use, is to apply for credit at twice as many banks as you actually accept loans from. For example, if you applied for credit from ten banks for $1,000 each and then accepted loans from only five, after thirty days, assuming you needed that $5,000 on a particular investment, you could borrow $5,000 from the banks that you initially did not accept loans from.

By using this method, you could actually borrow money and never pay it back out of your own pocket. You could continually pay back loans with other loans; your only cost would be the interest incurred. Some might consider this a highly aggressive or unsound way to finance. You should be aware that this is precisely what our government has been doing for several decades. Our huge national debt will no doubt never be paid off.

When the money becomes due periodically, all that the government does is issue more bonds, notes, and other financial instruments to borrow money to pay off the old debt. Many corporations do the same thing; they borrow money to pay off old loans. Then at that future due date, they borrow again to pay off that loan.

As you continue to execute this program, you will find that your credit rating will become stronger and stronger (assuming that you always meet your obligations on time). The result will be that you are able to borrow more and more money.

Of course, you *must* use the borrowed funds carefully. *Repeat: only use such funds for investments and appreciating assets.* If you do this, you will be using leverage as it was meant to be used.

Remember that leverage can be the best tool in the financial world or the worst. It can eat you alive or it can make you a millionaire, depending on your ability to make sound and wise judgments.

> NOTE: It should be noted that applying for a lot of loans at a lot of banks can have a negative affect on your credit report, inasmuch as your credit score is lowered by a very small amount each time you apply for credit. So, be very careful and judicious in how you handle this. Additionally, understand that your credit report will list each bank that you have accounts with and have borrowed money from, so all the other banks will be able to see what you're doing. But that's okay as long as you're totally up front should the subject ever come up with any of your bankers.
>
> As an alternative, and one that has worked miracles for Dell Loy Hansen (see his story in the addendum and also read Chapter 8, entitled *THE QUICKEST WAY TO A BILLION – Beyond SUPER LEVERAGE*), I have found that searching out and acquiring partners is an excellent way to leverage yourself and to raise hundreds of thousands of dollars that can be used in investments where you put little or nothing up and profit from the wise purchase of such properties.

NOTES AND THOUGHTS

CHAPTER 21
WINNING THE NUMBERS GAME

"Lucky Ted Williams!"

That's a sentence that's been repeated thousands of times. After all, the guy grew to be 6'4", weighs 210 muscular pounds, and has great eye-hand coordination; in short, he's a born hitter, right?

Glen Tuckett, an athletic director at Brigham Young University, knew Williams personally.

"I've seen Ted Williams stand in front of a group and absolutely pound the podium, he was so mad," remembers Tuckett.

"'Lucky Ted Williams!' he would explode. There's no such thing as lucky Ted Williams!' Then he'd go on to tell how he learned to play baseball."

When the custodian arrived each morning to unlock the school, the air was hushed and cool with that early morning feel. The sun was beginning to dry the dew; birds were chirping. Quiet and uninhabited? No, the boyish Ted Williams had arrived at the school playground, even before the janitor.

Ted was there swinging his baseball bat, hitting the ball — again and again. At recess he would rush to grab his bat, go out to the schoolyard, and hit some more. At noon he gulped down his lunch and was out in the hot sun for more practice.

Other kids went to the park after school to daydream or talk. The Williams kid went to the park after school to practice some more hitting. He practiced so much that his hands often blistered and bled. Glenn Tuckett remembers what Williams said, "There's never been a guy who hit as much as I have."

Sports authorities are fond of arguing the heredity-versus-environment theory. Is it background or training that makes a good athlete? When it comes down to it, most believe that great athletes, including homerun hitters, are born. Ted Williams is enraged by that, too. "They're 'born' all right — after 2,000 hours in the batter's box!" he fumes.

"You see," explains Tuckett, "he was saying that 2,000 hours of hitting is the gestation period. Only then can a good hitter begin to grow to greatness."

Of course there are many prerequisites for success in any field, but again and again in successful people, and Ted Williams is an example, we see one quality.

According to the law of probability, a man who buys a thousand lottery tickets has that much greater chance of winning than the man who only buys one. So Ted Williams, even though he had undeniable natural talent, was not content to buy just one ticket in the success lottery. Or ten. Or even a hundred. By his own estimate he paid as high a price as anyone ever has in order to *increase his odds* for winning.

"Ted Williams is as great a hitter as anyone who ever lived," says Glenn Tuckett. "If his career hadn't been interrupted by four years in the military service, he would have set even more records than he did."

Anyone who wants to be successful should absorb the *numbers game* into his life. If you want to be a success, you must be willing to make the necessary investment.

After reading stories like this, I not only approached my business of buying properties by making dozens and dozens of offers using the concept of the Numbers Game (I even made hundreds of offers on properties to increase my chances of winning), but I decided some years ago, when I took up tennis, to also apply the Numbers Game to that endeavor. This was the first time I ever really played tennis, starting somewhat late in life.

I decided I was going to become an excellent tennis player, and to do that I reasoned that I had to approach tennis from a Ted Williams mentality of numbers. (Especially since I basically had to "catch up" with all those people who had been playing for many years.)

The bottom line of it all was that within 24 months I had not only caught up to the guys who had been playing for 20 years, but I also passed most of them.

I simply did it by the numbers.

First, I had a dozen or so lessons from very good teaching professionals. Next, I bought many books and tapes and learned all I could learn from them. I studied the sport, and I studied the great players of the sport.

Next, I watched and I watched and I watched people playing tennis. I watched them on TV, and at local tennis matches from high school to college...I even traveled to London, Paris, Australia, and New York to watch the best of the best at what they called the Grand Slam Events of Tennis.

BUT, most importantly, I practiced and drilled over and over again. I bought a tennis ball machine that would hit every kind of topspin, sidespin, and under-spin ball with just about any speed you wanted to set it to hit to my backhand, forehand, or into my body.

I decided in my little brain that I needed to hit at least two thousand balls a day using that maddening machine (it always won!). And I did it – sometimes hitting as many as three thousand balls a day.

The results – wow! I became a darn good tennis player, if I do say so myself, in a very short period of time.

The lesson learned, once again, was that the Numbers Game worked…and, at least in my mind, I had won the Numbers Game of tennis.

The numbers principle applies, of course in every aspect of life. Take book publishing, for instance. Erich Segal taught at Harvard for years, and prepared some scholarly research articles.

In a sudden turnaround, he wrote a sentimental, romantic novel. He sent the book off to a publisher and awaited the reply. It must have been galling to receive a noncommittal rejection notice from that first company.

There are undoubtedly thousands of authors, unacquainted with the *numbers game,* who pack their stories away forever after one rejection notice. Segal, however, sent his novel on the rounds of the publishing houses.

In all, that novel was turned down many times before Hollywood discovered it. The novel was made into a film entitled *Love Story* and was published in book form as well.

The film was a box office sensation and made its delighted author a regular fixture on television talk shows. Needless to say, *Love Story* made a lot of money for Erich Segal. He had been willing to make the numbers investment. He made not one try, but dozens, in order to *increase his chance* for success.

Even fishermen rely on the numbers game. On 4 March 1977, Bob Bringhurst of LaVerne, California, his brother, and their father got up before dawn and launched their fishing boat into the cold waters of the Flaming Gorge Reservoir in Wyoming. The three men were trolling an area of the water known as Sheep Creek Bay. Bob had just let his ten-pound test line, baited with a three-hooked gold rapalla lure and hand painted to look like a rainbow, into the water, when it was struck.

Bringhurst set the hook and began to work the fish, reeling in carefully. The minutes ticked away. In the boat, excitement was building. This was one big fish! Using all his skill, Bob played the fish for ten to twenty minutes, his heart pounding, before he finally landed it.

Aboard the boat, the thrilled Bob Bringhurst surveyed his catch — a beautiful brown trout, fully forty inches long and twenty-five inches around! The men sped to the marina and then to the grocery store. It was only 6:40 a.m. and most of the world was still asleep.

They finally found signs of life at the Manila post office, which in this fishermen's hamlet was equipped with an official scale. Thirty-three pounds and ten ounces! A world record lunker!

Many a fisherman dreams about that kind of a trophy mounted in his den. Bob Bringhurst had done more than dream. He had made the investment that *increased his odds* for success. He has made four or five extended fishing trips each year — a couple to Flaming Gorge Reservoir and the others to the High Sierras. He has not missed opening day in years. Any free time Bob Bringhurst has, he can usually be found fishing the lake near his hometown of LaVerne. He is consummately interested in fishing.

Here are three entirely different examples: a professional sport, a bookish project, and an engrossing hobby. Each is different from the others, yet the same numbers principle contributed to the mastery of all three.

Before being named athletic director, Glenn Tuckett was head baseball coach at Brigham Young University. His experience with hundreds of athletes has led him to generalize that about ten percent of them are sparklers. Like Ted Williams, they have the character traits to make them stars.

Another ten percent he describes as those who "have memorized every excuse there is for losing." He believes the same percentages extend out of the sports arena into the rest of life. As evidence, he points to results of Korean brainwashing of American prisoners of war. Only about five percent of the men captured seemed to be independent minded. The rest were relatively easy to influence. He extends the Shelley quotation to say that athletics and any other endeavor of life are "through time and change un-quenchably the same."

What then about this great majority who comprise the remaining eighty percent? Tuckett's prognosis for them is good. They may not have learned about the rules for success yet, but his experience tells him that this eighty percent can learn to be consistent winners.

Take the example of Johnny Huart, for instance. In his junior year at Notre Dame, he was a rather ordinary football player. He only made the traveling squad for one field trip, and played a very unspectacular seven minutes at quarterback during the entire season.

One of the eighty percent? Definitely. Yet Huart determined to make the numbers investment required of a standout player. Countless grueling practice hours, grinding hours of learning tactics, hours and more hours of building strength — all improved his chances for success.

The next year, as his team's quarterback, he led Notre Dame through an undefeated season to the championship. He was voted the Heisman trophy winner, and signed a $300,000 bonus contract with the New York Jets. Had he learned how to be successful!

Sure, but he was born with exceptional talent, you say. Well, how about George Mikan? As a sophomore at Joliet (Illinois) High School, he showed up at the gym to try out for the basketball team. The coach threw him the ball — Mikan wasn't even coordinated enough to catch it! He had determination though; he made the extraordinary investment in hours and effort to develop what a champion needs to have.

The results: Mikan was a three-year all-American at LaSalle and later played twelve years for the then Minnesota Lakers. At Minnesota he received the National Basketball Association's outstanding player award.

Tuckett believes the main reason more people do not make the investment and become as great as they could be is the fear of failure. "It is the greatest 'de-motivator' there is," he claims. "Fear is a paralyzing thing." Fear immobilizes you so you cannot do what you need to do. Tuckett offers some suggestions for overcoming the fear of failure.

First, expect a certain natural percentage of nonsuccess experiences in your efforts. No one is completely successful all the time. This is where those who have big numbers investment have the advantage over those who do not. If you try ten times more than anyone else, you can afford to fail many times and still end up a super success.

Two sales representatives for Lear Jet Corporation might be able to sell one of their classy planes to one prospect out of every five hundred contacts. (These figures are purely speculative.) If one salesman is afraid of being turned down, so he falteringly talks to only five hundred people during a year, he will only sell one jet. (Incidentally, he probably won't be a salesman for long.)

If the other salesman expects a certain number of rejections and does not allow himself to be frozen by worry, he may enthusiastically contact several thousand prospects and sell eight planes in a year. This is a direct example of the law of probability, easily seen, yet the first man's potential for success was strangled by his fear of failure.

Second, cultivate the awareness that even great men fail. Tuckett goes beyond this, in fact. He has noticed that the men who have contributed most to the world were also "the world's most proficient failures."

George Washington, for example, had some abysmal failures as a general. Abraham Lincoln ran for political office over and over, but the gangly lawyer was repeatedly defeated. A list of his losses is impressive indeed.

Babe Ruth held the world's record for home runs, until Mickey Mantle came along. Babe was and still is loved and revered by thousands. Scarcely anyone remembers that Babe Ruth also struck out more times than any other batter in the history of baseball.

The St. Louis Cardinal base-stealing champ, Lou Brock, successfully stole an incredible 118 bases. The crowd roared with delight when he picked off another one. Yet a scrutiny of the records tells us that Brock was thrown out thirty-three times! Another record! He failed thirty-three times. Thirty-three times Lou Brock made his way back to the dugout knowing he had failed, knowing that even if the next batter hit a home run he (Brock) could not add a run to his team's score by crossing home plate.

It is obvious that a sometime failure does not automatically dump a person into a pile of misfits and undesirables. On the contrary, virtually all of the world's greatest are counted among those who have failed.

Do not be afraid to try for fear of failing. Instead, force yourself to try more times. Remember: It's a numbers game!

Third, it helps to keep in mind that "failure is the ignition to all greatness," as Tuckett puts it. If you were successful at everything you tried, your life would be a shallow satisfaction. You would never develop the resiliency, perseverance, character, and deep satisfaction that grow through the constant effort to improve and adapt.

Paul Ehrlich's name is not widely known in our time. Yet this man exemplifies recurring effort in the face of defeat. A

German bacteriologist and immunologist, he was determined to find a way to combine several elements with arsenic. Ehrlich combined the elements in every combination and under every condition he could think of. In fact, he varied his experiment 605 unsuccessful times! The 606th time he succeeded.

The resulting substance was marketed under the appropriate title of "606". Chemically, it was arsphenamine. Later trademarked Salvarsan, "606" became the specific cure for the dreaded syphilis. What an enormous numbers investment this Nobel prizewinner made in his experiments, failing often and learning from his mistakes until he inevitably accomplished his goal.

Glenn loves to pluck these interesting but little-known stories about champs from the obscurity of old records. George Mikan, Johnny Huart, Babe Ruth, Lou Brock, Washington, Lincoln, Paul Ehrlich — each man's story is an example that others can learn to be successful if they will learn the success rules. The fear of failure is the main reason most people never learn.

Once the fear of failure has been dealt with, anyone who successfully uses the principle of "greater investment equals greater returns" must be willing to work. To put it another way, "The only thing that stands between some people and the top of the ladder is the ladder."

Tuckett points out that a hundred years ago, most of man's work was done by sheer muscle power. Today technology has changed all that. Appliances do everything for us. Some people never learn the lessons of work and discipline that the physical nature of our forebears' lives automatically taught them. "If we don't watch out, we're going to completely lose the privilege of working," he says, "and it is a privilege, not a curse.

"I'd prefer to have farm boys show up for my teams," he says. "They're used to doing chores, and they know how to work. I send some of the other guys out to the field to work out, and they don't know what I mean."

Of course, response to our technological world is a matter of outlook. The ten percent who "have memorized every excuse there is for losing" may continue to get by. They will do as little as possible on a boring assembly line job and spend their evenings watching other people "really" live on TV.

Look back at any of the success examples used here and it is clear he was willing to work hard in order to achieve greatness in his field. These winners will find numerous opportunities to get more and more done. In fact, they will find all kinds of mechanical aids to help them be more efficient in their work.

Given an understanding of the numbers game, the control of fear, and a willingness to work, it simply remains to discover the most innovative and workable ways of putting numbers to work for you. It's a matter of running around versus creative thinking.

Time is precious. No successful person wants to spend his day doing something ineffective when he can pack it with vital, useful, productive activity.

Different types of problems are helped by variations of the numbers game. Asking "How can I get this job done in less time?" can stimulate creative solutions to problems

In the real estate field, simple numbers do not bring success. Few buy the first property they see. This is even truer of the investment buyer in search of a super deal. You need to look at dozens of properties, compare the possibilities, their histories, financing, etc.

Once you are conscious of the numbers game you will see its implications in all areas of life, even in emotions and human ties. Speaking of personal relationships, Max Gunther says in his book *The Luck Factor* that the luckiest people are usually those who form many friendships. They go out of their way to strike up conversations, to learn about the lives of their acquaintances, and to become friendly with people who fascinate them.

By taking every chance to get to know interesting people, lives can be enriched and many doors opened. On the other hand, fearful people who have impoverished social lives rarely turn out to be successes.

There are countless facets to life. Each person wants success in his own individual way. No two people want exactly the same thing out of life. Choose your field. Set your goals. Decide what *you* want to accomplish. Tuckett says, "The greater the dedication and commitment we have, the harder it is to surrender."

Use the numbers laws creatively to accomplish your goals in the fastest and best way possible. Anyone can do what he really wants to do. It is possible to pack more living (enjoyable, fulfilled, and pleasant living) into fewer days, and in essence live a much longer life.

That is what it's all about. People were meant to succeed. You, too, can put the laws of probability to work to enrich your life, as champions in every field have done. Says Glenn Tuckett, expressing the feelings of most of us, "These are the kinds of guys that are enshrined in my own private Hall of Fame."

PLANS AND GOALS

_____

_____

_____

_____

_____

PLANS AND GOALS

_____

_____

_____

_____

_____

_____

_____

_____

_____

_____

_____

_____

_____

_____

_____

_____

_____

_____

_____

_____

_____

_____

CHAPTER 22

HOW TO MAKE YOUR DOLLAR WORK HARDER FOR YOU

Where will our money work the hardest? Where can we consistently receive the highest rate of return?

In today's world, the answer to that question is real estate. By making wise purchases and by using leverage, a person can make a million dollars in a relatively small amount of time with real estate.

Real estate is *the* money-making approach — but it works only for those who are willing to take action. We all have a friend who says, "You know that property up on Third Street? The one with the old six-unit flat on it? Why, I could have bought that four years ago for $240,000 and now it's worth nearly $600,000!"

Our friend is right, of course. But he isn't rich. He failed to *act* on the opportunity when it presented itself. None of us can make any money from opportunities that have passed and gone.

But there are plenty of people who *did* act, who have made their fortune through wise real estate investments. Even now, hundreds of thousands of people are getting rich from properties they own.

Why is real estate such a good investment? Why do experts predict that the real estate market may slow down but will probably never fail?

Real estate is a basic need. People always need a place to live, a place to work, a place to farm. Improved real estate is especially in demand — apartment units, single family houses, duplexes, and the like.

Each kind of real estate has its own unique characteristics. Each has different risks and rewards. Of all the different types of real estate available, I am biased toward rental units, either apartments or single-family homes. They are such a basic need that it's hard to go wrong with them. Naturally, you have to buy right with any kind of real estate, and use utmost care in the management of the property but — apartments are in short supply in many markets and rents are constantly going up.

I made my first million with rental units.

But if you don't like rentals, there are plenty of other ways you can get rich with real estate. You can put your money in everything from farm land as an investment to recreational land for development and future speculation. You can buy such income-producing properties as shopping centers, apartment buildings, office buildings, medical complexes, hotels, motels, or industrial buildings. Or you might want to create condominiums by purchasing apartment buildings and converting from a rental situation to a sale situation, selling each unit individually.

Whether you decide to get into apartments or some other form of real estate, though, you'll find it difficult to fail.

But how does one get started? I remember the hard time I had taking that first step. Part of the problem is fear; part of it is inexperience. I remember how I worried about losing money through vacancies; how I worried about all my tenants moving out at once. What if the furnace stopped working? I wondered. What if the roof started leaking? Will the value of real estate continue to rise? Will I be able to meet my payments?

These worries and fears kept me from doing anything for almost a year. That year cost me many thousands of-dollars.

But finally I made up my mind to move ahead and not look back. I'm glad I did. My wealth has grown.

There are many ways to buy real estate. Usually, the greater the leverage the greater the profits. That usually means income properties that are bought for low or no down payments.

Other than leverage, one thing that can help the careful investor is the fact that real estate is an imperfect market. It is unique in that there is no one central place of exchange where all properties are bought and sold. You could pay $200,000 for a four-unit apartment building that sits right next door to a four-unit apartment building that I paid $320,000 for. And they could be identical in every respect. There are many reasons for this discrepancy: the seller may not have gone to the trouble of getting an appraisal; he may have paid $100,000 and would be absolutely delighted to get $200,000 for the property. The seller may need to unload the property fast — he may be divorced, or need cash, or may be fed up, or moving out of the area.

Whatever the reason for the difference in price, the smart investor has much to gain by shopping around for bargains. If he is persistent, he will eventually find a property that is listed far below the market value.

But looking around for properties takes a lot of time, and most of us don't have a lot of time. I don't have a lot of time, so I developed a method whereby I can find the bargains without a major expenditure of that commodity.

I call it the shotgun method, because it goes off in all directions like a shotgun does. Here's how the method works:

First, I go through the multiple-listing book or look on the Internet for the area that I'm interested in. These books or Internet listings are available for almost any city in the United States. I look in the book for the kinds of properties that I would be interested in. I mark down all those that look promising. That is, if I want four-or five-unit apartment dwellings, I look only at those, and mark down only those.

It usually takes just a few hours to go through the entire book or view the Internet web pages. I am able to come up with anything from a dozen to five dozen potential properties.

Next, I make offers on dozens of the properties that I listed, offering the owner twenty, thirty, or even forty percent less than he listed the property for.

The offer I usually make up is fairly standard. An offer on a $300,000 piece of property might read like this:

"Offer Price: $240,000

"Down payment: $25,000

"Seller to carry contract on balance for thirty years at six and-a-half percent. This offer is subject to the buyer inspecting the physical premises and accepting the same."

If I think the seller needs cash I may put in a balloon payment. That is, the contract balance would all be due and payable after say, the tenth year. This gets my monthly payment down low, and, of course, I figure I can either sell the place or get refinancing within ten years.

I also include in the offer the size of the monthly payment, an agreement on who will pay taxes and insurance, and all the other small details that are normally contained in the standard purchase offer form.

In the next step, I call in one or more real estate agents, give them the offer and the earnest money, and ask them to handle the deal. They take the offers to the sellers and try to convince them to accept my terms.

As you would imagine, most offers come back "not accepted." Out of thirty offers, normally twenty-five will not be accepted. But on the remaining five a counter-offer will be made, usually at a price somewhere between my offering price and the seller's original price.

And occasionally, much to my delight, the original offer is accepted.

Finally, I go to inspect each of the properties that seems to have the right price. If I like it, I can proceed with the closing. If I don't like, I am not bound to continue, even if my original offer was accepted. Remember, the offer was "subject to the buyer inspecting the physical premises and accepting the same."

This method multiplies your effectiveness many times. With this approach, you can make hundreds of offers in a short period of time, and you can quickly find which sellers are motivated to sell their properties for low prices.

Using this method, I was able to purchase over twenty-four properties in only a matter of months. I did it virtually by myself, using only brokers and agents to present the offers. Many of the deals were well under true market price, and I was thereby able to catapult my net worth into hundreds of thousands of dollars in a very short time.

I sincerely hope what you have learned or re-learned from reading this book will help catapult you to your own financial goals—I know it is possible—it will work but only if you do. The road to riches is simple but not easy—it takes effort and discipline—were it not so, beggars, winos and bums would all be millionaires.

But believe me developing your own potential through discipline is well worth the effort. What's more the rewards are much more than the great financial rewards you'll receive. So be a tough taskmaster on yourself and you'll not only acquire a vast estate for your own security and your families but you'll vastly improve yourself as an individual and productive human being contributing to the wealth of others. I guarantee you'll find as much or more satisfaction in that than in the money.

NOTES AND THOUGHTS

CHAPTER 23

THE FEAR FACTOR: OVERCOMING YOUR FEAR OF RISK

Fear is the opposite of courage. It is useful only if it motivates us to overcome fear through direct action. In financial matters, being fearful of risk undermines one's courage to act. With inaction, fears multiply through negative worries and over-imagined dangers. Be brave. Pursue your financial goals with confidence. Remember what Bertrand Russell said: "To conquer fear is the beginning of wisdom." If you have carefully considered all aspects of a deal and it looks mostly possible, go ahead. If you have to have a guarantee that everything will be all right before you take a risk, you will never ever get off first base: the future is promised to no one. I have never forgotten what a friend said to me many, many years ago when I was in a great debilitating state of fear. He said, *"Never forget this: A coward dies a thousand times, a brave person only once."*

ACTION WILL GET YOU MORE THAN $100

Many times in my lectures I take a $100 bill from my wallet and hold it up and say, "Action is really the great separator – it separates the wealthy from the poor, the dissatisfied from the frustrated, even the happy from the unhappy. But most of all, action gets things done, action overcomes fear." Then I ask who would like the $100 bill.

Typically, with 300 or 400 people present, only about 100 hands will appear. Sometimes three or four people will use their voices. "I do!" they'll shout. Holding the $100 bill absolutely still and staring straight ahead, I do absolutely nothing. I just stand there like the Statue of Liberty, but with a $100 bill instead of a torch in my hand. I stand there for as long as it takes for someone to take action.

SOMETIMES WE NEED A PUSH

The action that I want is for someone to get up, walk to the front, come up on the stage, and take the $100 bill out of my hand. It is amazing to me how long it takes sometimes. Recently a lady walked up and reached for the bill, but she didn't step up onto the two-foot stage and she couldn't quite reach it. She continued to stand and reach for it as I stood motionless. She looked around at the audience, very embarrassed. She seemed to be caught in the middle. She didn't know what to do. Finally someone in the audience yelled, "Go ahead and take it!" So she stepped up on the stage and finally grabbed it out of my hand, then went back to her seat. Sometimes we need a push from someone else, even from those who aren't brave themselves.

I told the guy in the audience, "Boy, you were really brave to sit there all safe and secure in your seat and yell out to her what she should do. Why didn't you come up and take it yourself?"

Obviously he (and everyone else) was somewhat fearful. It was an embarrassing situation, full of temporary risk, but the lady who got out of her seat and eventually took the money out of my hand admitted her action did help to overcome her fear.

She almost blew it at the last minute by not taking that one last step to get what she was after. And so it is with many people. They get right to the edge of success and they freeze.

They choke. They don't know what to do. They don't have quite enough courage to go over the edge, to make that final lunge or step to accomplish their goals.

ACTION GETS THINGS DONE

Besides overcoming fear, action does a lot of other things too. It gets things done; and, after all, that's the whole ball game. Without action you can be the greatest financial thinker, have the highest IQ, and end up broke.

The husband of the lady who came up and got the $100 bill was embarrassed. I asked him what he thought was happening to him. He said, "I don't know, but I didn't want anybody to know that I was with her." She admitted that she felt foolish, too! But as she sat down she won the applause of the entire audience, so who really turned out to be foolish? Her, or the 399 people in the audience? Remember the wall plaque in Chapter 9: *THE WORLD WILL STEP ASIDE FOR THE PERSON WHO KNOWS WHERE HE/SHE IS GOING.* Wasn't that demonstrated by the $100-bill incident? The audience stood aside while the woman walked forward and took the $100. Then, after she accomplished her task and sat down, they applauded. They were proud of her. No, they didn't do it themselves, but they were impressed by her courage to do what anyone of them could have done.

FEAR OF STARTING

Getting started is really the most frightening and the hardest part of virtually any task. *But* even *if* you *do something wrong,* at *least do something.* I am not saying take risks larger than you can afford. I don't believe in that. I don't think that that is good. One should take risks gradually, whether they are financial risks, social risks, or any other kind of risk. But one does need to *take* risks. To face fear. Then, when you have mastered a small fear, you can go for the bigger ones.

FEAR AND TENSION

Recently, while making the final approach on a flight (I wish they wouldn't call it the *final* approach), I noticed that the lady sitting next to me was very nervous. Thinking that by diverting her attention I could ease her stress, I began talking with her. Then the captain lowered the flaps and the landing gear. She gasped and gripped the armrests of the seat. Talk about a white-knuckle flyer, this lady was it. I quickly explained to her what had just happened, which gave her only temporary relief because then we hit a little turbulence and bounced up and down. She was obviously very distressed.

I suddenly realized that I was in the same plane, in the same situation, but my heart rate and blood pressure were normal. I patted her hand, but the only thing that came close to helping was each time there was a sudden movement or noise, I explained exactly what was happening, which seemed to calm her a bit. At the end of the flight she was very terribly uptight and not at all rested.

CHRONIC FEAR, NOT FEAR, IS YOUR REAL ENEMY

It was easy to understand how she felt since I had been there too. I knew the damage that fear could do because it had done damage to me in the past. The same thing used to happen to me, but once I realized that I was letting fear dominate my thoughts I decided to do something about it. Since I travel a great deal, and since being relaxed and rested at the end of a flight is important to my performance, it was important not to waste so much energy wrestling with fear.

It didn't take much thinking after that to figure out that the fear factor entered into many of my decisions that had far greater implications than did flying. Why should I let myself be fearful about flying or anything else? After all, does that fear change the outcome of the flight I'm on or my financial conditions? People who are the real doers in life face frightening situations almost every day, but they don't let those confrontations with fear scare them to death or slow down their progress or stop their actions.

PILOT, PRIEST, AND POPE ALL HAVE FEARS

Realizing that everyone has fears is a big first step to overcoming yours. Remember that Buddha's first of the four noble truths is, "Life is suffering." Life is difficult; it really is difficult, not just for you but for everybody. Fully understanding and realizing that can be a major breakthrough in anyone's life. Life is difficult for everyone, rich and poor, fat and skinny, beautiful and ugly, male and female, old and young; and everyone has fears, fears that make life harder. No matter what a person's position is, attorney, CPA, judge, pilot or priest; yes, even an astronaut, the President of the United States, and the Pope have fears. But those people who learn to confront them, try to understand them, and take some action to overcome them, are the people who are truly the successes in this world. They have courage. You see, courage does not exist without fears but it is facing them with actions so you can overcome them.

We have all been in situations where someone has said, "Don't worry, it will be okay. Calm down. There is nothing to worry about." And we all know those words usually don't help.

I totally overcame my fear of flying by understanding the facts and the dynamics of flying. I took action to have understanding. I even took flying lessons. I really confronted my fears. I learned, for example, that it is absolutely impossible for an airplane to fall out of the sky if it's flying faster than stall speed. So no matter how slowly the plane seems to be going, as long as it is flying faster than stall speed, that won't happen.

THE NUMBER-ONE FEAR

Speaking in public is the greatest single fear of Americans. It tops the list way above the fear of dying. I did two things to overcome this fear. First, I gained an understanding of the dynamics of speaking. I learned what makes a good speech. I came to understand both the empathy and the criticism that an audience can and will have. In addition, when I realized that virtually everyone is scared to death of standing in front of an audience and speaking, for some reason that was very, very comforting to me and helped me squarely face my fear.

Second, rather than being frozen in my tracks, I purposely and forcefully pushed myself to apply action to overcome that fear. That is, I began to give speeches and did so many, many times until the fear diminished. In fact, it diminished to the point that I could really be totally myself onstage. And that is when any person really becomes good, for he can then express himself by using his own personality.

SIX COMMON FEARS

Most of us, at one time or another in our lives, experience many or all of the following fears:

- Fear of making a fool of yourself.
- Fear of winning. Many times you will see people choke up right at the end and go on to lose. This is sometimes an indication of the fear of winning. If you win now, you might always have to perform on the same high level.
- Fear of losing all your money.
- Fear of losing your friends.

- Fear of losing the love and respect of someone you love.
- Fear of criticism.

FIRST-TIME FEARS

I remember back when I bought my first apartment building. It was a run-down twelve-unit building that needed a lot of time and attention. I almost backed out of the closing because of fear.

When we do something for the first time, it's almost always a frightening situation. Why, even going to a restaurant for the first time can be more than a little bit bothersome. You don't know what the menu is or what the prices are (it might be too expensive); you don't know the layout of the restaurant or whether to seat yourself or wait to be seated. All this can produce some anxiety—consequently many people get in the habit of going to the same restaurants, and so, because of trivial fears, won't try new and different places.

Multiply these small anxieties by ten or more, and you have the fear factor I had when buying my first apartment building. Even though it was a super deal with only 6% down payment, at a very low price, I almost backed out at the last minute. What were my fears? I was afraid of everything: from all the tenants refusing to pay the rent, to all the plumbing going bad the day that I bought it. When you have never bought a building before, your imagination can go wild. Mine did. When you haven't ever bought a $100,000 property before, it scares you to death. The first time I ever bought a $500,000 property, the same thing happened. Ditto with my first million-dollar purchase and again with my first five-million-dollar acquisition!

WHAT TO DO WHEN YOU'RE NOT BRAVE

So what do we do about these fears? Well, first remember that fear is a natural emotion, one that must be understood, confronted, and controlled. In other words, this is an appropriate place to *fake it till you make it.* But you need to do it with action.

WHISTLE A HAPPY TUNE AND NO ONE WILL SUSPECT I'M AFRAID

If we pretend to be brave, acting the way a brave man would act, the results are amazing. Consider the many times you have lain in bed thinking about some tough assignment, something that you are slightly or very fearful of doing. If you've never done it before, quite naturally you are reluctant and anxious. For example, if you are giving a speech for the first time to some important people, or asking a banker for a loan, or presenting an offer to buy a particular property. Or it may be visiting a new state or country, or being a master of ceremonies. In any case, whatever you have to do on that particular day as you lie in bed, if you have a few fears of doing it, they will only intensify the longer you lie there and think about it. What will overcome those frightening thoughts and imaginings is action. *Even if* it is incorrect *action,* get up, get *going, and get the blood running.* Take a shower, get on the phone, write letters, go see people, make things happen.

I HAD TO PUT ACTION WHERE MY MOUTH WAS

Even though I have a much higher level of confidence now, I find that I still harbor some fears. I was recently in Indianapolis to consult with a young, recently divorced mother of three. She didn't have a job and she didn't know how or where to start to get one. She was obviously very much afraid of going out into the marketplace. I was explaining to her how action overcomes fears and how she needed to go out and make things happen. I found myself telling her that she merely needed to get on the phone and start calling people, asking for a job. I said, "All you need to do is pick up the phone and call a business and ask them. It's as simple as that. That's how you overcome fear."

After saying that, I suddenly realized that if it were so easy to do, why didn't I do it and show her how to do it instead of telling her how to do it? So I asked what kind of business she would like to work for. She said she had always wanted to work in a floral shop. I grabbed the phonebook, turned to "florists" in the Yellow Pages, and dialed the first number I saw. As soon as the phone rang I could feel my heart rate increase and I was actually nervous, very nervous in fact. I was surprised at my nervousness and the fear I was experiencing. As the phone rang, my "self-talk" went something like this: "I can't believe that I am afraid of making a phone call to some dumb little floral shop. But heavens, I can't stop now, she's watching and I'm trying to prove something to her. I am onstage."

About that time, a young man answered and asked if he could help me. I began by saying, "I understand that you have been looking for some extra help in your shop, and I have a friend who would be excellent for the position." The young man hesitated a bit and said, "Well, I'm not sure that we do. Well, I guess. Well, I don't really know. . . let me have you talk to the manager." In a few moments the manager was on the line. I said the same thing to him and to my amazement he said that he hadn't really been looking for anybody, but he could use an extra person. So I proceeded to describe the young mother to him and actually set up an appointment then and there for her to come and meet him and apply for a job. I wrote down the time and his name and hung up.

I then turned to her and said, keeping a straight face the whole time, "See how easy it is-you just have to do it." Later, I did tell her that I had had some fearful thoughts as I dialed and as I spoke to the shop owner, but that action helped me overcome being scared as I got into the conversation with him. I could easily have made the next phone call since I was successful on the first one and feeling quite sure of myself by then. What I was doing was faking it until I made it. I was acting as if I had courage when actually I had some less-than-brave thoughts.

FEARS ARE MENTAL

Action overcomes fear because most fears are in your mind and action lets the physical part of you dominate for a while. The physical side of you needs to dominate because the mental side, in cases like this, becomes too introspective and too analytical. We tend to analyze to death. We have all heard of "analysis paralysis," which is more than two cute rhyming words.

Sometimes we think too much. In today's educated, deep-thinking, and analyzing world, we have a lot more planners and thinkers and analyzers than we do action people. Obviously we do need some kind of plan, but the greatest plan in the world is worthless without action. I would much rather have a mediocre plan and some real action people to carry it out than the most phenomenal plan in the world and a bunch of inactive people.

Try to always remember this, burn it into your brain so it will be there permanently: **"Action is nature's way of counteracting fear."**

I HAVE A CAREER TO BUILD

On a flight to Dallas, Texas, I eavesdropped on a conversation between two musicians sitting in front of me. One was telling the other how eager he was to have more of his music published. He had gone to a publisher who told him there would be an eighteen-month delay but they would nevertheless publish his music. He told the publisher that he couldn't wait that long, and he wouldn't, so he turned them down flat, saying, "I have a career to build." What a great line. It was like he was building the newly designed World Trade Towers that are going to replace the ones destroyed on 9/11, and he had a deadline he had to meet.

If all of us looked at our own projects, financial and otherwise, with this same attitude and intensity; if we looked at each thing we did as a stepping-stone or building block in our own career and thought that we had to build it within twelve months (or twenty-four or forty-eight), we would be so much better off. Most deadlines, however, are set by others, and if we don't have the deadline we don't get the work done. Maybe now is a good time to recall or go back and re-read *MAKE YOUR DEADLINE A DEAD LINE*, in Chapter 9, entitled *SETTING GOALS AND THE ENERGY THEY CREATE*.

EGO MUSCLE

To go to the top financially you have to have a fair-sized ego, but that ego can't be so large that it gets in your way. When you recognize you have weaknesses, you certainly don't want your ego to foolishly stop you from borrowing someone else's talents, talents that can shore up your weakness.

I have never met a person in my life who has total confidence in himself or herself. There is not one of us who won't have some serious questions about our own ability to succeed as we start a new venture.

We can gain great courage by looking at others and seeing what they have done. As we realize we can do it too, we start to grow.

OVERCOMING YOUR FEAR OF RISK

Fear keeps us from doing many things that can potentially bring great rewards. The most easily discussed and least understood phenomenon in the investment world (whether it's real estate, stocks, bonds, etc.) is that of risk. That term is bandied about to describe the quality of investments, the kinds of yields, and to define certain investment situations.

But in all of this, the most important definition of risk is often overlooked. This definition does not deal directly with the investment at all, but relates more to the investor, the person who is about to hand over hard-earned cash in the hopes of getting a return. It is not the risk associated with the investment that is so important, but rather the risk the investor is willing to assume.

FEARING RISK

We are all different. We have different ambitions, different objectives. We are motivated by different things. Risk, however seems to be something of a common denominator: each of us is willing to take a certain amount of risk. The difference is in how much we are willing to risk, and this comes from a variety of factors peculiar to the individual. An investment counselor's responsibility is to help an investor find an investment with an acceptable amount of risk.

A lengthy discussion of the mechanics of investing as they relate to risk is beyond the scope of this book, but I wish to emphasize how risk can be used as a tool in achieving financial freedom. It is easy to equate risk with fear.

A friend of mine took up the hobby of hang gliding. He told me of the thrilling, almost euphoric sensation of soaring over the open spaces. He said it was probably something I would never know. I replied that there was not any "probably" about it.

The risk involved in that venture could not justify its potential return. This does not mean that I was a coward.

Many confuse fear with good judgment, but fear has a negative connotation. But if fear is thought of as an expression of good judgment, it can have a positive effect in our lives. Understanding how good judgment relates to fear and risk is a key in considering any investment.

Many people have asked me, "With the publicity that you are giving investment real estate, aren't you afraid that everybody is going to get involved in it and thus diminish its potential?" My response is, "Not at all." The potential is so vast that even if everybody with an interest were to get involved, the impact would be minor. But there is never a threat of everybody getting involved because so many of us, limited by apprehension and fear, do not temper our fear with good judgment.

THE DECISION IS YOURS

Let's create two situations to explain this: The first finds a man standing before two doors. Behind one door is a fortune in gold and jewels, and behind the other is a man-eating tiger ready to spring. The doors are identical, and the man has no way of knowing which to choose. This is what you would characterize as a high-risk situation. The man may decide to choose between the doors, thus exposing himself to risk, or he may walk away, avoiding the risk but also losing the reward.

For some contestants, the risk is beyond the reward, and they choose to leave the arena. When a contestant finally decides to open one of the doors, he does so in spite of fear, perhaps, but he also shows his lack of good judgment. The odds of his choosing the right door are only 50-50, and the wrong door promises no second chance.

The second situation involves the same two doors, the same reward, and the same man-eating tiger, but now the man is permitted to do one thing before making his choice.

He is allowed to ask questions. You can imagine the possible questions the man can ask to improve his chances of making a correct choice, or reducing the risk. This gives him the opportunity to employ better judgment than was possible in the first situation. Fear comes from the unknown, and fear can be tempered, as in the second situation, by gathering more information. Fear can be replaced with good judgment based on correct information.

TRANSFORMING FEAR TO JUDGMENT

Now, why is all of this so important? Let's return to the question of why so few people pursue the dream of financial freedom. The answer depends on the relationship between fear and risk. No investment is completely void of risk, and investments with minimal risk usually bring minimal rewards. The adage, "The greater the risk, the greater the reward," tends to be true. But many people hesitate in taking that first step in real estate investment because of what they imagine to be risk. The so-called risk, however, is often their own failure to gather sufficient information upon which to make a well-considered judgment.

It is important to assess the risk associated with every investment decision. But that assessment needs to be made on the basis of good judgment, using the facts at hand, and not on the basis of blind fear. Yet most people who fail to take the first step, who fail to avail themselves of opportunities, do so because of fear, not good judgment.

Fear is an emotional response to a situation, while good judgment is a logical and practical response. Fear is a reaction; good judgment is a conscious action based on logic. If you are unwilling to take the time to gather the information that will enhance your judgment, then you will hesitate to take the steps necessary to achieve your objectives, and you will find your life will be controlled by the emotion of fear.

Preparation and a desire to succeed will help you gain control of yourself and your situation. Preparation will allow you to discern risk in investment opportunities and will permit you to understand the level of risk you are willing to take. Preparation will place you in control of the fear that might otherwise reduce your objective to a wish.

NOTES AND THOUGHTS

_____

_____

_____

_____

_____

_____

_____

_____

_____

_____

_____

_____

_____

_____

_____

_____

_____

_____

NOTES AND THOUGHTS

_____

_____

_____

_____

_____

_____

_____

_____

_____

_____

_____

_____

_____

_____

_____

_____

_____

_____

_____

_____

_____

_____

CHAPTER 24
PROFITS FROM PROPERTY MANAGEMENT

THE SIX F'S VERSUS THE LONG-TERM HOLD

Even though I personally prefer the four F's of making money from real estate – that is: Finding, Financing, Fixing, and Flipping properties – Many times I have ended up owning and keeping properties for the long term. The four F's is the quickest way to financial freedom, which you could now add two more F's to make it the six F's, i.e. *Financial Freedom.*

There are some real big advantages to long-term holding. Among them are the advantages of not paying any taxes, plus the fact that unlike stocks and bonds, you are not tempted to sell quickly, because to sell a property is certainly a lot more involved than picking up a phone and calling a broker or going online and executing a trade.

Good property management now comes into play if you're going to hold long-term and is very critical to your success.

Generally speaking, I think the very best overall strategy for super success is beginning with enough four F's to have a big enough net worth before you move into the long-term hold mode.

Ideally, your long-term mode property should be the ones that are as problem-free and as low-maintenance as possible. Why? Because, like shaving, no matter how well you shave today, you have to do it again tomorrow, and the next day, and the next day, and so on.

Property management, at least to me, is the un-fun part of the whole picture. But, as already stated, it is critically important!

What follows now is some very good helpful hints on property management – some very general guidelines, as well as some very specific things you need to do. Certainly, what follows is not a full course on property management, but I think you'll find some real jewels on how to go about it.

What follows is:

- Work Smart and Stay Ahead of Negative Cash Flow.
- Rent! A Landlord's Challenge.
- 11 Tips for Landlord Survival.

◆ WORK SMART TO STAY AHEAD OF NEGATIVE CASH FLOW

Proper management of residential investment property is a tricky business. Many investors are not aware of the liability they assume when becoming a landlord and property management agent. Inexperienced landlords falsely believe, running a rental property is nothing to be concerned about. They see other people living off of investment income and are sure they can do it, too.

These uninitiated investors fail to see the work going on behind the scenes. There is much more to property management than driving to the bank and depositing huge amounts of effortless, rental income. Successful investors, who manage their own property, must work hard, and smart, to stay ahead of any negative cash flow.

The laws pertaining to rental policies and landlording are constantly becoming more stringent. This is no longer a business of casual effort and high profits. The profits are still possible, but you have to know the right way to obtain them.

GETTING THE GOOD ONES

Buying the right property and controlling expenses is important. Arranging attractive financing is imperative and organized record keeping is essential.

As important as all these factors are, finding, and knowing how to deal with good tenants is more important. Without good, prompt paying tenants, you will not have to worry about the other details for long. The absence of good tenants will drive you out of the landlording business fast. Renting to bad tenants will make the trip to financial depression even faster. Tenants are the cornerstones of your investment.

PREPARING YOUR PROPERTY

If you want a high quality tenant you have to offer a rental unit with attractive features. Good tenants can take their pick of available properties. You must set your building or house apart from the competition. Ask yourself these questions:

1. Would you live in your rental property?
2. Is the exterior appearance of your building alluring?
3. Are the grounds of your property clean and neat?
4. What condition are your hallways in?
5. Are hallway light fixtures or light bulbs missing?
6. Is the hall littered with bags of garbage?
7. Are the halls and grounds well lighted?
8. Do you receive numerous inquiries to your advertisements, but little follow-up interest?
9. Use strong, but understandable, Lease Agreements that have been approved by a real estate attorney.

If your lighting, exterior appearance, and hallways are less than the best, you will undoubtedly answer question eight with a resounding, yes! When prospective tenants call to inquire about your property, they will frequently ask for the address. Once they have the address, many of them will do a drive-by inspection, before scheduling an appointment to see the inside of the apartment or house.

SCREENING TENANTS

The biggest mistake made in renting apartments is the lack of adequately investigating the prospective tenant. Many property managers require the prospect to complete an application and they make a few phone calls. This is not enough. References given may be friends or relatives. Bad tenants know every trick in the book. If you don't want to be duped, you have to invest a little extra effort in the screening process. And always, always, always do a credit check. That's one check that even professional deadbeats have a tough time cheating on.

The lease is where the battle for control is won or lost. If you have a weak, ambiguous lease, the tenant has the upper hand. Never let this be the case. Always insist on a strong lease to protect your best interest. This single document can have a massive effect on your rental income and success.

Have a qualified, real estate attorney prepare a master lease for you. Give the lawyer an outline of the items you want included. Ask for recommendations from the lawyer on additional language to include. A written lease is essential in maintaining control of your rental property.

THE PR OF LAND-LORDING

Landlord-tenant relations play a vital role in profitable landlording. Be receptive to your tenants. Listen to their complaints and try to eliminate their objections. If it means replacing a faucet or fixing a broken window, do it. Build a level of respect with your tenants. Responding to their reasonable requests will make your management job easier.* Happy tenants don't create problems.

Eviction is the worst word in the glossary of rental terms. This one word can cost you thousands of dollars and months of aggravation. The best way to deal with eviction proceedings is to avoid them. Here are some suggestions to stay in control and out of court:

1. Keep accurate records.
2. Make written responses to tenant complaints.
3. Don't allow past-due rent to build up.
4. When tenants break the rules, follow legal methods in dealing with the problems. Don't set yourself up for being sued by breaching the tenant's rights.

---

* *Responding in a timely fashion to your tenants is noticed by all of your tenants and is greatly appreciated and remembered. It's critical to get just the right person to manage your properties, in case onsite property management is not your strong suit or not practical for you to handle. The perfect property manager is a unique blend of dependability, consistency, timely attention to details, and the understanding of people and responding to their legitimate needs…and one who also has great follow-through. I know that's a lot but people fitting this bill can be found.*

My son, Mark E. Haroldsen has all these qualities and has done a brilliant job at managing many of my multi-million dollar properties, properties as diverse as office buildings, recreational parks, apartments, and small retail malls. There are a lot of people like my son out there, you just have to find them.

Your key to being successful here is this. Take your time to choose a property manager and choose wisely. Observe people carefully; don't just take other people's word for the quality of the person you are considering. Be smart and choose cautiously. If your manager is not working out to your satisfaction, be decisive and let the manager go. This is one of the biggest problems in any organization when you hire a person who's not doing their job. Most managers and owners are not decisive enough and think a person will change. Plain and simple – they don't! You need to start over. That manager position is critically important, so you must have the right person in that position.

5. If eviction seems inevitable, talk with the tenant. Try to work out a compromise without going to court.

6. If talking is not working, offer to make concessions to the tenant. Forgive their debt, and if necessary, pay them to move. This is not a palatable option, but it may be your best choice. The cost of going to court and time lost, without rental income, could far exceed the cost of buying out the tenant.

7. As a last resort, turn the situation over to your attorney. Evictions should be handled by a competent lawyer. There are many rights and repercussions involved in the process. Don't risk your future and assets by playing lawyer.

MAKE LAND-LORDING A PLEASURE

Being a property manager requires good people skills. Gaining and maintaining control of your property is mandatory for a happy, successful career. Landlording can be a pleasant experience when it is done right. The rewards offer outstanding income and with a little effort, you can be the coveted landlord with all the good tenants.

◆ RENT! A LANDLORD'S CHALLENGE

Now we're going to talk about the real thing, the cash flow of your real estate business — rent from your properties — how to collect it and how to raise it.

You've dared to take the risks involved with owning real estate. You've made calculated guesses, and thrown in a little bit of luck investing in your future. You've decided how much you need to rent a piece of property for in order to bring you either to a break even, or better yet, a positive cash flow.

LOOKING FOR A GOOD TENANT

Screening the tenant is a vital step in the process toward collecting the rent. A good rental application is important and there are certain key questions that must be answered on the application. You are looking for stability in the tenant. You should have a place on the application for the previous landlord and the current landlord. A check with the previous landlord will be more rewarding than a check with the current landlord. Ask questions such as: Did they pay the rent on time? Why did they move? And would you rent to them again?

You'll find that hard working families who fit into the category you want for your properties stay put for longer periods of time. If you treat your tenants right and they fit this description, you'll keep them for a long time and they will enjoy renting from you.

Another criteria you should adopt is that you prefer people from the trades to rent your properties. You will look for the plumbers, electricians, the carpenters and air conditioning trades people as your number one priority tenant-types. I had this type of tenant in one of my single-family homes. He worked for a general contractor and got good deals on many types of home improvement items. While he lived in the property, he installed new kitchen cabinets, a new kitchen countertop, a new bathroom vanity and upgraded the wall treatments in several rooms. I was really sorry when he took a job in another state and moved on. But to get to the point, because of his care and upkeep of the property, it allowed me to raise the rent easily on the next tenant.

AFFORDING YOUR PROPERTY

In order to keep up with your obligations on the property, you need to know whether the prospective tenant can afford to live in your unit. According to the FHA statistics, people will not, and usually cannot, pay more than 35 percent of their income for rent. So this becomes a very important thing to check out on the rental application.

When vacancies arise, and they will, you should send out letters to your tenants and tell them of the vacancy you have. They have friends just like themselves and if you've treated them fairly they will recommend you as a landlord. Neighbors are also very good sources for filling a vacancy. Since they have to live next door to the tenants, they might be more selective than you could be. And don't wait to advertise your rental after the tenants have moved out. This will put you behind in the rent collection game. Even though your property may not be fully ready for occupancy, it's a good idea to make the availability known. Also, when prospective tenants see you at the property repairing and upgrading, they know you are a caring landlord and the rental rate is justified.

FIRST IN LINE

One of the biggest misconceptions most new landlords have concerning tenants is that they have to rent to anyone who applies or they stand to be in violation of the anti-discrimination laws. You cannot discriminate because of race, religion, or national origin, but you can turn down a smoker for instance, or someone with too large a family for the property space, or people with waterbeds, or pets, or tuba players. None of these reasons are discriminatory reasons. Therefore, you don't have to rent to the first person who shows up on your doorstep.

Keeping good tenants is just as important as avoiding bad tenants. Once you get good tenants, keep them, work with them and understand that they are people who have problems from time to time just like everyone else. Read and understand the tenant-landlord act and the fears of rejecting an undesirable applicant will come to rest. Knowing legally how to evict a tenant is also important, it doesn't have to be a nightmare as most landlords assume. There is an orderly procedure to follow in the eviction process.

TENANTS IN TRAINING

Landlords need to train their tenants in rent paying from the beginning of their tenancy. They should know what is expected from them every month. A heavy-handed approach isn't necessary. A light, but firm touch is generally the most productive in any relationship. A smile and a generous sense of humor are helpful, so don't forget these important tools in dealing with tenants.

Inform new tenants both verbally and in writing exactly when their rent is due and how it is to be paid. Even though this information should be included in your rental agreement, provide each tenant with a separate copy of this information in large print, and have him/her sign a copy. If there are late penalties or bonuses for advance payments, make sure this information is included and highlighted.

If rent is due on the first of the month, and it has not been paid by the second, it is overdue. Because many landlords don't consider rent late until the tenth, they often don't receive it until then or later. If it is truly expected on the first, it is more likely to be paid on the first. Personal collection is really the easiest way to get your money on time. It's a simple habit to develop, and the pay-off is high. Even if you have a resident manager, showing your face once a month is more likely to produce on-time rent.

WARNING SIGNS

Even an excellent long-term tenant can become a collection problem. Major warning signs include:

1. Marital problems — failure to pay bills is often used to punish errant spouses.
2. Check problems — even if a check isn't NSF, it may be returned because the tenant "forgot" to sign it.
3. Frequent complaints — a tenant may be seeking justification for his failure to pay.

If you observe any warning signs, call the tenant personally to inform him you do not expect future rent problems. This can be done in a subtle and friendly manner.

A TIME FOR EVERYTHING

As it says in the Bible, there's a time for everything, including raising the rent. One of the best times to up the price, according to many landlords, is when a tenant moves out. This has been called the "turnover" method. Its advantages are obvious: you'll completely avoid having to ask a tenant for more rent than he's been paying. It's a very painless technique.

There is one major flaw, however. What if your tenant stays in your unit for ten years? Some tenants do become permanent fixtures, and if you use the turnover method, you'll come out on the short end of the stick while they are getting the deal of the century. In this instance, and others, a periodic raise is best. In other words, you let everyone know that once every so often (a year is a good interval), there will be a rent increase. This way, it comes as no surprise to your tenants, and eliminates many complaints.

Another excellent time to raise the rent is when you make improvements to the property. Tenants feel like they're getting something in return for the extra money they are being asked to pay. It seems to make it less painful to come up with the extra money when the rent is due.

KEEP IT FAIR

A good tenant can be a long-term asset. But you must treat them well, and that includes keeping the rent at a fair level and handling increases in a way that will not rub your tenants the wrong way. Remember, renting out property is your business and it must be treated as such. Doing the right things in rental management assures your financial success.

◆ 11 TIPS FOR LANDLORD SURVIVAL

Owning rental property is a business. And as with any business, it's a matter of survival of the prepared, especially when you manage it yourself.

Here are some tips designed to save your sanity and your pocketbook.

#1 — Checklist

Always use a checklist when new tenants move in. Have them fill it out, room by room, listing anything that's broken, dented, chipped, or damaged. Have them sign and date it and send it to you. Attach it to their rental agreement. Then when they move, use that checklist to determine if there has been any additional damage. If you hold back some of the security deposit, be sure you take pictures and document the damage in case the tenant decides to sue.

#2 — Credit Check

And last, but certainly not least — be sure and run a credit check on *all* prospective tenants. There are bureaus where you can sign up for a nominal fee and then you're charged by how thorough a check you want. People with bad credit almost always make lousy tenants. Don't be swayed by their hard luck stories. Don't be tempted to rent to the first person who comes along with the money. Hold out for a credit worthy tenant — they pay on time, stay longer and take better care of your property. Just the kind of people you want as a tenant for a little peace of mind.

#3 — Paint

Instead of jumping around from sale to sale, find a brand and a color (like Navajo White) that you like and stick with that product. That way you won't find yourself with partially filled cans of paint in different colors and shades cluttering your garage or storage area. It's easier to touch up and you'll save bucks in the long run. If tenants don't like your color scheme — let them paint at their expense, with the understanding that when they vacate, they will repaint the walls to the original color. Get the agreement in writing so you aren't stuck for the cost of covering enameled electric blue walls.

#4 — Gardeners

Tenants aren't going to take care of the yard and the plants (I don't care what they promise). Believe me, nine out of ten times, they won't do it. So if you must have grass be smart and split the cost of a gardener with your tenants. Make sure the arrangement is written into the rental agreement. You don't have to have a full-fledged landscaping service — you can usually get by with a day laborer. If you have a large yard or lots of plants, consider paying the water bill yourself. That way tenants won't hesitate to water and it'll save you the cost of having to replace the landscaping every time there's a vacancy.

#5 — Carpet Cleaning

Contact the manager of your favorite carpet cleaning company and cut a deal. Explain that you have rental property and you'd like to establish a business relationship with his/her company. Negotiate to get their best rate — regardless of when you call for service. This saves you having to clip coupons and bounce from company to company.

#6 — Verticals and Mini-blinds

When it's time to replace drapes — don't! Get vinyl or plastic verticals or mini-blinds. They will cost a bit more initially, but they will last considerably longer. They are almost indestructible, easy to clean and give the place a more modern look. Look for ads in your local newspapers for places that offer price breaks.

#7 — Appliances

Get rid of the refrigerators. Let your tenant buy or rent one. Then you won't have to pay for repairs. It's an appliance you really don't have to provide.

#8 — Utilities

When tenants do vacate your property, contact the utility company to have the gas and electric switched into your name. Ask to have the bill pro-rated. That can save you the cost of having someone sent out to read the meter.

#9 — Pets

Consider renting to people with a dog or cat if you own a single-family residence or a condo where pets are allowed. Because it's hard for them to find housing, when they do find a place they like that takes pets, tenants tend to stay awhile. Just make sure you write into the rental agreement that when they vacate they will have the house and yard professionally fumigated for fleas. Also, I have always made it a practice to insist on a much higher initial cleaning and/or security deposit for people with pets. In fact, I usually double the normal amount of their deposits to cover all possible problems that may be caused by their pet. I also charge a monthly pet fee (or pet-rent). In most cases, people with pets do not hesitate to pay the higher deposit or monthly pet fee.

#10 — New Tenants

When your tenants do give notice, set up a time to inspect the property. If it's in decent condition, cut a deal with them to show it while they're still there. Offer them $100 if you rent the place to someone they've shown it to. Make sure you give them rental applications and a list of requirements. Then run an ad with both their phone number and yours. Make sure they are actually showing the property so you're not wasting your advertising budget.

#11 — Security Deposit Refund

Don't be pressured into doing a walkthrough with your old tenants with the idea of returning the security deposit on the spot. Take the time allowed by law. Be sure and run the appliances — the dishwasher, garbage disposal, oven and stovetop burners. Make sure the garage door openers still work. Flush the toilets and run the showers to make sure drains are properly working. The property may look good, but don't take any chances.

I would like to thank my son, Mark E. Haroldsen, who has brilliantly managed several of my multi-million dollar properties for many years, and for contributing to creating these 11 TIPS FOR LANDLORD SURVIVAL.

PLANS AND GOALS

_____

_____

_____

_____

_____

_____

_____

_____

_____

PLANS AND GOALS

PLANS AND GOALS

_____

_____

_____

_____

_____

_____

_____

_____

_____

_____

_____

_____

_____

_____

_____

_____

_____

_____

_____

_____

_____

_____

CHAPTER 25
MOTIVATION + FORMULA = SUCCESS

Belief, drive, desire, a positive mental attitude, determination, discipline, enthusiasm, excitement, and motivation are all vital ingredients of success. But each quality is only gas or fuel to power the vehicle.

Although a vital commodity, fuel is worthless without something to use it in. Belief, drive, desire, and the other ingredients of success must have the vehicle — a well thought-out plan — to lead one to his goal. After that, the proper methods must be used to execute the plan.

Motivation is the high-octane gas, and the plan or specific formula is the performance race car.

It is unfortunate that millions of those who want to enter the race of success in wealth have only one can of gas. To make things worse, many empty that can of gas into a dilapidated or unsafe vehicle.

YOUR FORMULA 4 CAR IS NOW READY
You, the reader, are standing there with a full or nearly full can of fuel. Do you realize that the vehicle I have shown you is capable of winning first place in the race? Only you have the power to dump the gas in, jump in and steer to the finish line.

Once you get going don't stop. It is your future and the outlook for real estate investment looks brighter than ever before.

I can't help but remember what Mr. Billion Dollar's Worth of Real Estate Man, Dell Loy Hansen, said in his letter in the beginning of this book; "When people ask, 'can I still do this,' I smile. I truly believe it is actually easier today with better information, computers, more cash in the economy, and obviously, a great deal more real estate to choose from. I sincerely think I could do "better" today with an average intelligence and above average desire than twenty-five years ago."

THE FUTURE LOOKS BRIGHT — BUT YOU MUST MAKE A DECISION

In addition, many states and areas will benefit from increases in population, both from birth rate and the influx of people from other states. But even more important is your determination, your drive, and your desire to accomplish what you set out to do. With a strong personal determination, absolutely nothing can stop you. Without it, you will fail in the *best real estate market* in the world. Regardless of how good your formula is, without the motivation and the determination to make it work, you have nothing.

Charles E. Jones has said many times that, "You must make a decision, make it *your* decision, and you must die by it." It is sad that few people can make decisions, and even fewer are willing to stick by their decisions, regardless of the consequences. Make your decision now, and make another decision to stick by that decision. When you apply the formula contained in this book, when you see that it works, don't stop there! Make it work again, again, and again.

Don't let your vehicle run out of fuel. Reinvest your profits so you can get the benefits of compounding. Later you will be able to spend huge sums without even denting your capital. But don't do that at first.

Even the Bible speaks of compounding and the good it can do. Read Matthew 25:14-30.

As you compound your money, don't forget to work on yourself. Increase your abilities through your own effort. Let your brain and soul compound at the same rate as your assets.

YOU SHOULD GROW WITH YOUR ASSETS
On the wall of the office of Larry Rosenberg's brother, Lew, in Denver, Colorado, hangs a plaque with this inscription:

> Why build these cities glorious,
> if man unbuilded goes? In vain
> we build the world, unless the
> builder also grows.
> — E. Markham

As you ascend the ladder of growth in both assets and personally, unless you also help build others, you really have not learned to live. You will no doubt end as the men in the story below:

In 1923, a group of the world's most successful financiers met at the Edgewater Beach Hotel in Chicago. Present were: the president of the largest independent steel company, the greatest wheat speculator, the president of the New York Stock Exchange, a member of the President's Cabinet, the greatest "bear" on Wall Street, the president of the Bank of International Settlement, and the head of the world's greatest monopoly. Collectively, these tycoons controlled more wealth than there was in the United States treasury, and for years newspapers and magazines had been printing their success stories and urging the youth of the nation to follow their examples.

Twenty-five years later, let's see what happened to these men. The president of the largest independent steel company, CHARLES SCHWAB, lived on borrowed money the last five years of his life and died broke. The greatest wheat speculator, ARTHUR CUTTEN, died abroad, insolvent. The president of the New York Stock Exchange, RICHARD WHITNEY, was recently released from Sing Sing. The member of the president's cabinet, ALBERT FALL, was pardoned from prison so he could die at home. The greatest "bear" on Wall Street, JESSE LIVERMORE, committed suicide. The head of the world's greatest monopoly, IVAN KREUGER, committed suicide. All of these men had learned how to make money, but not one of them had learned how to live.

In fact, it is questionable whether they really learned how to make money, for they did not keep it. Don't forget the advice from *The Richest Man in Babylon.* These men obviously never learned the lesson from that story.

In learning to live as you go, you must realize that money is not the end product. It is only the tool that shapes, forms, and molds that product or goal. The goal is to build yourself and others as you travel along the path.

Never forget that those who are confused and think that money is the goal will end up like the men that met that day at the Edgewater Beach Hotel.

DON'T LOVE MONEY — LOVE THE GOOD IT CAN DO

Many people think wealth is bad. They quote the Bible that money is the root of all evil. But that is not what the Bible says; read it for yourself. "For the *love of money* is the root of all evil." (1 Timothy 6:10; [italics added].) That is the big difference. It is not the money that is evil; it is the love of money that ruins people. In fact, money is good, very good, if used for the right things.

Suppose for a moment that your child was blinded in an accident. You are told that his or her sight can only be restored by a very delicate and difficult operation. There is only one man in the world who can perform this intricate surgery. His services are expensive and it will cost $100,000 for the operation. Is money now good or evil?

WHAT IS MONEY?

A great author and a great man, Sterling W. Sill, says this about money:

Someone once said that money can't buy happiness, but his friend pointed out that it does enable one to pick out the particular kind of misery that he enjoys the most. Money may not buy happiness, but it's pretty difficult to be happy without it. It is hard to send children to school or to maintain a proper standard of living without something to use as a medium of exchange. Someone said, "Money ain't everything." His friend said to him, "Just name me three things that it ain't." Suppose that we name a few things that it *is:*

1. Money is the medium that we exchange for other things.
2. It is planning and industry made negotiable.
3. It is preserved labor.
4. It is stored-up accomplishment.
5. It is food, clothing, and education for children.
6. It is comfort and peace of mind for elderly people.
7. It may serve as the thermometer of our industry.
8. It may be used as the scorecard for at least one branch of our success.
9. It builds churches and fosters righteousness.
10. It has helped to win wars and preserve national security.
11. It has built comfortable homes and high educational standards.
12. It fosters research and helps to build up our national health.
13. Through money we may contribute to the welfare of other peoples.
14. By its proper use, we can multiply our own usefulness.

Through money one may store up the results of his own labor in such a way that it will go on working long after his own life has come to its end. With money we may send out missionaries, hold homes together, provide children with fulltime mothers, and do many kinds of helpful scientific research. *(The Miracle of Personality* [Salt Lake City: Bookcraft, Inc., 1966], pp. 165-66.)

Now implement the specific methods and formulas of financial success. Begin achieving your goals one by one, but also give plenty of hard thought and action to learning to live and enjoy life along the way.

YOUR GREAT OBLIGATION
TO THE WORLD

Build others with your wealth. Use your assets for good so your wealth will benefit the future generations. This is more than your task; it is your obligation. The eternal laws that govern the universe demand that you give more than you receive. You will receive in abundance, so prepare yourself to make even larger contributions to build yourself and the world.

NOTES AND THOUGHTS

_____

_____

_____

_____

_____

_____

_____

_____

_____

PLANS AND GOALS

PLANS AND GOALS

_____

_____

_____

_____

_____

_____

_____

_____

_____

_____

_____

_____

_____

_____

_____

_____

_____

_____

_____

_____

_____

_____

BONUS SECTION
BEST DEALS, GOOD DEALS, HAPPY DEALS

In this next section of the book, I'm going to tell the stories of some of the people who used what they learned from my first book to secure a little bit of financial freedom. They are people from all walks of life and all parts of the country. This once again reiterates how simple the formula for success can be when applied with a little work and imagination.

Keep in mind that these deals were transacted after reading "Financial Genius" when it was first written. The numbers in the - stories may seem low to you, but plug in the same deal with today's numbers and you'll see that the formula and ideas still work.

THE CHURCH CONNECTION

"A 3-bedroom home built around 1890 had been occupied by an elderly woman who was a member of our church," explains James Koski, a real estate investor in Saginaw, Michigan. "She was an only child, had been born in the house, and had lived there all her life. Until the last 30 years, her father had lived there with her. She had set things up in her estate in a way that the church would get the house when she died or became incapacitated and had to be put into a rest home."

When she was 93, she moved into a rest home. The church was given the property, but wasn't equipped to assume the responsibility of taking care of it. Knowing that

James bought properties, the minister contacted him and asked if he'd be interested in taking it off their hands.

James went over to inspect the home. "It was in rough shape," he recalls. "It looked like it hadn't been decorated, painted, or even given a thorough cleaning in 30 years. And although it was livable, it wouldn't have measured up to the local codes for rentals because it needed some plumbing, electrical, and other work to be done.

"I made the church an offer of $8,500, with $8,250 in a land contract, and $250 down. It was an 11 percent interest, six-year contract with monthly payments of $184. There were no closing costs. Since it didn't meet the codes for rentals, I could have had the work done, but that was my Plan B. Plan A was to "flip" it on another contract to someone else who wanted a house to live in and would be willing to go in and pour some sweat equity into it."

The object of the game, at that point, was to find someone who fit that description. The daughter of an acquaintance of James — a single mother of three on social assistance — fit the bill perfectly.

"I offered it to her for $24,000 with no down payment," he recalls. "Her payments were set at $300 per month which included her taxes and insurance. That was about $50 less than what she had been paying to rent an apartment. In her case, because of her restricted income, that payment would remain the same even if taxes and insurance were to go up, unless her financial situation changed.

"We wrote another land contract at 11 percent interest, with a 30-year term. (Eleven percent is the maximum interest rate that can be charged on land contracts in Michigan.)"

In short, James purchased a home for $250 and $184 monthly payments for six years. He turned around and sold it for 30 years" worth of $300 monthly payments (from which taxes and insurance would be paid, amounting to a total of about $50 a month). That means he would net approximately $55 per month.

Leaving it right there, this would qualify as a happy ending to an extremely easy, inexpensive, no-hassle deal. But that's not the end of the story. It gets better.

"I went to my credit union," James explains, "refinanced the property, paid off the church, and put $3,500 in my pocket. I did this by mortgaging the property for $12,000. With that money, I paid the church the balance on the land contract of $8,250 (for which the church gave me the deed to the property), paid myself back the $250 I put into the down payment, and pocketed the remaining $3,500."

The monthly payment on the 10 percent interest, 10-year refinancing loan was about $150. This meant that James was paying $34 per month less than before, and although he'd be making those payments for four years longer than if he hadn't refinanced, he now had $3,500 more to play with than if he hadn't pushed the deal the extra step.

The foundation of the deal was buying low and selling for a good price. "I was able to buy at a low price," says James, "because the church was a "don't-wanter". It's in the business of saving souls – not real estate.

James did a bit of soul-saving in this deal himself. . . at least in the material sense. He was able to take a problem off the church's hands. And he helped the young single mother, even though he sold her the house for a relatively high price. "This lady was on welfare," he points out. "She had no possibility whatsoever of ever buying a house under normal circumstances. Although I didn't give her a low price, I did give her very attractive terms — terms that fit her budget and her situation. It was a good deal for her."

Clearly, it was a good deal for everyone involved.

RELATIONSHIPS YOU CAN
TAKE TO THE BANK

Moving on to another part of the country, Craig Horton's deal involves a duplex and several good relationships. This Medford, Oregon real estate entrepreneur had a few years' worth of experience under his belt when this deal came along.

It was his wife, Jane, who found this gem of a deal. "Being born in the Philippines, my wife knows a lot of Filipinos in this area," says Craig. "One of them, a lady, owned a duplex here in Medford that she wanted to sell. It was a townhouse duplex with wood siding and a total of 1,800 square feet. She talked to my wife about buying it because she wanted to be cashed out. She needed money and felt that we might be able to come up with it.

"So we negotiated with her, and as it ended up, we told her that we'd pay $30,000 cash for the duplex, contingent upon a property inspection. She agreed."

In accordance with the contingency, Craig asked his father to go over to the property and inspect it with him. "My dad has been in the business for a long time," explains Craig. "He has owned a lot of units, and has helped me in the business. We went through and he inspected both units completely. We found that the seller had put a new roof and nice, new wood siding on the building and had rewired it within the previous two years.

Craig's father confirmed what Craig had suspected all along: that the duplex was worth substantially more than the $30,000 cash purchase price.

The next step involved getting the $30,000 to make the cash payment for the purchase. This was no real problem. "I talked to my local banker at Valley of the Rouge bank," recalls Craig. "I made arrangements with him to get a $33,000 first mortgage loan on the duplex. It would be an interest-only quarterly payment loan with a one-year term.

"My father and I had done this several times before with this particular bank. We had a large line of credit, and we would go to them and say, 'We're buying this property at a heavy discount. We want you to put a first mortgage on the property, and we will refinance within a year.' The bank loves those loans."

Next, Craig drafted an earnest money agreement for the $30,000 cash purchase and took it to the title company, along with a small deposit. A closing date was set.

At the closing, the $33,000 first mortgage loan Craig received from the bank was used to pay the seller her $30,000 sales price plus closing costs. When everybody and everything was paid, Craig walked away with a check for $1,141. He now owned the duplex and had money in his pocket, but he couldn't rest on his laurels.

First, he had to turn his attention to the duplex itself. One side of the property, which housed the granddaughter of the seller (who wasn't paying rent), had to be filled with a solid, rent-paying tenant. Plus, a few improvements had to be made, such as the replacement of a refrigerator and stove. All in all, this cost about $2,000. But by the time he was finished, he had a duplex that was in top shape and filled with solid tenants.

Craig's second task was to find long-term financing to take the place of the one-year mortgage note from his local bank. "It was kind of a quirk," recalls Craig, "but a friend of mine who had just gone to work for a mortgage company called me and asked if I knew anyone who wanted to refinance a non-owner occupied property. He said his company had mortgage money available for that type of property. This was well in advance of when the one-year note would be due. I told him the criteria that I needed — what I had to have and what the restrictions were.

"You see, the problem was — and is — that it's tough to get decent financing if you own a lot of rentals. Because If you own more than about five or six units, your loan isn't salable on the secondary market. They really frown on it unless they 'portfolio' your loan, which means they keep the loan in their loan portfolio and don't try to sell it on the secondary market.

"My friend did some checking and found out that the loan *would* be a portfolio loan, so they could give me what I was looking for — a fixed-rate, long-term mortgage."

The loan was for $35,000. This was based on the mortgage company's appraisal, which had come in at *$50,000.* Remember, Craig bought it for only $30,000 just a few months before. The loan was a 30-year first mortgage loan at a fixed interest rate of 10-1/2 percent. Principal and interest would be $320 per month.

When Craig walked out of the closing for the $35,000 refinance mortgage, he had a $35,000 mortgage and had spent a total of $2,000 of his own money on the project since the inception.

Craig now owned a property that was worth $50,000. (With the $35,000 mortgage, this gave him an equity position of $15,000 — a figure that would grow larger as the mortgage was amortized and the property value increased.) In addition, the duplex was generating a positive cash flow each month.

Says Craig: "One of the major reasons why this deal came about was that my wife and I have a good working relationship in our real estate investments. She did a lot of the groundwork on this and helped put the transaction together.

Another key to this deal was the $33,000 loan Craig received from the Valley of the Rouge Bank. Without it, he wouldn't have had the cash to purchase the property when the deal was hot.

"You've got to have a good relationship with a lender," Craig points out. "Not everybody can walk in and get that kind of money and get it that quickly, with so little hassle. If you really cultivate a relationship with a bank, it can be done."

The bank relationship was not the only one that contributed to making this deal work. His relationship with his father, an experienced veteran of the business, allowed him to call on his expertise when he needed to inspect the property. And his relationship with a friend resulted in a call that led to an excellent long-term mortgage loan.

When it comes right down to it, relationships are what the real estate investing game is all about. If you doubt it, ask Craig.

CDHORTON@aol.com

http://www.mrlandlord.com/mbhousing

SNATCHING PROFITS FROM THE JAWS OF FORECLOSURE

"The big thing around here was to buy properties just before they went into foreclosure," explains Sue Brawn, a real estate investor from Dayton, Ohio. "My partner found a series of properties owned by the same person that were in pre-foreclosure in Miamisburg, Ohio." (Miamisburg is located very close to Dayton.)

One was an old seven-unit building. Another was a two-unit apartment. There were also two houses. But the property that most captivated Sue was a brick commercial building that housed a pizza place that was going out of business, a carry-out that was hanging on by its teeth, and two three-bedroom, 1,400 square-foot apartments upstairs. The building was located on a corner right out of downtown Miamisburg where the main bridge is located. It sat on 1.2 acres of land, but much of that was on a hill.

"This property particularly interested us because it had the potential of becoming an office building," says Sue. "We own a company called Tenant Chek, and were looking for a larger space for our operation."

The seller wanted $155,000 for the corner building. Even though that was what it had appraised for, Sue didn't think it was worth that much. So she made an offer of $90,000 in pre-foreclosure. "The seller liked that," she states, "so we went and talked to his attorney, and got involved in the biggest mess in the world. We couldn't get the property out of foreclosure even though the lending institution, which held the mortgage, was willing to have us buy it. The whole series of properties finally went into foreclosure.

"The city condemned the old seven-unit building and we decided not to try to get it. Someone else bought it, but hadn't done his homework, and the city tore it down. One of the houses and the two-unit apartment building went up for foreclosure, but we passed on those, too, because we discovered they weren't very well made.

"But I lusted after that corner office building and the house behind it on the hill, which was now a separate package."

At the foreclosure sale, several people bid on the building, but not enough to cover the outstanding mortgage balance owed.

By this point the pizza house and carryout business were gone. The tenants in the two upstairs apartments were not paying rent. So, Sue was ready to make her move. She had done her homework, and had talked to the people at the lending institution. Having done business with her before, they were more than willing to help her take it off their hands. She offered $58,000.

Says Sue: "I talked the lenders into giving us what I call a 'Bud' loan. Bud was the president of the lending institution. 1 got an adjustable-rate loan for the full $58,000 for 20 years at 9-1/4 percent interest. And believe it or not, they gave me a six-month moratorium on payments! Plus, they gave me a loan to fix up the building for $10,000 at 10 percent interest, renewable yearly, with interest-only payments.

"We went in and did everything we could. My partner rehabbed the old pizza house for less than $1,000. Of course, that didn't include our labor. We turned it into a very beautiful office for Tenant Chek with a reception area, storage area, a room where we could screen tenants, and a large private office.."

To make a long story short, the entire building was soon renovated. The non-paying tenants in the two upstairs apartments were evicted and replaced with good, solid paying tenants. The side of the downstairs that had housed the carryout operation was converted to three attractive offices and rented out. The building became a real credit to the community.

Best of all, it's now worth upwards of $200,000 — a far cry from the $58,000 purchase price Sue negotiated. The bridge in front of the building has been rebuilt, so the property is the first thing to be seen by the increased traffic that is entering the town from that direction.

What happened to the house behind the office building that Sue also wanted to buy? Well, she and her partner bought that too in a separate transaction. But that's a whole 'nother story.

MAKING BEAUTIFUL MUSIC IN REAL ESTATE

John Bayer, a high school music teacher, makes beautiful financial music on the side by investing in income-producing real estate. He and his wife, Sylvia, heard about a three-unit apartment property in the small rural village of Perry, New York, just eight miles away from their home in the similarly small village of Warsaw.

The Victorian-style property was comprised of three residential flats, one on top of the other. It was located on the main street running through town. Overall, the building was in good shape. A tax assessment had placed the property's value at $60,000, and the seller was asking $59,900. The rents at that time were on the low side for the area and the type of property.

"I asked the real estate agent if the seller would be willing to carry a second mortgage if I came in with a first mortgage," says John. "The agent said he thought he'd be willing to carry some paper, since he'd been trying to sell the property for over six months. He also indicated that he had two other appointments to show the property. He said somebody was quite interested. Now, I didn't know whether he was just trying to get me to move faster, or what, but he'd been straight with me in the past, so I had no reason not to believe him. Besides, I had the advantage of being able to run the numbers on the property quickly on my own computer.

Says John: "I wrote an offer that said I would go to the bank and get a first mortgage for $45,000, if the seller would be willing to hold a second mortgage for $15,000. It also said that the purchase price would be $57,000."

The real estate agent wasn't used to this sort of addition. He pointed out that $45,000 and $15,000 didn't equal $57,000. "I know that," said John. "They add up to $60,000." The agent scratched his head.

"It's okay," John assured him, "as long as nobody has any hang-ups with it. There's nothing wrong with this as long as the property appraises high enough to cover both mortgages." So it was written into the offer that it was contingent on the bank appraising the property for a minimum of $60,000. (The appraisal actually came in at $62,000.)

The offer and a $500 deposit were accepted after a little negotiating. John had asked for a six-month moratorium on the second mortgage, during which time no payment would have to be made and no interest would accrue. The seller didn't like this, and offered to drop the 10_ percent interest rate he had planned to charge to 10 percent if John would forget the moratorium. John agreed.

The $45,000 first mortgage, however, was a horse of a different color. John explains: "The only commercial loans we have around here are one-year, renegotiated interest loans. So they really socked it to us that first year. The loan is amortized over 20 years.

As it happened, both John and the seller had the same attorney. He agreed to represent both parties and lower the closing costs. And he had no problems with John borrowing $60,000 for a $57,000 purchase.

"It was interesting," John remarks, "that our banker didn't mind the fact that we weren't putting any of our own money into the purchase. And it didn't bother him that there was a second mortgage on the home worth $3,000 more than what we needed to make the purchase." These things didn't bother him because of the professional, organized presentation that John made.

Because John had financed the property for $3,000 more than the sales price, he walked away with $2,198 after paying closing costs. Of course, $500 of that went to pay him back for the deposit he had made with the offer. This still left him with a nice $1,698 profit on a deal in which he had put none of his own money.

He plowed the $1,698 back into the property in the form of improvements, including painting, almost all of which he hired out. In fact, he had a contractor go over the building from top to bottom to make sure everything was in good shape — from the roof to the baseboards.

The property generated a slight negative cash flow for a little less than a year. "But I knew that up front," adds John. "The computer told us exactly what the building was going to do and that's what it did. It helped to know ahead of time what we could expect." As forecast, the negative cash flow soon turned into a break-even and then a positive position as John inched up the rents. The positive cash flow will grow each year, and their equity grows each time a tenant pays rent.

In addition, this tidy, well-managed, three-unit building is appreciating in value. John and Sylvia bought smart, fixed up and manage the property well. When this equity — which will grow over the years — is combined with the positive cash flow that they'll be receiving, it becomes obvious that the $2,500 or so of their own money that they put into the project (in improvements and to cover early negative cash flow) has indeed been money well spent.

SWEATIN' WITH THE OLDIES

Building up equity in your rental properties is what real estate ownership is all about. It's not just the monetary additions, but also an often-neglected ingredient called "sweat equity."

WHAT IS SWEAT EQUITY?

A simple illustration: If you were buying a house that was under construction you might want to cut costs in order to reduce your mortgage *or* to upgrade some feature *of* the house. You might ask your builder if you could do some *of* the work yourself, such as painting, tiling, *or* doing the grading and clean up. As you might have a licensed friend *or* relative do sheet-rocking, electrical *or* plumbing — anything the builder could allow and still pass inspection. All that labor would become part of the value but not part *of* the mortgage. It would add to your equity due to the "sweat" *of* your brow.

Equity is the dollar value to the owner that lies over and above any mortgage or other liability against the property. It is that value which is due rightfully to the owner because of such things as his initial cash down payment, his subsequent payments (mortgage reduction), the influence of inflation, neighborhood upgrading, and the improvements he adds.

No two *owners* of income property will invest the same amount of time and effort to maintain their properties.

For example, the computer technician with one rental unit can wisely budget his time in order to keep that unit sharp, up to date and running efficiently. Whatever he does — repair, repaint, remodel, landscape – with his own two hands, his time and his talents to increase his cash flow and to enhance the value of his property is called "sweat equity." On this equity he pays no salaries, no interest charges, no discount fees, no commissions or carrying charges. He receives an added bonus of increased pleasure and pride of ownership.

THE NAME OF THE GAME

Cash flow is one *of* the main economic reasons for investing in any type of real estate. Sweat equity plays into a most crucial element of income property ownership namely: income must be produced at the lowest possible cost.

Most wise investors look at income property with an eye to improving efficiency, cutting costs and increasing cash flow. The owner who succeeds today in maximizing cash flow and market value is usually the one who is personally involved in the cutting of those costs. You may well ask, "With the price of everything going up, how can we talk about cutting costs?"

The answer: Because this is the time to be "superior to circumstances."

It may be that we are not so short of money as we are short of inventive ideas about money. . . that we are not so short of time as we are short of self-discipline. . . and we are not so short of opportunities as we are short of determination to create them.

There are bargains out there! There are sellers who must sell. There are buyers who must buy. There are terms that will work.

Take a good look at that prospective property or at the property you now own. What can be done by your own efforts to breathe some exciting new strategy into your property ownership portfolio? If you're a ho-hum owner you are neglecting your investments. You have lost sight of your initial goal.

THE KEY TO PROFITS

Buying right is the key, of course, to most success stories. There is a hidden potential for income in obsolete buildings, which are now being bought and restored as offices, apartments and condominiums. Old houses of charm with that unmistakable mark of quality so often lacking in modern construction are becoming more and more attractive to affluent renters and purchasers.

It is important to note the distinction between restoration and renovation. Restoration requires faithful attention to historic detail. The work preserves the original style. Renovation simply puts a building back into sound condition without regard to original style. Shopping for an historic rehab calls for patience and a strong constitution. It takes an intrepid spirit to hold up through one old depressing area after another. You may be combing neighborhoods where every house is totally disheartening. Or you may be looking at the very worst house on the block. Can you see through years of neglect, decay, rubble, coat after coat of garish paint to a structural gem?

SWEAT EQUITY RECYCLING

The net result for sweat equity recycling of old structures is among the highest in the remodeling business. Added to this is the bonus of finding a building that qualifies for the government financing incentives.

Some rules of thumb that apply here as well as to any purchase are:

- Borrow maximum
- Buy only property that needs improvement
- Make only those improvements that increase value
- Do not overkill for the market.

Find out the rent competition in the area and keep in line. Overall costs should be kept low enough so that new construction in the area cannot compete, since lower rental is often the chief competitive advantage of older housing.

Bear in mind, however, that in the current trend, the old-world charm of high-ceilings, large rooms, elaborate crown moldings, carved mantles, stained-glass windows and all such features of historic flavor more than carry their weight in the marketplace. Such homes have become so sought after recently that it requires luck and timing as well as hard work to find them.

FIRST LOOKS

Often, the landscaping is the motivating factor that gets the renter or buyer out of his car and inside the property. That first glance can be decisive. There are captivating tricks to landscaping that can far outweigh more basic advantages and can often offset serious disadvantages. The miracle of landscaping can be proven again and again in quick turnovers that reflect over 50 percent increases in selling prices.

Tom and Donna Brown drove to a good residential neighborhood and stopped at a weathered old For Sale sign. What they saw was a jungle of weeds, ungainly bushes, and trashy elm trees. But somewhere down in that jungle, the

Realtor had assured them, was a decent four-bedroom brick rambler. It was an estate sale. The surviving heirs lived 3,000 miles away and wanted to be rid of it. The Browns got it for $80,000 with ten percent down and the balance at ten percent with a balloon note due in one year. It was a gamble, but the Browns believed in miracles. Then they went to work to create one.

Tom took his summer vacation early and Donna put her two younger brothers to work. They cleared the weeds and plowed up the old grass. They cut down all but a few of the elms and trimmed the bushes.

They put down new sod, balled and burlapped some good sized pine trees and assorted bushes from a wholesale nursery. They transplanted from friends' overgrown gardens a variety of trees, shrubs and ground cover. Along the foundation they arranged the planting to enhance the pleasant lines of the house to soften the sharp corners.

They put up a low white split rail fence along the front by clusters of aspen that they had planted in beds among large rocks, flowering annuals and spreading junipers. They painted the outside trim, added shutters, a lamp post, did minor roof repair and within two weeks, three unsolicited offers had been pressed into their hands. They waited until they had finished their project and by the end of the month they had closed the sale with a cash offer of $150,000. Their cost - $12,400. They simply made the house irresistible by putting in their own sweat equity.

USING YOUR POTENTIAL

Are you asking yourself where your opportunity is? Will there be backaches, stiff necks, black and blue thumbs? You can almost bet on it. But financial security is a rather musical phrase. Repeat it over and over a few times. And repeat it to yourself as you dab on the alcohol and the band-aids. With wit, wisdom and "sweat" you'll make it just as countless others have.

Regardless of the level of your present skills you have more potential than you can ever use up in a lifetime. Who knows? Perhaps "sweat equity" is the key that will unlock that genius inside you.

So there you have it. Stories from real people who made real money from their real estate deals. They used the success formula they learned from my first book, added their own imagination and "tweaked" the circumstances to make their own financial freedom.

PLANS AND GOALS

_____

_____

_____

_____

_____

_____

_____

_____

_____

_____

_____

_____

_____

_____

_____

PLANS AND GOALS

_____

_____

_____

_____

_____

_____

_____

_____

_____

_____

_____

_____

_____

_____

_____

_____

_____

_____

_____

_____

_____

_____

_____

ADDENDUM "A"

While struggling in college as an undergraduate student in accounting in a small Northern Utah college, the dream to own investment real estate kindled in Dell Loy Hansen's young mind. He had seen two small homes for sale in his hometown of Smithfield, Utah (a town of less than 5,000 people). He thought these homes were priced right to earn positive rental income, but how would he buy them with a minimum part-time wage of a college student? It looked impossible – no capital, just a good idea.

His fervent search for how led him to purchase a copy of "*How To Wake Up The Financial Genius Inside You*" by Mark O. Haroldsen. He applied the techniques taught in the book and both homes were purchased and held for over 12 years using less than $200 of Dell Loy's limited, or better stated "non-existent," capital.

He consistently bought and traded homes for the next ten years, building a net worth and cash flow that allowed him to tackle large apartment communities and office buildings as the next level.

The basics learned in "*How To Wake Up The Financial Genius Inside You*," followed by years of practice, allowed Dell Loy and his partners to buy a twenty-four story office building (the largest in Salt Lake City) for half of its construction cost. Eight months later, with only fifty percent of the building rented, the owners are enjoying its positive cash flow knowing that as it fills to capacity, it will pay millions of dollars a year to the fully "awake" owners – It's your turn to wake up!

The best part is that you can start small and gain new, positive cash flow now, with the knowledge that if you are persistent, there is no limit to your own financial future. Your persistence is much more important than your education or intelligence. Learn the basics. Then get busy creating the secure, comfortable life you deserve.

See Salt Lake Tribune article on Mr. Hansen below:

Company Hits It Big With Skyscraper Deal
Skyscraper a Milestone For Logan Company
BY LESLEY MITCHELL THE SAL T LAKE TRIBUNE

The 24-story high-rise on Main Street near 200 South in downtown Salt Lake City had been largely vacant for more than two years when Dell Loy Hansen decided he had to have it.

Within 48 hours, Hansen and several friends had assembled a down payment of $17 million in cash to buy the building, owned by Boise-based grocery chain Albertson's Inc. A bank loan and a commitment from Albertson's to sell the building for $78.5 million soon followed.

The fact that Hansen and his company, Wasatch Property Management of Logan, were able to pull off a deal of such magnitude — in just a few weeks, no less — surprised many people in Utah.

But it did not surprise those who know Hansen.

"There's nothing this guy can't do," said Daryl W. Hennick, a retired business owner from Utah now living in Sedona, Ariz. He has given Hansen more than $5 million over the past 10 years to invest in real estate.

Since 1990, Hansen and about two dozen investors such as Hennick have quietly built a real estate portfolio made up of 41 apartment complexes, seven commercial office properties and two retail shopping centers valued at more than $1 billion.

Hansen this year expects those properties, managed by 450 people in Utah, Arizona and California, to generate $58 million in profit.

The Salt Lake City skyscraper, now called Wells Fargo Center for its largest tenant, put the little-known Wasatch Property Management on the map in Utah. Hansen, whose other tenants include the Salt Lake Organizing Committee, has ambitious plans to quickly fill most of the building with office and retail tenants.

The purchase of Wells Fargo Center is Hansen's largest deal to date only by a small margin. Three years ago Wasatch Property paid nearly as much — $78 million — for five apartment complexes in Sacramento, Calif., totaling 2,017 units.

Hansen, who loves to joke around — especially at his own expense — is considered an expert deal-maker.

"He's a very interesting negotiator — he's quite upfront with what he wants," said Bill Martin of Colliers Commerce CRG. "A lot of people beat around the bush. He's very straightforward. It's refreshing."

Hansen, who grew up in Logan, founded Wasatch Property Management in 1989, the year after he lost $35,000 building 28 homes in northern Utah. "I thought, I could have sat at home and done better than this," he said. "That's when I decided I didn't want my future to be building homes."

A 1971 graduate of Skyview High School who went on to earn a degree in political science from Utah State University in 1981, Hansen saw opportunity in a number of properties being unloaded by the Resolution Trust Corp. and other organizations as part of the real estate collapse of the late 1980s.

"I saw the government selling things for 40 cents on the dollar and I wanted a part of that," he said.

As luck would have it, Hansen had several high school and college buddies who were not only interested in making such investments, but through successful business ventures collectively had millions in cash to invest. Many of those who invested with Hansen in the early 1990s are still doing so, citing Hansen's eye for smart investments that have yielded in the range of 20 percent to 25 percent a year.

"Dell Loy is a real visionary," said Jonathan Bullen, one of Wasatch's major investors who grew up in Logan and attended Logan High School at the same time as Hansen attended Skyview. "We don't always agree, but our relationship and friendship is deep enough that we can move forward. And we all know each other well enough that we can move quickly."

Other investors who have joined Hansen over the years, such as Daryl Hennick, learned about him through friends.

Hennick's first investment, in 1991, totaled $400,000. He gave Hansen another $2 million after selling his company in 1995. "I've probably given him a total of $5 million and I haven't been disappointed," Hennick said. "That $5 million is worth more than $20 million today and that doesn't count the income I've earned each year."

Each investor contributes different amounts to each property and some pass on particular projects altogether. Hansen, however, makes an equity investment in each one. One of Hansen's first deals after becoming a real estate investor was an uncompleted 54-unit condominium project called Towne Park in Salt Lake City. Wasatch purchased the complex for $1.15 million in cash, recouping its investment after selling only 34 of the units.

Next came Broadmoor Village in West Jordan for $8.6 million. His third purchase, the Justice Building in Salt Lake City for $1.4 million, is the only real estate Hansen's company has ever sold.

"We want to buy and hold on to properties for income," he said. "We want to purchase a property, improve its operations and over time, increase the cash flow it generates."

Throughout the early to late 1990s, Hansen and his investors bought nearly three dozen apartment complexes — totaling more than 10,000 rental units — mainly in Arizona and California. The goal is to own and manage 15,000 rental units by 2004.

"Apartments are a lot of hard work," Hansen said. "There are a lot of details and collection issues. Commercial offices are easier in that regard but they take a lot more capital and it's much more expensive to replace a tenant who moves out."

Although the company specializes in apartment and commercial office buildings, it also has invested in companies that supply products or services to the company's properties.

For example, the company invested in a carpet company and a furniture company that supply apartment complexes. It also has invested in Atlas Disposal Inc., a Sacramento company, after Hansen realized he could save money by hauling trash out of its apartment complexes itself.

"We'll buy a company if it allows us to do something much better or much cheaper than we're paying someone else to do," he said.

lesley@sltrib.com

PLANS AND GOALS

_____

_____

_____

_____

_____

_____

_____

_____

_____

_____

_____

_____

_____

PLANS AND GOALS

A NEW WIN-WIN: FROM FORTUNATE TO FORTUNE

When I was young and had dreams of making a fortune, I was very fortunate to have three great coaches.

- A millionaire friend
- A billionaire acquaintance
- A down-to-earth spiritual leader who really cared about me as a person.

Boy, did I feel fortunate – and that feeling helped catapult me to my own fortune.

And now it's payback time – time to give back – and that kind of payback lifts me as much as it lifts others. Let me explain:

There's a time and a season for everything. Recently, I had lunch with a bright, young, very ambitious Olympian. Not a want-a-be, but a gold medalist and a very unique gold medal winner at that. He has the distinction of being in the family that became "the first family ever with three generations of winner Olympians all in different sports."

But here comes the payback part. It doesn't have anything to do with Olympics other than the Olympic mind and drive of gold medal winner, Jimmy Shea. He wants me to coach him as he changes his focus from making his mark in Winter Olympic gold to the gold that can be won in the world of real estate.

PAY IT FORWARD TO YOUR COACH

How could anyone say no to this enthusiastic young man with a new dream? I couldn't. It's payback time. I'm trying to payback by paying it forward to others – and by the way, if you've never seen the movie, *Pay it Forward,* you really need to! By helping Jimmy, I believe in some small way I'm paying back my three coaches and all the other people who helped me reach the top. (Actually, it wasn't the top I hit, because I'm still climbing – and enjoying the climb!)

At my age and stage in life, the coaching of others is an honor and it energizes my brain and my life – and when you can coach a winner who won't quit, no matter what, the coach wins as the player wins. It's a true WIN-WIN!

Jimmy Shea is already off to a stunning start.

Four months ago he bought some very expensive land at a ski resort. He paid $640,000 with $80,000 down. He now has signed an agreement to sell off a fraction of the land for $425,000. The balance of the land (because of the way he creatively divided it up) will be worth $1.1 million. I like coaching great financial athletes like this because it makes me look good. Oh, by the way, I really didn't coach him on this deal, except for the bit of tax strategy I gave him over lunch.

But Jimmy Shea* is just beginning to compete in the

---

* If you are thinking, "Wait a minute – I'm not like this guy, Shea. He probably had wealthy parents and a topnotch education. A real head start." Well, if you are thinking that, you're wrong.

Jimmy Shea never made more than $16,000 in his life up until the 2002 Winter Olympics. In fact, as he was in training for the Olympics, he lived in a cabin in the mountains of Utah that didn't even have running water. Plus, it was miles away from civilization where he had to go to train. As far as education goes, Jimmy was in special education in public schools during most of his educational life. But, Jimmy's grandfather taught him a lesson that he never forgot. (His grandfather died in an automobile accident 17 days before the 2002 Olympic games.) His grandfather taught him that when you go after something, you should go after it to win, not just to do well. A lesson Jimmy never forgot and is putting to good use in his financial world now.

world of real estate and I know he's going to be a gold medalist there too.

Note: See Chapter 9, entitled *goals and the energy they create,* and how Shea used them for his quest and success at achieving Olympic Gold.

PLANS AND GOALS

_____

_____

_____

_____

_____

_____

_____

_____

_____

_____

_____

_____

_____

_____

_____

_____

_____

_____

_____

_____

PLANS AND GOALS

ADDENDUM "C"
B-RAM
(BENEFITS, REASONS, AND MOTIVATIONS)
FOR THE CRON DIET

1. 150 Years…very possible – Live longer, and live younger.
2. Restore the energy of your youth.
3. CRON Diet – most Gerontologists agree probability bordering on certainty that CRON Diet can expand maximum lifespan.
4. Weight loss easy if you limit calories to high quality calories.
5. CRON retards basic rate of aging in humans.
6. Postpones the onset of late-life diseases.
   a) Heart disease
   b) Diabetes
   c) Cancer
7. Lowers overall susceptibility to many diseases at any age.
8. You will feel better.
9. Won't need as much sleep.
10. Less stress on lower back.
11. Less stress on knees, hips – because of weight loss.
12. Ability to run better and faster.
13. Greater flexibility, i.e. slows loss of collagen and helps joints.
14. Play better tennis.

15. Multiple careers possible.
16. More time with kids and grandkids.
17. Enjoy my own financial reward more and longer.
18. More time for compounding.
19. Look better.
20. Better eyesight.
21. Feeling of wellbeing – starchy carbs produce serotonin.
22. Better hearing.
23. Better sex life.
24. Lower cholesterol.
25. Lower blood pressure.
26. Slows bone loss.
27. Slows loss of dopamine receptors = better motor skills for a longer time.
28. Brain functions at a younger age level.
29. Possibly lowers risk of Alzheimer's and Parkinson's Disease.

*Important Note: I have prepared this B-RAM List for **me**. This list is not for everyone. Please take time to prepare your very own B-RAM List that is specific to your own **Benefits, Reasons, and Motivations**.*

APPENDIX A
*COMPOUND TABLES
(Based on beginning capital of $10,000)

Years	5%	15%	25%	30%
1	10,050	11,500	12,500	13,000
2	11,025	13,225	15,625	16,900
3	11,576	15,208	19,531	21,970
4	12,155	17,490	24,414	28,561
5	12,762	20,113	30,517	37,129
6	13,400	23,130	38,146	48,268
7	14,071	26,600	47,683	62,748
8	14,774	30,590	59,604	81,573
9	15,513	35,178	74,505	106,044
10	16,288	40,455	93,132	137,858
11	17,103	46,523	116,415	179,211
12	17,958	53,502	145,519	232,980
13	18,856	61,527	181,898	302,875
14	19,799	70,757	227,373	393,737
15	20,789	81,370	284,217	511,858
16	21,828	93,576	355,271	665,416
17	22,920	107,612	444,089	865,041
18	24,066	123,754	555,111	1,124,554
19	25,269	142,317	693,889	1,461,920
20	26,532	163,665	867,361	1,900,496
21	27,859	188,215	1,084,202	2,470,645
22	29,252	216,447	1,355,252	3,211,838
23	30,715	248,914	1,694,065	4,174,390
24	32,251	286,251	2,117,582	5,428,007
25	33,863	329,189	2,646,977	7,056,409

* For more information on Compound Tables, visit the Internet.

APPENDIX A
*COMPOUND TABLES
(Based on beginning capital of $10,000)

Years	50%	100%
1	15,000	20,000
2	22,500	40,000
3	33,750	80,000
4	50,625	160,000
5	75,938	320,000
6	113,907	640,000
7	170,860	1,280,000
8	256,290	2,560,000
9	384,435	5,120,000
10	576,635	10,240,000
11	864,979	20,480,000
12	1,297,468	40,960,000
13	1,946,201	81,920,000
14	2,919,303	163,840,000
15	4,378,954	327,680,000
16	6,568,431	655,360,000
17	9,852,651	1,310,720,000
18	14,778,976	2,621,440,000
19	22,168,464	5,242,880,000
20	33,252,696	10,485,760,000
21	49,879,044	20,971,520,000
22	74,818,566	41,943,040,000
23	112,227,849	83,886,080,000
24	168,341,779	167,772,160,000
25	252,512,668	335,544,320,000

APPENDIX B
ANALYSIS OF HAROLDSEN'S COVENTRY HEARTH SUPER-LEVERAGE DEAL

By James D. McClure, Albuquerque, New Mexico

Case A Original price = $102k, $10k down payment, $92k wrap-around contract. That is, the original owner was willing to wrap around the $68k first mortgage. The original owner had a total equity of $34k, $24k of which would be received through payment of the wrap-around contract. This $24k amount is what Haroldsen negotiates with the original owner in "subordination" negotiations.

Case B Upon purchase, Haroldsen performs $25k worth of property improvements-that is-he forces the inflation of the property value. The new or actual total property value shown in case b is $127k ($102k plus $25k). However, next step is to have the improved property appraised as in Case C.

Case C New appraised value is $175k. Haroldsen negotiates with original owner to subordinate the $24k equity interest of the original owner. Example, give original owner $4k cash, and/or increase interest rate from 8.5 to 9.5%, or decrease term of 2nd mortgage by years. Also obtain new first mortgage for $120k.

From the New First of $120k
$120k (New first mortgage)
$68k (Pay off original first mortgage)
$4k (Paid to original owner for subordinating ___interest.)
$48k tax-free dollars (borrowed money) for further investment.

Note—$ 175k property— Haroldsen's equity = $35k, break-even cash flow position with $120k first and $20k second.

OTHER BOOKS* BY MARK O. HAROLDSEN:

- **Courage to be Rich*

- *Goals, Guts, and Greatness*
- *The Beginner's Guide to R.E. Investing*

- *How to Wake Up the Financial Genius Inside You* (1st edition)

- *The Best Real Estate Deals I Ever Did...*

*Some of the concepts, formulas, and sections of the above mentioned books have been adapted and used in this book.

**Mr. Haroldsen's book, *The Courage to be Rich*, should not be confused with Suze Orman's book with the same name. Her book was published years later and apparently she was not creative enough to come up with an original title.

Author Contact Information:

Mark O. Haroldsen
4505 Wasatch Boulevard, Suite 350
Salt Lake City, Utah 84124
801-273-2374
moh@reincome.com